"We bought your book and I truly believe it was the best $30.00 I have ever spent...period. We read every page and followed your recommendations and sure enough...everything worked as you said it would. We purchased a new car and closed on our new house without getting robbed by the lenders. I look back now and recall us trying to figure out how we were going to wade through everything that people go through after a BK and I must say, we would have never figured out all that is necessary to successfully maneuver through it all. Thankfully for us, you arrived just in time to help us put everything in perspective. You provided critical information and also provided that super pep talk we needed. We are now 5 years into a successful recovery after bankruptcy. To you personally, and all the folks who work for and with you, a thousand thank yous and God bless you all."

Cecil Miller
Dallas, Texas

"I bought the book at your seminar and have used it to the T. I have 3 houses, 2 very nice cars and credit again. Life is good."

Lori Jovin
Atlanta, Georgia

"I read the book TWICE, followed all the steps in rebuilding my credit...and within a year after bankruptcy received 100% financing for a brand new $170,000 house in the suburbs. I first got the secured credit card, and was later approved for a regular one. Six months after having both, the credit line was increased. My score has gone from 486 to 607 in a year. Now that I have the mortgage, a car and two credit cards, I'm sure my score should now be above 620."

Shari Quinn
Chicago, Illinois

"I just wanted to share my good news with you. I closed on a house last Friday thanks to you and your books. I used all the information I got at your workshops. Thanks again."

Yvonne Dunkley
Phoenix, Arizona

"I received an invitation to your seminar and unfortunately I could not attend, but there was something about you I felt was different. I got on the phone with Borders and had them order me a copy of Credit After Bankruptcy. I could barely put the book down! I made my husband read it and I am passing the book around to anyone that will listen to me...By the end of this year I will have a good start on rebuilding my credit. I have passed on my wisdom in savings and spending money [to my children]...Thank you again. I just want to shout to anyone on how not to end up where I am. I know God places people in my life to help me and I thank Him for you. God Bless you and your wife."

Lisa Rogers
Houston, Texas

"I began reading your book prior to filing so that I could get a head start on recovery. Initially we filed Chapter 13, but converted to Chapter 7 after struggling to make payments. In August our bankruptcy was discharged. We had saved enough money to catch up on our mortgage payments and pay off our car. I ordered my credit scores 30 days later and went to work. By the end of September I had my first unsecured credit card. It was only for $300, but it was a start. In February, I leased a new SUV with 0% financing and had 2 additional unsecured credit cards. In September, I purchased my first rental property with 100% traditional financing and an interest rate of 7%. We celebrated our 2 year bankruptcy discharge anniversary date with an approved business line of credit for $25,000, credit scores in the low 700's and a contract to build our new home from the ground up. Thank you for the insight and motivation to not only recover from bankruptcy, but truly 'Improve Our Lifestyle.' May God continue to bless you in all your endeavors."

Linda Harris
Detroit, Michigan

CREDIT
AFTER
BANKRUPTCY

The easy-to-follow guide to a quick and lasting recovery from personal bankruptcy

STEPHEN SNYDER

Chapter 20 Publishing, Inc.
Jackson Hole, Wyoming

Thank you to Tyndale House Publishers for the use of *Success! The Glenn Bland Method* audio cassette, an abridgement of *Success! The Glenn Bland Method,* © 1972 by Glenn Bland. Published 1995 by Tyndale House Publishers, Inc. Used by permission of Tyndale House Publishers, Inc. All rights reserved.

Thank you to Nolo.com for the use of segments from *Stand Up to the IRS.* Reprinted with permission from the publisher, Nolo.com, from *Stand Up to the IRS* by Frederick W. Daily. © 2000. www.nolo.com

Thank you to Jim Rohn at Jim Rohn International for use of his great words and wisdom throughout this book. Jim Rohn's website is: www.jimrohn.com

Thank you to Perigee Books for the use of an excerpt from A KICK IN THE ASSETS by Tod Barnhart, copyright © 1998 by Tod Barnhart. Used by permission of Perigee Books, an imprint of Penguin Group (USA).

Publisher's Cataloging-in-Publication Data

Snyder, Stephen.
Credit After Bankruptcy : The easy-to-follow guide to a quick and lasting recovery from personal bankruptcy / Stephen Snyder. – Jackson Hole, WY : Chapter 20 Pub., Inc., 2008.

p. ; cm.
ISBN: 978-1-891945-25-0

1. Finance, Personal—United States. 2. Consumer credit—United States.
3. Bankruptcy—United States. I.Title.

HG3766.C74 S69 2008
332.7/5—dc22   2007921790

Printed in the United States of America
Vaughan Printing, Inc. • Nashville, Tennessee
First printing January 2008

Contents

Introduction

I was forced at gunpoint to update this book.

Well, not really...you see, soon after the new bankruptcy law went into effect in October of 2005, the national bookstores decided that ALL bankruptcy-related books were outdated.

Phooey.

Nothing could be further from the truth. Especially since the book you are holding in your hands only deals with the choices and decisions you make AFTER you file bankruptcy...not before.

So, to keep the book in bookstores I read it again to see what needed to be changed, if anything.

It's been years since I read this book from cover to cover. After 22 printings since 1996, with over 350,000 books sold, I'm proud to say it's *still* the best resource for anyone who has filed bankruptcy.

How do you improve on something that has helped so many people rebuild their financial lives?

That's why it's taken me over a year to carefully edit this new, fully-updated version of this book.

When I wrote the book, Michele and I were in recovery mode. I didn't want that sense of urgency and transparency to disappear.

This time around we're far from recovery mode. The first version of this book was just me with a yellow pad, in a 900 square foot condo, up every morning at 5 next to my fireplace with a Duraflame log keeping me warm.

Today I'm enjoying an oceanfront view of the Gulf of Mexico, and I have staff members smarter and more talented than me who have joined in my mission to help educate, enlighten, and encourage people going through financial crisis—several of whom have filed bankruptcy themselves.

Through their collaboration, coupled with the new information I share through my free weekly newsletter, *Life After Bankruptcy®*, I can honestly say, the book you are holding is even better than the original.

So, what started as a burden forced upon me by the national bookstore chains has become a blessing in disguise. It helped me make something already great even better. This is especially good for you, the reader. You get everything you need to know to recover from bankruptcy in one place.

So sit back, relax, and enjoy the journey you're about to embark on. You'll be back on track before you know it—just like the thousands of others who've used the information in this book to recover. You can read many of their success stories at: *www.afterbankruptcy. org/testimonials*. And when you're finished reading the book and putting this information to work for you—I expect you to have a success story of your own!

Enjoy the journey.

Preface

Bankruptcy is a powerful phenomenon. It can be both a financial death and a financial rebirth.

Personal bankruptcy has long been seen as a refuge for blue-collar workers, high school dropouts, and former high-fliers whose fortunes have turned and who are seeking to shelter their luxury assets.

That is no longer the case.

The average bankrupt debtor is a typical American—right down the middle. Bankruptcy has become the safety net of the middle class.

That's not to say that famous people do not file bankruptcy. They do. In fact, here are a few names you may recognize who have filed bankruptcy:

Larry King	T.L.C.
M.C. Hammer	Sherman Hemsley
Francis Ford Coppola	P.T. Barnum
Debbie Reynolds	Bjorn Borg
Kim Basinger	Buffalo Bill Cody
Redd Foxx	David Crosby
Dorothy Hamill	Charles Goodyear
Wayne Newton	Tony Gwynn
J. Ronald Getty	Isaac Hayes
Joe Gibbs	George Jones
Tom Petty	Jerry Lewis
Lorraine Bracco	Willie Nelson
Governor John Connally	Thomas Paine
Thomas Jefferson	Randy Quaid
Walt Disney	Burt Reynolds
Johnny Unitas	Nikola Tesla
Toni Braxton	Mark Twain
Abe Lincoln	Tammy Wynette

As you can see from this list, it's not about how much money you make. Bankruptcy can happen to anyone.

I wrote this book to help bankrupt debtors avoid bad financial decisions that threaten to cripple their financial future after bankruptcy. It seems so many companies today prey on bankrupt debtors. They think they're doing us a favor by financing a used car at 26% or extending a mortgage with excessive fees.

By avoiding these vultures, and making better credit decisions, a bankrupt debtor can recover from bankruptcy within months and build a strong foundation for a lasting recovery.

But the choice is yours. It can be tempting to take the easy path to what looks like recovery from bankruptcy with bad lenders when the better decision is just a few extra steps away.

Recovering from bankruptcy is more than just getting approved for an auto loan from AmeriCredit. It's more than a $500 credit limit from Capital One, or mortgaging your first home after bankruptcy at a double-digit interest rate through a sub-prime lender. That's the wrong way to recover. In fact, that's not recovery at all.

Throughout these pages you will find an easy-to-follow guide that will enable you to establish the right type of credit, from the best lenders, in the shortest amount of time. Unlike other books that dispense general financial recovery information, this book confronts the specific issues every bankrupt debtor must face after bankruptcy.

The following information was uncovered during years of trial and error as my wife and I personally learned the truth about establishing credit after bankruptcy.

This book was designed to be read by people who have already filed bankruptcy. The first 13 chapters act as a prerequisite to the second half of the book. Chapters 14 and 15 focus on personal development issues. And Chapters 16 through 31 deal with specific issues, like financing a car or mortgaging a home. The Bonus Chapter has been designed to guide Chapter 13 filers through issues that are specific to their unique circumstances. With that in mind, enjoy.

Stephen Snyder
January 2008

*"If you can believe, all things are possible
to him who believes."*

– Mark 9:23

"I have recovered from my bankruptcy and own nearly $2 million worth of property with much more in the pipeline."

"I would like to take a moment to thank you all for your price-less contribution to my financial life...I have recovered from my bankruptcy and own nearly $2 million worth of property with much more in the pipeline. The last time I checked, my middle score was 709 and I have been able to get many unsecured lines of credit from the likes of Amex, Discover and mortgages. I do not know what I would have done or where my fiscal life would be if I had not been blessed with your story, lessons and knowledge."

Frank Morales
Crestwood Village, New Jersey

Our Story

Our story is typical of people who file bankruptcy. We lived beyond our means and chose bankruptcy to avoid garnishment.

At a young age we experienced a high income. That income bought us luxury cars, a large home, fine furniture, new clothes, travel, dining out regularly, etc.

In December 1991, less than 6 months after we married, I decided to make a career change. Looking back, it's easy to recognize that we didn't change our lifestyle after my decision to change careers. The lifestyle remained, even when there was no income. Hard to believe, but true. We survived for over a year by simply selling things from around the house. In December 1992 it finally caught up with us. My wife made the decision to file bankruptcy to avoid garnishment against her wages. She advised me to do the same. She wanted a fresh start for us both. I didn't want to file bankruptcy, but my new wife didn't give me a choice—it was either file and start over, or she would leave me.

Like most bankrupt debtors, we couldn't afford to file bankruptcy. So our plan was to find an attorney who would work with us on a payment plan and allow us to do as much of the work as possible to lower the cost. Once my wife's bankruptcy paperwork was complete, I would have a template with which to file my own bankruptcy paperwork with the court. Our motive was saving hundreds of dollars. It worked. With a small loan from my parents, Michele's bankruptcy was filed on December 11, 1992. My bankruptcy followed on February 1, 1993. Both were Chapter 7 filings recorded in South Bend, Indiana.

Filing bankruptcy affected us in two ways. We felt relieved that with our automatic stay in hand the harassment was finally over.

Creditors would leave us alone. But later we experienced frustration with ourselves about decisions we had made that led up to the bankruptcy. We played the blame game with each other. It almost cost us our marriage.

During the 90 days of waiting for our bankruptcy to be discharged, we had a lot of time to think and reflect. We came to the realization that we were not bad people. Our problem stemmed from errors in judgment that we had repeated daily. Our thinking had been wrong when it came to managing our money and our credit.

Before our bankruptcy was discharged we made seven major decisions and put them in writing. They were:

- We would pay cash for everything, and not go into debt or apply for credit ever again.

- We would pay back our bankruptcy debt with interest, even though we had filed Chapter 7.

- We would radically change our spending habits and thinking about the proper use of money.

- We would begin to give away 10% of our gross income each week.

- We would open a savings account and begin saving 10% of our income.

- We would live within our means.

- We would find a home church and get "plugged in."

The decision to pay cash for everything and reject debt was an emotional decision. It didn't last too long. We realized that credit and debt were not our problem. We were our problem. I used the following illustration to explain it to my wife, who was opposed to any new credit: "A gun can kill. A gun can protect. The end result is determined by the person using the gun..." Credit and debt are not our enemies. With new thinking habits and a plan of action, they can be managed properly.

Since our recovery 14 years ago, we established the After Bankruptcy Foundation and deliver free seminars to show other bankrupt filers how to quickly recover during and after bankruptcy. I've authored several books, and I am currently the editor of the *Life After Bankruptcy*® newsletter, the weekly newsletter on how to recover after bankruptcy, which is read by nearly 92,000 people a week.

It's now 2008, over 15 years since our discharge dates. We've been successful in almost all of our goals. Our biggest success has been the peace of mind our new thinking habits concerning our finances have brought us. We are not concerned about next week's bills. We successfully entered into mainstream credit in a very short time, and continue to enjoy the peace that comes from managing our money and credit well.

∼

"You seem to be 'one of us.'"

"I trust you because you seem to be 'one of us.' Your face
is trusting and your words are truthful. Makes us (made me)
believe that if you can do it, I could do it too! And I did! I purchased my condo in February. My interest rate is 5%."

Rosalyn Burris
Yarmouth Port, Massachusetts

My Qualifications to Write This Book

There are numerous self-proclaimed gurus out there who want to help you improve a certain aspect of your life. And that's okay, but take the time to understand what makes them qualified for you to listen. Take today's marriage gurus for instance. An issue of *Self* magazine published a story on famous authors who give advice on improving marriages. All but one was divorced several times! The article pointed out that one of the most popular marriage gurus, Barbara De Angelis, is on her fifth marriage. And one of her divorces involved Dr. John Gray, the author of *Men Are From Mars, Women Are From Venus.*

It's important to know what a person's qualifications are before listening to their advice. The only qualifications I have are the results of our actions. Results speak louder than words.

- Two weeks after my bankruptcy was discharged we were approved for major Visa bank cards issued from a bank.

- Less than 60 days after my bankruptcy was discharged we established new accounts with another bank that extended to us: free checking accounts, Visa debit cards, and several bank loans.

- Less than 90 days after my bankruptcy was filed we mortgaged a beautiful home in Indianapolis through a reputable mortgage lender at 10.5% interest (this was in 1993 when 10.5% was a good rate).

- Six months after we closed on our mortgage we refinanced it to a 6% adjustable interest rate, reducing our mortgage payment from $663 to $441 a month.

- Less than 3 months after my bankruptcy was discharged we leased a brand-new car from a major car manufacturer at 2.9%. Six months later we leased our second brand-new car at a similar interest rate.

- We were pre-approved to receive a credit card from a major department store within a few months after closing our mortgage.

- Eighteen months after my bankruptcy was discharged I purchased new furniture on credit.

- Eleven months after my bankruptcy was discharged I received a small business loan.

- Twelve months after my bankruptcy was discharged a private investor invested into my new start-up business.

- Thirteen months after my bankruptcy was discharged a local bank approved me for merchant status—which enabled the new business to accept major bank cards as a form of payment.

- Less than six months after my bankruptcy was discharged we each obtained another bank card from a local bank.

- Less than 12 months after my bankruptcy was discharged I received store credit to purchase a Nikon™ camera system.

- Less than 14 months after each of our bankruptcies were discharged we were each able to gain cellular telephone service without security deposits.

- Less than 18 months after my bankruptcy was discharged I established my first brokerage account with one of the top brokerage firms in the country.

- Less than 12 months after my bankruptcy was discharged my credit limits began increasing automatically.

- Less than 17 months after my bankruptcy was discharged we were approved for our third brand-new car at a normal interest rate. Six months later we were approved for our fourth new car.

- Exactly 24 months after my bankruptcy was discharged we were approved for a home equity loan from a local bank at the same interest rate as a person with excellent credit.

- Thirteen months after my bankruptcy was discharged I turned a $500 secured bank card from a local bank into an unsecured bank card with a $5,000 credit limit at 9.9% interest. Six months later the limit was raised to $7,000 with just a four-minute telephone call.

All of these events occurred 24 months or less after discharge.

Since that time we've been approved for many car loans, leases, credit limit increases, mortgages, refinances, home equity loans, lines of credit, bank loans, and even a few retail accounts...you name it, we've done it.

Today we have a substantial estate and a sophisticated estate and asset protection plan. And of course, we strive to maintain excellent credit scores. Our scores are consistently in the top 1% of the population and we rarely carry any revolving debt. We feel blessed.

Can you reestablish credit after bankruptcy? Certainly. In fact, it's easier to reestablish credit after a bankruptcy than it is for a person who hasn't filed bankruptcy and has bad credit.

Let our accomplishments inspire you to reach your goals. Our "re-obsession" with credit was out of necessity. We needed a place to live. We needed cars to drive to work. We needed a bank card when traveling.

This book was written to encourage people who have real needs and have been told it can't be done. Or worse yet, you believe that your only options for new credit are high-interest finance companies. If all you get out of this book is hope, our objective has been accomplished.

By conducting free seminars around the country we have experienced first-hand what our example has done—it has changed people's lives. Don't underestimate hope. The hope of achievement is one of the greatest riches in life! Our example is proof that all things are possible.

"I started over 2 years out of a bankruptcy and today I own 6 properties, I am self employed, we went in 50/50 on a condo in Maui (and should close in 2 weeks) and today I got a call from my lender letting me know my score is 710."

"Today, January 31, 2007, is a great day. February 2003 was my bankruptcy discharge date. I started over with in a new state, new job, new life. After attending a seminar we decided it was time for a change. We moved and rented for six months from my brother. March 2005 I purchased my first home and have not looked back since. I have been working a full time job making about $40k a year and buying real estate under value and renting them out, this has worked out so well I was able to quit my 9-7 regular job and help others placing people into their investment homes full time. I started over 2 years out of a bankruptcy and today I own 6 properties, I am self employed, we went in 50/50 on a condo in Maui (and should close in 2 weeks) and today I got a call from my lender letting me know my score is 710. I would of never imagined all that hard work to pay off so big. One of the properties I own I was just able to qualify for a mortgage that will save me $1000 a month, just because my score went from 670 to 710. It is possible!"

Jay Sanders
Phoenix, Arizona

Bankruptcy Defined

Bankruptcy is a legal remedy for previous errors in judgment. Our founding fathers were smart enough to realize that there needed to be a "safety net" to catch people who attempted great things and failed, giving them a fresh start.

Bankruptcy represents both death and life. Death, in that bad habits leading up to the bankruptcy should die. Life, in that it gives another chance to take advantage of the opportunity this great country provides.

The goal now is to recognize previous errors in judgment and quickly correct them. Forgive yourself and move on with your life. Stop looking in the rear-view mirror. Look out of the windshield and move forward.

"At the time of my bankruptcy my scores were: Equifax 300, Experian 360, TransUnion 336... Our credit scores are; Equifax 850, Experian 840, TransUnion 843. Our gratitude to you and your program is boundless. Thank you."

"At the time of my bankruptcy my scores were: Equifax 300, Experian 360, TransUnion 336. After being discharged, and a lot of hard work cleaning up our record, we were able to replace our 11.1% mortgage with a more affordable 5.65% loan along with increasing our mortgage by $50,000 and improving the property and putting a pool in. We again refinanced to a 3.75% loan and again took out more cash. We now have over $100,000 in the bank and as an extra bonus the bank manager now knows my name. Wow! Who'd of thunk it four short years ago. Our credit scores are; Equifax 850, Experian 840, TransUnion 843. Our gratitude to you and your program is boundless. Thank you."

Charles Backman
Opa-Locka, Florida

Paying Your Bills on Time is Just Not Enough Anymore

Your parents probably taught you that as long as you pay your bills on time, your credit rating would be considered good.

Maybe you're thinking that's all you need to do to recover from bankruptcy.

Not true.

When it comes to our credit, what worked for our parents won't work for us. You see, our parents weren't scored. We are.

Over the last 15 years lenders have begun to rely on credit scoring to determine whether they will offer you credit and, if you qualify, what interest rate they will extend to you. In fact, paying your bills on time accounts for only 35% of your scores, which means 65% of what determines how good your credit is, has nothing to do with paying your bills on time.

Your credit scores are calculated from information appearing on each of your three credit reports. The most popular credit score is called the FICO® credit score. A FICO credit score is simply a three-digit number ranging from 300 to 850 that summarizes the information on your credit report.

The higher your scores, the better.

You have three scores. One score from each credit reporting agency. Lenders use these scores to measure your credit risk. Even insurance and utility companies have begun to use similar scores to deny service or to charge you more if your scores are low. Lenders have used FICO® credit scores to evaluate you for years. Created by Fair Isaac Corporation, FICO credit scores have long been a closely guarded secret kept from consumers.

However, since June 11, 2003 you have been able to (for the first time in history) purchase all 3 of your FICO credit scores, which enables you to quickly see how lenders see you.

By increasing your FICO credit scores you can:

- Lower your interest rates on your credit cards
- Increase your credit limits
- Save tens of thousands of dollars in interest on a mortgage
- Refinance at a lower interest rate
- Get approved when you would otherwise be denied
- Qualify for a lower car payment
- Get approved for no-money-down financing
- Lower your insurance premiums
- Get utilities at a lower rate or without a deposit
- Know whether you will get approved and at what interest rate before you ever fill out a credit application
- And more...

It's vital to your recovery after bankruptcy that you know your three FICO credit scores and learn how to increase them. If you don't know what your 3 FICO credit scores are, you can purchase them from: *www.myfico.com/12*. For more information on increasing your credit scores subscribe to my free email newsletter by going to: *www.lifeafterbankruptcy.com/subscribe*.

"Thank you, Stephen, for your program and the encouraging newsletters."

"I don't know if my story qualifies as a 'success,' but a year ago I wouldn't have thought I could qualify for a mortgage, let alone be able to actually buy a home. I declared Chapter 13 bankruptcy in September 1998 and the case was discharged in April 2003. In January 2004 I asked an acquaintance who is a mortgage broker if I could qualify for a mortgage. She told me I already qualified! I closed on August 24, 2005. If I hadn't attended your seminar I never would have thought to even ask about a mortgage, let alone be a homeowner. Thank you, Stephen, for your program and the encouraging newsletters."

Patricia Wicker
Pahokee, Florida

"We followed the instructions in your book to reestablish credit and we used the mortgage company from your seminar to get our home exactly 24 months after our discharge just like you stated in your seminar."

"I'm proud to say that my wife and I are now happy owners of a 2,400 square foot home, a new truck and we are on our way today to pick up our new car. I attended your seminar two years ago and the only reason I went was because it was free. Otherwise I would not have gone. But knowing what I know now, I would have gladly paid for the information. We followed the instructions in your book to reestablish credit and we used the mortgage company from your seminar to get our home exactly 24 months after our discharge just like you stated in your seminar. We were credit approved to buy a new truck one month after discharge, and we are now getting another loan from the same lender to purchase my wife's new car. I know with all of the scams out there today it is hard to convince someone of a legitimate way to improve their credit. Your information has been great to us and we just want to say thanks, from the bottom of our hearts."

Lamar Sherman
Dennis, Massachusetts

Why Reestablishing Credit is Important

There are a lot of people telling you to be debt-free. To avoid credit and pay cash for everything. Not to use bank cards. To purchase a used car. To wait 7 to 10 years before you can mortgage a home.

These people have valid ideas. But they are dead wrong.

They're missing one important ingredient—they probably have never filed bankruptcy. Therefore, they do not have a clue as to what you are going though. To them, adding $1,000 overdraft check protection takes one telephone call. For you and me, it takes time. Even then, we must beg and persuade our bankers to extend us even the smallest amount of unsecured credit.

These people mean well, but if they haven't experienced bankruptcy, they're not qualified to give you advice. Just ignore them.

My friend David wouldn't tell his pastor that he filed bankruptcy. Six years had passed living on a cash-only basis and he now wanted to mortgage a home and acquire a new car. His pastor gave him the best advice he had, which was not to go into debt. It was good advice—but not for that season in David's life.

We constantly meet people who filed bankruptcy years ago and never attempted to reestablish their credit. They pay cash for everything. When the time comes to purchase a new car or mortgage a home, no lender will extend them credit.

Why not? They are good people. It's been years since the bankruptcy. They earn more now than before and even have a nice savings account. But how can a lender extend credit to someone who hasn't proven they are creditworthy? They can't.

In fact, most mortgage lender guidelines dictate you must establish two or three new credit accounts after you discharge. So if you chose to be a cash-only person and wait 10 years to apply for credit, you will be in a similar situation.

You must have a history of paying on time before reputable credit lenders will extend you credit. A cash-only system provides no track record. It's just that simple.

After meeting thousands of bankrupt people through our free seminars, I've noticed that a "cash-only" mentality is very common among recent bankrupt debtors. After six months to two years, the emotion seems to wear off and they're ready to try again. But this time, with a new resolve.

What I am asking you to do is make some commitments to yourself. These are the seven commitments.

COMMITMENT 1: FIND THE PROBLEMS THAT LED YOU INTO BANKRUPTCY AND FIX THEM

The first step of this strategy is to make some life-changing decisions in how you handle your finances. Find the problems. Fix them. Remember, when you file bankruptcy, it doesn't fix the problem. Bankruptcy simply gives you a fresh start.

Think about it. There was something, maybe several things that led to your bankruptcy. Maybe it was a poor investing decision, poor credit management, a job loss, a divorce, a major medical event that zapped your savings, a lawsuit, a failed attempt at a small business, a death in your family, no cash reserve to weather a storm, or some combination of these circumstances.

Of course nobody can avoid the unavoidable, but you can learn from your experiences and take steps to make sure you are protected or have a "Plan B" the next time something unexpected happens.

COMMITMENT 2: GO BACK INTO DEBT STRATEGICALLY

Go back into debt using only mainstream lenders—no high-interest finance companies. Strategic debt is when you borrow money from a lender because you need it and can improve your credit rating at the same time.

Don't be afraid to go back into debt after your bankruptcy. It's just like learning to ride a bike. When you fall off you have to get back on until you figure it out. The same concept applies here. Get back into debt cautiously and on your terms, but don't avoid it. Stick with mainstream low-interest lenders and keep the amounts you start with manageable. As you get more comfortable, begin focusing on credit that gives you some sort of tax or net worth benefit, like a home or some other appreciating investment.

COMMITMENT 3: PAY YOUR BILLS EARLY OR ON TIME

Commit to paying your bills early or on time. This is the key for a strong financial foundation. One of the last things a lender wants to see on your credit reports is one or more late payments after your bankruptcy.

By paying early or on time you will guarantee that none of your lenders will ever report your account as being late. Late payments (and other negative credit items) account for 35% of your FICO® credit scores.

COMMITMENT 4: REMOVE INACCURATE INFORMATION FROM YOUR CREDIT REPORTS

Work hard to remove any inaccurate, incomplete, misleading, unverifiable, or outdated information from your credit reports.

This is nothing more than you exercising your rights as defined by federal law. The Fair Credit Reporting Act states that anything on your credit report that meets any of the previously mentioned conditions must be removed.

There are often inaccurate, incomplete, misleading, unverifiable, and outdated items left on your credit reports after bankruptcy, and these can have a significant negative impact on your FICO scores.

COMMITMENT 5: MANAGE YOUR CREDIT TO INCREASE YOUR CREDIT SCORES

Make a goal to increase your FICO® credit scores to 780 or above. This doesn't happen overnight. Along the way to FICO credit scores of 780, you should create more attainable goals for yourself. Maybe 700, and when you reach 700, 720, etc.

It's like training for a marathon. You don't go out and run 26.2 miles your first day out. You work your way up to your ultimate goal. You don't have to go from 550 to 800 in a week (nor is it possible). But, you DO have to start right away. The sooner you start, the closer you will be to reaching your goal.

Set a goal to increase your FICO scores by 50 points every 6 months until your scores are all above 780. Then change your strategy from an "improvement" goal to a "maintenance" goal.

To learn more about increasing your credit scores, you can subscribe to the free *Life After Bankruptcy®* newsletter by going to: *www.lifeafterbankruptcy.com/subscribe*.

COMMITMENT 6: LEARN TO LIVE OFF A PERCENTAGE OF YOUR INCOME

Just look around you and see how much money you're needlessly spending every month. Do you really need an HD cable television with all the premium channels? If you smoke, how much money are you wasting on cigarettes? How many $5 cups of coffee from Starbucks are you drinking every week? (All of the wealthy people I know refuse to pay $5 for a cup of java.) Look around and you'll be surprised at how you can cut back without affecting the quality of your life one bit—in fact, it will probably improve.

If you just invest the $5 a day you spend on coffee at 5% interest, after 40 years you could end up with $231,483! There will be more about how to invest your money properly in Chapter 31.

Try to save 10%, invest 10%, and give 10% to charity. It will be difficult at first, but be persistent. The reward you will get from this will be worth more than anything else you could buy with the money.

COMMITMENT 7: STRIVE TO USE CREDIT AS A CONVENIENCE, NOT A NECESSITY

America is the most "credit hungry" country in the world. It's the only country that views credit as a right rather than a privilege. That's not a good way to look at things—especially if you are bankrupt.

You should use the credit system to your advantage. Use your credit to invest in real estate. Use your credit cards to buy things in a way that will improve your FICO® credit scores.

An executive from one of the largest banks in the United States was once quoted as saying, "Our ideal customer is a person that carries a balance and only pays the minimum payment due every month." This is because they make the most money from someone who does this.

Don't become a prisoner of the credit system (e.g., purchasing more than you can afford on credit and paying the minimum balance due each month—you'll never get ahead that way). It's hard to escape.

COMMITMENT 8: CONSIDER PAYING BACK THE DEBT YOU FILED BANKRUPTCY ON

This step is optional, and certainly not for everyone. But, once you're fully recovered, look back at all the debts you discharged, and consider how you might pay them back, slowly.

Some lenders won't issue you credit again until you've paid them back. That means you can have FICO scores in the 700s but can't get a credit card from some banks because you discharged a debt that you owed them many years ago.

IN CONCLUSION

Some people think that bankruptcy is the final chapter of their financial lives. This is not true. Bankruptcy can be a new beginning. Remember the commitments. They've worked for us.

"...I own my first home, I recently paid off my car, I have 3 credit cards that are in excellent standings and I just found out today that my credit score is finally above 700."

"I attended one of your seminars about three months after my bankruptcy. I must tell you, I did not think that your methods would work...even while you were saying it. I was at the low point, believing the myths that no one would ever give me credit for at least 10 years. You gave us companies to contact for credit cards, mortgages, car loans and even where to open up checking accounts. Okay, I must admit, you were absolutely correct. After 3 years, I own my first home, I recently paid off my car, I have 3 credit cards that are in excellent standings and I just found out today that my credit score is finally above 700. It does take work and discipline. I just want people to know that bankruptcy is not the end, it could be a very wonderful beginning. I really wanted to thank you for the encouragement and important information. What you are doing for people...is priceless. I enjoy your newsletters. I still follow your advice. You're the man!!!"

Candace Booth
Bella Vista, Arkansas

Is Bankruptcy Wrong?

Is filing bankruptcy wrong? Yes. For you to believe otherwise would make you a fool. The best decision you can make right now is to come clean and say something like:

> *"I realize that what I did was wrong. I alone am responsible for my decision to file bankruptcy. It was no one else's fault but my own. Today I recognize this and accept it as the truth."*

How liberating. So many people neglect to accept responsibility for their actions. They experience denial. It's everyone else's fault. The first step to recovery is to take responsibility for your actions. John F. Kennedy did, and he became a great leader because of it.

Are there some circumstances where bankruptcy truly isn't your fault? Probably. But, aside from medical related financial crises, that percentage is so small it's not even worth considering. Walk on the wild side and take responsibility. You'll be glad you did.

Once you reach this point, all you need to do is ask forgiveness. Look at the Apostle Paul. He killed Christians, yet he was forgiven, and God used him to take His message to the world.

Then there was King David. This guy had an affair, strategically killed his lover's husband, brought a nation to war, lied, was a poor father—yet God said he was a man after His own heart. Wow.

The secret to Paul's and David's ability to move on with their lives was their ability to accept responsibility for their actions, ask forgiveness, and forgive themselves. They lived in the present, not in the past. Too many people I've met in our seminars go through life after bankruptcy looking through a rearview mirror. If you were to drive your car looking through the rearview mirror, how far would you get? Start looking ahead. Forgive yourself, learn from your mistakes, and move on.

We dealt with this issue in a unique way. We look at our bankruptcy debt as a long-term loan to be paid back with interest. Our part is to believe it will be done. God's part is to make it happen.

Our goal is to pay it back before the year 2020. Looking at it this way freed us from a lot of guilt.

I am not asking you to pay your bankruptcy debt back, I am asking you to consider it. It's pretty simple when you understand your role.

Look at the miracle of the seed. The farmer plants a seed, and over a period of time it produces in abundance many times over the amount of seed that was planted. Amazing. How does that happen? The farmer does the possible. God does the impossible. Do the possible—have faith.

"The mortgage company said that they have never seen anyone two years out of bankruptcy have such good credit."

"I have read your book and went to your seminar. Took 10 pages of notes. It helped me immensely to get my credit life back in order. I was able to buy a new car at 4.5%, get an unsecured Platinum Credit Card, and refinance my house for 15 years at 6.5%. The mortgage company said that they have never seen anyone two years out of bankruptcy have such good credit. I now feel like I have my life back and am on track for retirement in 10 years or less. Thanks to all your organization has done."

Mark Thornsburg
State College, Pennsylvania

"I now have a new car at 6.9% interest. I have two other friends that went through bankruptcy around the same time, and they are paying over 18% interest for their car loans."

"I attended your seminar and with much trepidation, I finally took the leap of faith and went out to speak with two of the lenders that were there. I test drove several cars. These two went above and beyond, and I now have a new car at 6.9% interest. I have two other friends that went through bankruptcy around the same time, and they are paying over 18% interest for their car loans. I have been following your advice, and will continue to do so. This has been a real eye-opener for me as to how credit REALLY works! Please keep up the great work, and spreading the news about how to recover!"

Elizabeth Rohde
Fort Myers Beach, Florida

Your Choices After Bankruptcy

Filing for bankruptcy for many people can be a very emotional experience. Making good decisions can be difficult when you're in the midst of a financial crisis.

Deciding the right path to take after you file bankruptcy is critical to putting bankruptcy behind you quickly.

There are shortcuts to a fast recovery...but there are also many stumbling blocks that could set you back months...even years. There are six initial choices a person may consider after being discharged from bankruptcy. They are:

- Paying cash—avoiding credit altogether
- Relying on another person's good credit
- Creating a new credit file by establishing a new identity
- Maintaining accounts through your bankruptcy
- Applying for new credit
- Using credit repair

Let's take a closer look at each option.

CHOICE 1: PAY CASH—AVOID CREDIT ALTOGETHER

On the surface, paying cash for everything seems like the most practical way to avoid getting back into debt. Don't do it...unless your goal is to build a log cabin in the mountains, live off the land, and cut yourself off from civilization. A cash-only lifestyle is just not realistic in the 21st Century.

As you will learn in upcoming chapters, establishing new credit after bankruptcy is critical to getting credit in the future. The sooner you start, the faster you will recover. Then you may enter into a cash-only lifestyle if desired. The fact is that lenders want to see if

you have learned how to responsibly handle your finances. No reestablished credit—no track record. No track record—no new credit.

CHOICE 2: RELY ON ANOTHER PERSON'S GOOD CREDIT (CO-SIGNING)

It can be tempting to rely on another person's good credit after
filing bankruptcy. Whether it's your parent, brother, sister, or close
friend. My advice would be if you're under 18 years old it's OK to
depend on someone else to help you. But if you're over 18—it's time
to grow up. It's not Mommy and Daddy's or anyone else's responsibility to take care of you anymore. You need to take responsibility
for your recovery. If you need help ask to borrow money, not to borrow someone's credit. If you fall short, it hurts them and you.

There is a time when relying on another person's credit can
work, and that's when you're married and both parties are working
together to improve their credit ratings. If you're a happily married
couple and both contributing to the household income, determine
whose FICO® credit scores are higher before applying for credit. The
spouse with the higher income will get better terms if their income
supports the request.

Many wives who stay at home have higher credit scores than
their husbands. But if their income doesn't support the request it
won't work. In most situations lenders will consider the "major
breadwinner" the primary borrower.

And don't confuse this with "piggybacking." Piggybacking refers
to the practice of paying an individual to be added as an authorized
user on another person's credit card. I think this is wrong. Fair Isaac
and Equifax® agree. They announced that they will close the loophole in the credit scoring formula that allows for this to happen.

CHOICE 3: CREATE A NEW CREDIT FILE BY ESTABLISHING A NEW IDENTITY

Shortly after I filed bankruptcy I looked into changing my identity as a strategy for recovery. I remember paying $600 via cashier's
check for 2 large, 3-ring binders filled with information about what
to do.

When I ordered those manuals, I remember thinking that these were the true secrets to repairing my credit. As I was reading them, I felt like a secret double-agent. I envisioned changing my name...my identity...heck, my whole life.

As I read more and more about the "techniques" the manual suggested for forming a new identity—I felt a little queasy. My gut told me something wasn't right about what the manual was telling me to do. Ya think?!

For example, one technique was to apply for an Employer Identification Number (EIN) and use it in place of my Social Security number. To me it seemed like fraud. And I didn't want any part of that.

Later I discovered that what the manual taught was indeed illegal.

It's a federal crime to make any false statements on a loan or credit application, misrepresent your Social Security number or obtain an EIN from the IRS under false pretenses.

Further, you could be charged with mail or wire fraud if you use the mail or a telephone to apply for credit and provide false information. Worse yet, establishing a new identity in this manner would constitute civil fraud under many state laws.

Now let's take at look at some better options.

CHOICE 4: MAINTAIN ACCOUNTS THROUGH YOUR BANKRUPTCY

The purpose of filing bankruptcy is to get a fresh start. A lot of people make the mistake of reaffirming (or maintaining) too much of the debt they should have let go in their bankruptcy.

For instance, if you cannot afford your house payment and you have no equity in your home—why try to keep it?

If it's because of emotional attachment—you're headed for a bumpy ride. I recently spoke to a young gal who used to work with us. She's regretting she ignored my advice not to become emotionally attached to her home with no equity. In fact, she filed a Chapter 13 bankruptcy after her Chapter 7 just to save it. Now she's wishing she hadn't tried to save the home and is looking for a way out. She's a smart gal. She'll come out on top. It's just the experience would have been a lot less bumpy had she let go of the emotional attachment and started fresh.

When I filed bankruptcy, I included everything in the bankruptcy. I paid off two small credit card balances before the bankruptcy petition was filed, which allowed me to legally exclude them from my bankruptcy petition.

Be sure to consult your bankruptcy attorney for specific advice for your situation. Otherwise, reaffirming debt you cannot afford is not a good idea.

CHOICE 5: APPLY FOR NEW CREDIT

Getting approved for new credit after bankruptcy is critical to a fast recovery.

I realize that you may think credit is what forced you into bankruptcy in the first place, and it may seem like you're throwing yourself back in the fire, so to speak. Just remember that credit wasn't the cause of your problem. You were most likely the cause of your problem.

One of the first questions lenders ask after you are discharged is, "Have you reestablished credit since your bankruptcy?" They usually don't lend money to people who do not show a history of financial responsibility on their credit reports. Fortunately, bankruptcy is a great opportunity to start over. It makes it easy for a lender to look at your credit report and say, "This person has paid on time for 'x' months after bankruptcy."

The secret to rebuilding your credit after bankruptcy is to build a few new, positive credit references to outweigh the old ones. The less negative references you have, the better.

CHOICE 6: CREDIT REPAIR

When done properly, repairing your credit reports can have a dramatic and lasting effect. There are plenty of books on how to accomplish this but most are outdated and teach theories that no longer work. There are also "credit repair organizations." The mission of a good credit repair organization is to remove inaccurate, incomplete, misleading, unverifiable, and outdated information from your credit reports.

As you probably know, there's a lot of incorrect information appearing on credit reports these days.

In fact, there was an independent study done in 2004 by the National Association of State Public Interest Research Groups that concluded over 79% of credit reports contain inaccurate information.

Inaccurate information on a bankrupt person's credit report can mean the difference between being approved or turned down for credit. It's vital you take this seriously.

However, there are a lot of journalists in the popular media who will tell you to stay away from all credit repair organizations.

They're just not telling the whole story. They report only the most sensational examples of the worst credit repair organizations and spread around the credit reporting agencies' propaganda without checking the facts first.

To state that every credit repair organization is bad is just ridiculous.

The fact of the matter is...there are a few very legitimate and quite good credit repair organizations, and there are many bad ones.

There is a way to spot a reputable credit repair organization. The secret is a piece of legislation called the Credit Repair Organizations Act—CROA for short. CROA was created by Congress to establish guidelines for organizations that provide credit repair.

And what the credit reporting agencies don't want you to know, is that Congress legitimized the practice of credit repair when they created CROA. Removing inaccurate information from your credit reports as outlined in CROA is perfectly legal and your right under federal law.

However, the credit reporting agencies and the popular media will still try to convince you otherwise. They will do everything in their power to make you think all credit repair organizations are evil because credit repair organizations expose how inaccurate the credit reporting system can be.

There are two types of credit repair organizations.

1. Fly-by-night operations that ignore CROA and advertise using spam emails and flyers on telephone poles.

2. Legitimate law firms that follow CROA and are fully compliant.

Here are some highlights to help you determine if a credit repair organization is legitimate:

- A legitimate organization cannot guarantee the results of their services.

- A legitimate organization must provide a written disclosure separate from the service agreement.

- A legitimate organization can only charge for services after they are performed. In other words, they cannot take money in advance.

- A legitimate organization will give you three to five days to cancel their service without charging you any fees.

- Unless they are a law firm or a non-profit organization they must be licensed in each state they do business in.

Go to: *www.ftc.gov/os/statutes/croa/croa.shtm* to read the Credit Repair Organizations Act online.

Once you read the guidelines, you can decide what's right for you.

What you'll find is most small credit repair companies do not follow CROA—let alone know what it is. And if that's the case I would suggest you keep looking for a CROA-compliant organization to help you.

One excellent law firm I've been watching closely for years is Bradley Ross Law located in North Dakota. You may reach them Monday through Friday at: *(701) 355-0123*. They charge you a small monthly fee for their services after work is complete. If you can afford their small monthly fee this firm is hard to beat. For further reading, go to their website: *www.bradleyrosslaw.com.*

WHAT WORKED FOR US

1. We used a combination of a few of the strategies outlined in this chapter to rebuild our credit after bankruptcy.
2. We maintained a few credit accounts through the bankruptcy.
3. We engaged a law firm to remove inaccurate information from our credit reports.
4. We opened new credit accounts.

However, today I'd recommend you modify our strategy.

I'd suggest retaining a law firm first (even if you're not discharged yet) to help increase your credit scores. I wouldn't wait. There's no reason to. Chances are you have inaccurate information appearing on your credit reports. The sooner you correct that information the sooner your scores may increase! Higher scores mean getting approved instead of being denied—not to mention, you pay less for everything you buy with credit.

Remember as long as inaccurate information remains on your credit reports, you will be limited in what you can get approved for.

You must then reestablish mainstream credit. Commit to make early or on-time payments. After you have a few major bank cards, secured bank loan, new car, and mortgage, then consider using credit only as a convenience. Make it a goal to minimize your debt.

Is it possible to recover from bankruptcy? YES. All you need to do is decide on a good plan, and then simply follow the plan. This book will get you started.

*"I am truly thankful for your help. Thanks for help-
ing us change our paradigms in how we approach
our finances and credit—I actually have a plan and
am working at implementing other strategies you
shared at the seminar."*

"I wanted to let you know some good news. It has been eight
months since I received the discharge for my BK and four
months since I attended your seminar. Two weeks ago, I used
your strategy for purchasing a new auto. I didn't even set foot
on the premises of the dealership until the deal was all but
signed. I dealt only with the Finance Manager by phone. He
actually complimented me twice and said, 'It was a breath of
fresh air to work with someone so prepared.' I was able to
lease a new car at 3.5% from a mainstream lender with nothing but the 1st payment down!!! I just set the car payment up
on EFT from my checking account two weeks before it is due
to show an early payment every month. I am truly thankful for
your help. Thanks for helping us change our paradigms in how
we approach our finances and credit—I actually have a plan
and am working at implementing other strategies you shared
at the seminar. UDA MAN!!"

Robert Ashcraft
Wilmore, Kentucky

The 6 Questions Lenders Will Ask After You File Chapter 7

When I first began applying for credit after my bankruptcy I noticed a trend. Lenders asked me the same questions over and over again. They all seemed to care about a few key things. Of course, now I realize they were trying to quickly assess if I was creditworthy or not.

You see, after you file bankruptcy, lenders will be very cautious when considering if they should extend you credit (and rightfully so).

Can you blame them? After bankruptcy your number one mission is to prove to lenders you're now a low credit risk.

So what do they want to see from you? The right answers to the following six questions:

1. Are you discharged?

2. When was your bankruptcy discharged?

3. How have you paid your bills since your discharge?

4. What new credit have you established since the bankruptcy?

5. How much do you have for a down payment?

6. What are your FICO® credit scores?

QUESTION 1: ARE YOU DISCHARGED?

Reestablishing credit after bankruptcy starts after you receive your discharge letter from the court, not a minute before. With a copy of this letter in hand, many lenders will welcome you with open arms the very day you receive it. Especially bank card companies and car dealers.

The reason lenders want to know that you're discharged is because if your bankruptcy is still "open," then you could technically still add accounts to your bankruptcy (including the lender you're applying with). Not many lenders are going to grant you credit when you still have the ability to include them in your bankruptcy.

Make sure you don't confuse the term "filed" with the term "discharged."

Filed means your bankruptcy is in its beginning stages. Your filing date is the day your bankruptcy attorney puts your bankruptcy petition on record with the court.

Discharged means your bankruptcy is complete or finished, meaning that any debt included in the bankruptcy is no longer your responsibility.

Another bankruptcy term that is important for you to know is "dismissed." Hopefully you haven't had a bankruptcy dismissed. In 2006 alone, there were 232,742 dismissed bankruptcies. Having a dismissed bankruptcy is bad, bad, bad. You basically receive most of the negative effects of filing bankruptcy—but none of the benefits—since your bankruptcy was not completed.

HOW TO KNOW IF YOUR BANKRUPTCY IS DISCHARGED

How do you know you're discharged?

The bankruptcy court will send out a discharge letter that is usually one piece of paper that simply shows the date your bankruptcy was discharged.

If you filed Chapter 7 bankruptcy, you usually receive your discharge 90 to 120 days after you file.

If you filed Chapter 13, you'll usually receive your discharge letter within 6 months after you complete all your payments to your trustee.

Be sure to put your discharge letter in a safe place. You will need this little piece of paper, as well as the rest of your bankruptcy paperwork, in the future. In fact, you may want to make a few copies and store them in a file folder.

Whatever you do...never...ever...under any circumstance give a lender original copies of your bankruptcy paperwork. You'll never see it again. It has happened to me many times.

If you're not sure if you're discharged or not, you need to find out.

Contact your bankruptcy attorney or the bankruptcy court where your bankruptcy was filed and inquire as to how you may acquire a copy of your discharge letter.

When a lender asks if you're discharged you need to be able to honestly say, "YES" and tell them the date of your discharge.

QUESTION 2: WHEN WAS YOUR BANKRUPTCY DISCHARGED?

This is very simple. The more time that has passed since your discharge—the better.

You see, each lender has different credit guidelines. A lender's credit guidelines are essentially their minimum requirements that you have to meet in order for them to approve your application.

For instance, you won't be able to finance a new car at a low interest rate until you're discharged. Being discharged is a basic credit guideline for most auto lenders when financing a car after bankruptcy.

Mortgage lending requirements are more complicated. How much time you have after your discharge will determine what type of mortgage financing you qualify for. Anything less than 24 months after your discharge and you're considered a sub-prime borrower. If you have more than 24 months after discharge you may qualify for more conventional mortgage programs.

In addition, banks will want several years of perfect credit before they will extend unsecured credit to you again. And in some cases, as long as your bankruptcy still appears on your credit reports, certain banks will not extend credit at all.

QUESTION 3: HOW HAVE YOU PAID YOUR BILLS SINCE YOUR DISCHARGE?

A lot of lenders are willing to give you a second chance. But, if you neglect to pay your bills on time after a bankruptcy, you'll have a hard time establishing credit with reputable lenders.

Late payments appearing on your credit reports after a discharged bankruptcy will extend the dark cloud of bankruptcy hovering over your head for years.

You might as well walk around with a sign over your head that says, "I don't pay my bills on time—please charge me the highest possible interest rate."

Let's be clear. You want to keep late payments from appearing on your credit reports. Lenders will look to see how you've handled your credit since your discharge. And if you think late payments hurt you...collection accounts, judgments, and other nasty things like those will be much worse.

You need to be able to tell a lender that you've paid everything early or on time since your discharge. When they review your credit reports they will see what you're saying is true.

QUESTION 4: HAVE YOU ESTABLISHED NEW CREDIT SINCE YOUR DISCHARGE?

Avoidance is not recovery.

Some lenders need you to reestablish credit after bankruptcy. In fact, most mortgage guidelines dictate that you must have at least three new lines of credit to qualify for a mortgage. You must give lenders something to work with. Show them new lines of credit. Show them timely payments. Show them mainstream lenders on your credit report. Show them a down payment. Show them one or two accounts carried through your bankruptcy.

The types of new credit you need to strive for are:

1. Secured credit cards
2. Retail credit card
3. Secured bank or credit union loan
4. Car loan or lease
5. Home mortgage
6. Unsecured credit card
7. Home equity loan
8. Gasoline credit card
9. Overdraft protection

The catch-22 is that the lenders you really want to work with may not want to be the first ones to grant you credit. It can be frustrating trying to open that first account—which is why you need a strategic plan of attack. In other words, don't apply for an unsecured platinum credit card if you can't even qualify for a secured credit card yet.

However, not all new credit is good for you. Stay away from: finance companies, high-interest auto loans, rent-to-own, and other high-interest companies. Using a lot of this type of credit will label you—not to mention cost you a lot more. Stick with mainstream lenders.

QUESTION 5: HOW MUCH MONEY DO YOU HAVE FOR A DOWN PAYMENT?

It will be necessary in most cases to be able to come up with a down payment or deposit. So start saving!

As a general rule of thumb, if you made all your payments as agreed on your last car, you should plan on no more than $500 to finance a new car at a normal interest rate.

On the other hand, if you made late payments on your last auto loan, your only option will most likely be 20% down at a high interest rate through a finance company.

If a car dealer is telling you to come up with more money, you're either at the wrong dealer...or you need to wait until you've increased your credit scores a little more.

If you want a good secured credit card—plan on depositing around $250 to $500. There are some secured credit cards that you can get that have lower deposits, but I don't recommend them. Most of the lower-deposit cards have hidden fees...don't report to the credit reporting agencies properly...and usually have hidden problems you find out after the fact.

A down payment on a home will obviously depend on the purchase price. Although 3% to 5% of the purchase price is considered the norm—it's more than possible to get a mortgage with no money down. And I'm not talking about predatory lenders or some crazy television infomercial that's promising you the world. I'm talking about real, bona fide mortgage programs—the same ones people with good credit use.

So be prepared. Have a little money down to show you're serious.

QUESTION 6: WHAT ARE YOUR FICO® CREDIT SCORES?

When I was recovering from bankruptcy, credit scoring was just starting to become popular. You couldn't even purchase all 3 of your credit scores before 2003.

Today credit scores are used by nearly every lender in the United States and Canada. You should be able to recite all three of your FICO credit scores at the drop of a hat.

Do you know your three FICO credit scores?

It's important to know which credit reporting agency has your:

- HIGHEST credit score

- MIDDLE credit score

- LOWEST credit score

To gain the most leverage over any lender you should choose to work with the lender that uses the credit reporting agency that has your HIGHEST FICO® credit score. This way you receive the lowest interest rate and best terms.

As a bankrupt person the absolute most important action you can take is to immediately begin working to increase your credit scores after you've been discharged.

These are the six major questions any lender will ask you. Sure, there will be more questions. But these are the foundational questions that everything else will be built upon.

*"I got my FICO scores on April 21, 2007.
To my surprise, they are: Equifax—806, Trans-
Union—817 and Experian—824!"*

"I was laid off from my job as a medical technologist in 1996.
I had to sell my home. Because my next job paid less than
half of what I was earning, I declared Chapter 13 bankruptcy in
1998. It was paid off about four years later. Meanwhile, I was
turned down for store credit at Best Buy and Circuit City. That
was before I attended your seminar. I qualified for a mortgage
in 2005 and bought the condo I was renting. Long story short,
I got my FICO scores on April 21, 2007. To my surprise, they
are: Equifax—806, TransUnion—817 and Experian—824! I
have never had such high scores, even before bankruptcy. My
income is still lower than it was when I was working at the hos-
pital, but I don't feel deprived financially and I can pretty much
have whatever I want. (Fortunately, I don't have fancy tastes.) I
enjoy your newsletters and just wanted to share with you and
your readers that by just hanging in there and making sure no
payments are ever late, you can be successful in overcoming
you worst financial situations."

Patricia Wicker
Robstown, Texas

The 4 Questions Lenders Will Ask After You File Chapter 13

For the most part, lenders are going to ask a Chapter 13 filer similar types of questions to the ones they ask Chapter 7 filers. However, there are some unique characteristics that Chapter 13 filers have that require additional information. Here are the 4 questions a lender will ask a Chapter 13 filer.

1. Are you discharged?

2. Have you made your trustee payments on time during the bankruptcy?

3. Will your trustee approve the loan?

4. How much time do you have left until you are discharged?

QUESTION ONE: ARE YOU DISCHARGED?

With the exception of a mortgage, most everything for a Chapter 13 filer starts after the discharge date. Most lenders will not touch you until that date. The ones that will approve you (with a few exceptions) are going to offer you very high interest rates, and probably will be frowned upon by your trustee.

That's why this question means something a little different to Chapter 13 filers, because a discharge indicates that you: (1) no longer have to get permission from your trustee to apply for credit and (2), have completed your bankruptcy, which lenders like to see.

If you filed Chapter 13, your discharge papers should arrive within 6 months after you complete your payments to your trustee.

QUESTION TWO: HAVE YOU MADE YOUR TRUSTEE PAYMENTS ON TIME DURING THE BANKRUPTCY?

For most Chapter 13 filers, their trustee payments are their only payment record from the time they file until they are discharged. In fact, many lenders will look at how you made payments to the trustee as one way of reestablishing credit.

QUESTION THREE: WILL YOUR TRUSTEE APPROVE THE LOAN?

When you are in a Chapter 13, everything runs through your trustee. It's his or her job to make sure that you do not get overextended again, and that you meet all the obligations you've agreed to with your creditors. When you apply for new credit, you must get it approved by your trustee first. Here's the legal "mumbo jumbo" from section 1305 of the bankruptcy law that explains this:

"§ 1305. Filing and allowance of postpetition claims

(a) A proof of claim may be filed by any entity that holds a claim against the debtor—

(2) that is a consumer debt, that arises after the date of the order for relief under this chapter, and that is for property or services necessary for the debtor's performance under the plan.

(c) A claim filed under subsection (a)(2) of this section shall be disallowed if the holder of such claim knew or should have known that prior approval by the trustee of the debtor's incurring the obligation was practicable and was not obtained."

Basically, this means that you must obtain permission from the Chapter 13 Trustee or the Court any time you want to apply for credit while you are in a Chapter 13 bankruptcy. Approval is extremely difficult before the bankruptcy is confirmed, which usually occurs two to three months after filing.

I'm not an attorney, so you'll have to speak to one you trust to get the real deal. Bottom line: if approval is not likely, most types of lenders are not going to work with you.

QUESTION FOUR: HOW MUCH TIME DO YOU HAVE LEFT UNTIL YOU ARE DISCHARGED?

There are options for you, even while you are still in your Chapter 13. You may be able to do a "buyout." This is often done through refinancing your mortgage and paying the balance of your Chapter 13 debt. The best programs for this type of deal are through FHA and VA. Speak to a mortgage lender you trust first.

The thing to be cautious of is that every state handles "buyouts" differently. In some states you could stir up more problems just by asking your trustee. In addition, each trustee may have a different belief system as to what's "right" and what's "wrong." For that reason, it's important you start with the lender. Ask if they've been able to do what you want with others in your state. Then get approval from your trustee.

These are the 4 additional major questions any lender will ask you if you have a Chapter 13 bankruptcy. Use these with the questions in Chapter 8 to develop a game plan when applying for a loan.

"I am glad to be able to write you because it means I have a success story to share. Because of unwise 'investments' I found myself filing for Chapter 7. Once I filed, my attitude was 'no more credit cards' and to live on a cash-only basis. Two months after I was discharged, I got in the mail a credit card offer for $400. Then another offer came for $200. Finally in the Summer, I got another card for $1000. All of these cards were unsecured but at high interest rates. My wife and I were buying using only cash. Then I got the best invitation I had ever gotten in a long time, that is, an invitation to your seminar. My first question was: What is he selling? As I listened to your seminar, I was more than happy that I attended. I learned so much, from FICO scores to fake credit scores that the credit reporting agencies want to sell us. I bought your book *Credit After Bankruptcy*. I read it and applied everything in it. We started paying our bills early, keeping a low balance on our credit cards, buying our FICO scores on a regular basis from Myfico.com/12 and monitoring our credit report from the company you suggested. Our scores began to ascend at a nice pace. We began thinking about purchasing a new home, thus we began to clean up our financial home. Having practiced your principles we began to search for a house. In December we got an approval letter for a $250,000 mortgage. While searching for a house, we began counting the 14-day credit inquiry clock so that any inquiry for mortgage would be counted as one inquiry and our FICO scores would not suffer. At that time my scores were 678, 711, and 719 and my wife's middle score was 701. With those scores every lender we went to was approving us. They said not to worry about the BK on my credit reports. At this point, we found a house, we got approval and all we needed to put down was $1000, since the builder was going to pay all closing costs (about $7,000). We signed all the documents and were going to have our house in about 8 months or about in August. But my wife's sixth sense told me, No, No, get your money back. And I did. The house was not worth it. A 1610 square feet house for $280,000. No way. In addition, today that builder is not doing well, not many sales, poor materials. It is good to listen to that super sixth sense. We were a little disappointed, but we did not give up. However, in January, we signed a contract for a 2,500 square feet two story house which costs us $280,000. My wife's sixth sense said: 'this is it.' Last Friday we closed on the new construction house at 6.5% with 0% down. Before our closing I again used the 14-day inquiry period to see who could beat our current lender. During the 14-day inquiry period, I got my truck refinanced at a lower rate which has cut down my monthly car payment by $50. I also applied for a credit card during that time and got approved in 1 day for $10,000 at 0% on all balance transfer and purchases for one year and a low interest rate there after. My mortgage company, auto lender, and recent credit card company are all MAJOR BANKS. They are some of the top banks in the nation. I have so much to thank you for, Stephen. You have changed our lives in a great way. When people hear me talk about finances, they think I am some top notch financial expert that works on Wall Street. You cannot imagine what 'monster' you have created since I am not satisfied with our FICO scores only being over 700 (my wife's has reached 735). We want to go above 750 and will try to even join the 800 club. I am sure we can if we continue to practice what you have taught us. I enjoy reading your e-mails along with the success stories. I have heard you been called God sent, priceless, the man, etc. These are all true. To me you are to BK and Financial recovery what Jordan is to basketball, what Tiger Woods is to golf, what Pelé is to soccer, what Bill Gates is to money, what Maria Sharapova is to tennis, what Peyton Manning is to football; you get the point. You are the man all the way. Thank you again and keep up the excellent work."

Shawn Shaiman
Osceola, Arkansas

The 34 Things You Must Know After Bankruptcy

There are certain things you must know in order to speed up your recovery from bankruptcy. The following is a list of the 34 most important.

NUMBER 1: CHOOSE MAINSTREAM CREDIT OVER HIGH-INTEREST CREDIT

The only credit that you should consider obtaining is what I call "mainstream" credit. This is the type of credit you are proud to have on your credit reports. Mainstream lenders also tend to offer single-digit interest rates.

A student in our very first seminar in April 1995 raised his hand and complained that no one would give him mainstream credit. I asked him about his current credit situation. He proudly explained that his car was financed at 26% and his mortgage was at 21%. His credit cards were north of 21%. His new computer was also with a high-interest finance company. He went on and on. The lesson is that lenders consider you a prime high-interest customer if you already have a lot of high-interest credit. Avoid high-interest credit like the plague. By sticking to mainstream lenders, you shorten the amount of time the dark cloud of filing bankruptcy follows you. If you're offered high-interest credit—just say, "No."

Some examples of mainstream credit are:

- Major credit cards issued from a bank
- Secured bank loans
- Car manufacturer financing
- Reputable mortgage lenders
- Bank loans
- Credit union loans (if the credit union reports to all three national credit reporting agencies)

Pick the companies you do business with just as closely as a movie star would select a movie role. You don't see Harrison Ford starring in B movies. He has a reputation and public image to uphold. The same goes for you with mainstream credit. High-interest financing is tempting, but it will lead you to ruin.

Then there are the sneaky kinds of high-interest finance companies hidden within large retail companies. Home Depot is a national home improvement supply store with financing programs provided by high-interest financing companies. Not good. However, a trend is developing among newer retail stores to provide bank financing (spelled b-a-n-k). A great example of this is Target, which offers financing through Target National Bank.

So what's the big deal? For starters, high-interest financing is very expensive. You're trying to recover, not go deeper into debt. More importantly, mainstream financing attracts more mainstream financing. High-interest financing attracts more high-interest financing.

Some examples of high-interest financing are:

- Buy-here-pay-here auto companies
- Finance companies
- Rent-to-own companies
- Department store finance programs
- Investor financing for mortgages
- Sub-prime auto financing through car dealers

It's difficult to turn away from high-interest financing. We were tempted many times. Thank God we didn't do it. We wouldn't be where we are today if we had. Mainstream credit is worth waiting for. It really is. It's the difference between recovering in months or years. The choice is yours.

NUMBER 2: PURCHASE YOUR CREDIT SCORES

Unlike your credit reports, which you can get for free, you must purchase your credit scores. Your credit scores are based on the information appearing on your credit reports. However, you must be careful and purchase your *real* credit scores.

There is a huge scam being perpetrated on the American public today. TransUnion™, Experian®, and their affiliated companies are selling you consumer credit scores, instead of your FICO® credit scores.

What you need to know is that when you apply for any credit-related transaction, the lender or bank will look at your FICO credit scores. They will NOT look at consumer credit scores. Consumer credit scores are useless.

These companies know that most folks don't understand the difference between a useless consumer credit score and a real FICO credit score. So they created these fake consumer credit scores to increase their revenue. They often offer these useless consumer credit scores to you free if you purchase one of their products or services.

If you've ever been on a website and it says something like: "Order today, and get your FREE credit scores..." the scores are FAKE!

Here's how to tell the difference between a fake consumer credit score and a FICO credit score...if it doesn't explicitly say it's a FICO score...it's fake.

FICO is Fair Isaac Corporation's registered brand name and they are very proud of it. If it's a real FICO score, trust me, it's going to say "FICO" all over the place.

Now, let's expose a few of the fake score sites.

If you want to purchase your real FICO credit scores don't use any of these sites:

Experian.com	FAKE
Transunion.com	FAKE
Creditexpert.com	FAKE
Consumerinfo.com	FAKE
Freecreditreport.com	FAKE
Truecredit.com	FAKE
Truelink.com	FAKE
creditXpert.com	FAKE

If you've ever ordered your credit scores from one of these sites, you've been ripped-off! And these are only some of the more popular sites. There are many more sites that offer consumer credit scores. Ignore all the flashy television commercials, radio spots, internet come-ons, and propaganda from companies offering credit scores. If they promise you free credit scores...something fishy is going on. Either they're not real FICO® credit scores...or the fine print tells you you've just subscribed to a service that charges a monthly fee.

If you purchase a consumer credit score, and take it to a lender, you'll become frustrated.

I hear about this from lenders all the time. A person comes into their office with their credit scores. But when they compare their real FICO credit scores with their consumer credit scores, they're different. In some cases the scores are very different—to the point they cannot qualify for what they thought they could, based on their consumer scores.

And worse, predatory lenders will know they have someone who doesn't really understand credit scoring, and they may try to take advantage of you.

The best place to purchase your 3 FICO credit scores is from: *www.myfico.com/12*. At: *www.myfico.com/12* you not only get all 3 of your real credit scores that lenders actually use, you also get your 12 negative reason codes, which tell you exactly what you have to do to increase your scores.

NUMBER 3: ASK LENDERS FOR THEIR CREDIT GUIDELINES

Every lender establishes minimum credit requirements to determine who gets approved and who gets denied for credit. These are called credit guidelines.

Credit guidelines can be as simple as...

- Must have 2 years after bankruptcy and a FICO credit score from Equifax® of 678

Or as complicated as...

- Middle score of 600

- 12 months of bank statements to average deposits to calculate monthly income
- No more than 30 days late on mortgage or rent
- 3 old or new tradelines, 2 with a 24 month history and 1 with a $5,000 credit limit
- No foreclosure in the last 12 months or discharge at least 12 months old
- Debt-to-income ratio of no more than 45%

By knowing your credit scores and details of your bankruptcy, it's possible to know if you'll get credit approved before you ever fill out a loan application.

You accomplish this by asking a lender what the credit guidelines are BEFORE you apply for credit. Not after.

But be careful when dealing with lenders who hire telephone operators to take applications over the phone. These innocent people do not know anything about credit guidelines. In fact, the only thing they usually "know" is completely wrong information.

If I had a dollar for every time a telephone operator told me something in error, I could retire to Beverly Hills.

Shortly after my bankruptcy was discharged I was ready to switch my cellular telephone service from a "pay-as-you-go" plan (which was popular back then) to a normal credit plan. I never exceeded the $125-a-month cap on the account, but I was tired of paying a premium per-minute rate. I felt that I had established an excellent payment record with them over the last six months. So I called customer service. A woman answered and informed me that I must wait until my contract was up for renewal in 18 months. I begged and pleaded. She insisted I had to wait 18 months. I ended the call.

A few minutes went by. I didn't want to wait 18 months. I called again. I spoke with another woman. This time I received a different answer. She told me to wait six months. I hung up and waited a few more minutes, then called back. A man answered the phone this time. He told me it takes up to 48 hours to determine whether the company would put me into a normal account. I put in my request and waited for his return call. They approved me. The next day I received a new phone, a new number, a lower monthly payment, and a cheaper per-minute rate. The best part was my monthly cellular phone bill was cut in half the following billing cycle.

Remember, you may talk to people who are paid minimum wage for answering a telephone. They usually are not paid for their knowledge to understand the whole operation. They are paid to answer only certain questions. Anything out of the norm, they typically guess. Keep calling until you get what you want or at least the same answer more than three times.

NUMBER 4: PAY YOUR BILLS EARLY, WORST CASE ON TIME

Paying your bills early after bankruptcy is important. Mainstream credit lenders will first look to see if you pay your bills on time after bankruptcy. After all, it's a pretty good indication of whether you have truly redeemed yourself from previous bad habits. It's your strongest asset when you apply for credit. It is one of the essential keys to reestablishing new credit after bankruptcy.

Before our bankruptcy, I refused to allow my wife to handle our checkbook, thinking it's a man's job! I finally gave her control, and now I enjoy not having to deal with it. She handles it better than me, anyway. So if you're not good at managing the checkbook, find someone who is.

You must also understand which bills, if paid late, will not affect you negatively. For us, it was our fitness club membership dues, long distance phone bill, and internet service provider. As a general rule, if a company reports to the credit reporting agencies, pay on time. How do you know if they report? Get a copy of each of your three credit reports and look to see if they report.

Falling short now and then may seem normal. It's not. I challenge you to take a serious look at your finances. Falling short is a financial red flag. Where there is smoke there is fire. Quickly determine what is causing this problem, and fix it before it gets out of control.

When you pay your monthly bills for your revolving credit accounts (e.g., Visa, MasterCard, Shell, Victoria's Secret), always pay more than the minimum payment due. The Sears Tower in downtown Chicago was probably paid for by people who pay only their minimum payment due. When we began our recovery from bankruptcy, my wife and I always paid more than the minimum amount due, sometimes even four to six times the amount due. Today we rarely carry monthly balances at all—we usually pay the entire amount off each month. Worst case scenario, you should pay at least one dollar above the minimum payment due each month.

NUMBER 5: UNDERSTAND THE DIFFERENCE BETWEEN YOUR FILING DATE AND YOUR DISCHARGE DATE

Don't confuse the term "filed" with the term "discharged."

As I explain in the last chapter: filed means your bankruptcy is in its beginning stages. Your filing date is the day your bankruptcy attorney puts your bankruptcy petition on record with the court. Discharged means your bankruptcy is complete or finished, meaning that any debt included in the bankruptcy is no longer your responsibility.

This is important. Unless you filed a Chapter 13 bankruptcy, everything begins from your discharge date. For example, if a mortgage lender's policy is to extend credit to people with a bankruptcy after two years, what that really means is two years after the discharge date. Memorize your discharge date. If you don't know it, call your attorney or local bankruptcy court and ask how to obtain a copy of your discharge letter. If you filed Chapter 7, your discharge letter should take no more than 120 days to arrive.

Chapter 13 filers will have to wait approximately 3.5 to 5.5 years to receive their discharge letter. Essentially, they must get approval through their trustee to acquire most types of new credit after bankruptcy (which can be done) or wait until they receive their discharge before reestablishing credit.

Regardless if you filed Chapter 7 or Chapter 13, it would be a good idea to make two copies of your entire bankruptcy paperwork. One complete set for you and one for lenders to borrow—especially if you want a mortgage. Some attorneys will gladly give you a copy. Others will charge you. You will need it sooner or later, so do it now. The longer you wait, the more difficult and expensive it may be to obtain.

The majority of lenders base their lending decisions on how long it's been since you've been discharged. There are exceptions, especially if you filed Chapter 13, but they're rare.

So when a lender tells you they need two years after your bankruptcy to approve you...what they're really saying is they need two years after your discharge date.

NUMBER 6: AVOID THE TEMPTATION OF HAVING A CO-SIGNER OR BECOMING A CO-SIGNER

You may become tempted to have a friend, grandparent, or Mommy and Daddy co-sign for you.

Big mistake.

Having co-signers weakens your position to gain new credit in your own name.

Once a lender sees you've had a co-signer before, they'll want you to get a co-signer for any loan they offer you. They'll be looking to protect themselves. They'll want someone else on the hook in case you default—just like your previous lenders. It's best not to have co-signers so lenders don't get any ideas.

In addition, a co-signed loan may not even help your credit scores if you're not the primary borrower (the person whose name is first on the credit application). If you're the primary borrower the account should show up on your credit reports, and if it's paid on time it will help you. If you're not the primary borrower, it may not report and you'll be out of luck. Each lender determines how they report. Only information appearing on your credit reports helps you reestablish your credit.

Also, if you happen to be in a position to become a co-signer for someone else, be careful. My friend Jim Rohn (America's foremost business philosopher) learned the meaning of the word "co-signer"... to the tune of $250,000.

He co-signed for a business line of credit for some young businessmen he knew very well. Later the bank called asking when he was planning on making the loan payment. The word "c-o-s-i-g-n-e-r" cost him over $31,000 for each letter. You can hear Jim's story and many others in his inspirational audio course called *The Weekend Seminar* (my favorite).

I have a core belief...and it goes something like this, "Lend people money only if you can afford not to get it back and you won't hold a grudge if you don't—but never ever lend people your credit."

If you're thinking about co-signing for someone...

Don't do it. There is too much at stake. If the borrower defaults on the loan, two things will happen to your credit reports and FICO® credit scores:

1. If the loan goes into default, the lender looks to you to make the payment(s)...so have your checkbook ready.

2. Each time the loan becomes 30 days past due, a late payment will appear on your credit report(s) for up to 7 years...and as a result your credit scores will be lower than they could be.

Additionally, when you co-sign...

- The payment you co-signed for is calculated in your debt-to-income ratio. So going in debt for someone else could actually prevent you from getting the credit you need when you need it. And it could increase the cost of credit since your scores may be lower.

- When each lender reviews your credit report(s) to consider the loan, they will post a credit inquiry that will lower your credit scores.

- Your own credit card interest rates could skyrocket. In what is becoming a more common practice, credit card issuers are reviewing your credit reports and looking for how you manage credit with other companies. This is called a "universal review" of your credit reports and if the outcome is bad, your interest rates can dramatically increase with little notice (this recently happened to one of my employees).

- The added debt could lower your insurance credit scores to the point where it could impact your ability to get or keep homeowner's and auto insurance or cause your premiums to increase.

As you can see, there is very little value in either getting a co-signer or co-signing a loan. But there is a lot of downside risk.

Just one final note, don't get co-signing confused with co-borrowing...that's something different altogether. Co-borrowing is a common practice among married couples on a loan for a car or mortgage. And there is nothing wrong with co-borrowing. The goal, however, would be not to have everything held together. You need to build individual and joint credit so you can weather a storm (e.g., death, loss of job, serious illness) on your own if need be.

NUMBER 7: UNDERSTAND THE DIFFERENCE BETWEEN W-2 AND 1099 INCOME

w-2 income is when you are employed by a company. 1099 income is generally when you are self-employed or an independent contractor.

w-2 income is easier to verify. It's less work and less paperwork for lenders. Your chances of reestablishing credit will be greatly enhanced if your income can be supported by w-2s.

Mortgage lenders generally look at the last two years to qualify you. Most other lenders primarily look at your FICO® credit scores. Each lender is different. An auto dealer may not even check your income. A mortgage company or bank will want everything documented and may check all three credit reporting agencies. A credit card company, if they have time, may simply do a telephone verification of employment.

Here's a word of caution if you plan on changing jobs at the same time you're looking for a mortgage or refinancing—make sure you talk to your mortgage lender before you change jobs. It will save you headaches and stress.

For example, my friend Luis and his wife, Lee, were interested in refinancing their mortgage. Luis had been a w-2 employee for years and recently became self-employed. Although he was in the same line of work, he no longer qualified for refinancing because he went from w-2 to self-employed. Much to Luis's surprise, he discovered he needed to wait two years after his employment change. Many entrepreneurs face this same problem.

So if you're intending to start a new business right after bankruptcy, you may want to start part-time and eventually move into full-time over an extended period. That isn't to say that reestablishing credit after bankruptcy with 1099 income is impossible. It's very possible. As long as you can prove your income through your tax returns and/or pay stubs, you should be OK.

My wife and I were both self-employed while obtaining the majority of our new credit after bankruptcy. It can be done.

NUMBER 8: KNOW THE BENEFITS OF LIVING IN A LARGE CITY VERSUS A SMALL CITY

I was born and raised in a very small town. I could count the stoplights on my two hands. Our entire family was within a 20-minute drive. There are benefits to small towns, but establishing credit after bankruptcy is not one of them.

As adults, my wife and I made a decision to move from South Bend, Indiana, to Indianapolis in February 1993. It was a tough decision, but it became one of the best decisions we've ever made. It's true, the larger the city, the more options you will have. Lenders in smaller towns seem to be more rigid. There are always exceptions to the rule, but this is important to consider.

What does this mean, exactly?

- It could mean that an innovative banker is more likely to be located in a larger city than a small town

- It could mean a car dealership in a large city has enough volume of business to convince their underwriters to take marginal deals from bankrupt people

- Or maybe there are more homes available in a big city and it's easier to find a motivated seller (who wants to get out of the big city to move to a small town)

- It might mean having access to a wider variety of creative mortgage lenders other than your hometown bank

- Not to mention, bigger cities usually have higher paying jobs

In summary, you will probably have many more options in a larger city. It worked for us.

NUMBER 9: BANKRUPTCY IS ONLY A SEASON IN YOUR LIFE

Summer starts and sadly ends. Fall begins and turns into winter. Winter turns into spring. Just like each season plays a part in the course of a year, the effects of bankruptcy are just a season in your life as well.

So resolve in your mind that the effects of your bankruptcy aren't permanent. Bankruptcy is only a season in your life. This too shall pass. Remember, if you do the right things after bankruptcy... you can speed up your recovery.

NUMBER 10: EMBRACE TIER SCHEDULES

In the old days, you were either approved or denied credit. It was either YES or NO.

Today, thanks to the widespread use of credit scoring, lenders rarely just say, "No." They say, "Yes," but at higher interest rates to compensate for higher risk.

What lenders use to match your FICO® score to the rate they will charge you is called a tier schedule.

The higher your credit scores—the lower your interest rate. It's just that simple.

So, while credit scores have allowed more people than ever to qualify for low interest rates, they have also justified lenders charging higher rates as well. It's a two-way street.

You must work to obtain the highest scores possible. Then use your high scores to leverage the best deal for you. It's all about your credit scores.™

NUMBER 11: YBF

Sometimes people who file bankruptcy have an attitude. They feel they should be treated like everyone else. Well, yes and no. You need to build up to that. You need to start small and prove that you are financially responsible. Within months you will begin to regain a portion of the respect you deserve. But to completely recover takes time. Your first credit purchases after bankruptcy are important. Unlike most people who get to shop and make decisions based on what they want, you're buying the financing (YBF)!

So what does this mean, exactly? It means you ask the car dealer which car you should be looking at. It means that when shopping for a house you go to a mortgage lender to get pre-approved before you go house-hunting. It means ignoring the high interest rate on your credit card for the first year or so. Your whole approach to credit will change for the next 12 to 36 months. You're buying the financing.

The real question is...can you get financing at an interest rate and terms you can afford? The same is true for anything else you want to purchase on credit.

So many people get this turned around. They want a new car. So they decide exactly which one they want, talk to the salesperson, and take a test drive. Then they get frustrated when they are unable to obtain financing. I would encourage you to remember the YBF formula. It's really simple. Determine whether you can obtain financing first. Talk with the person who controls the money, not a salesperson—then apply.

NUMBER 12: WHAT THE WORD, "NO" REALLY MEANS

Parents will understand this. What does the word, "No" mean to children? That's right, absolutely nothing. At times they keep doing what you told them not to do.

As you begin trying to reestablish credit after bankruptcy you may hear the word, "No" a lot. Car dealers...mortgage lenders... credit card companies...banks...credit unions...you name it, they'll all tell you, "No." That's okay. Remember your children. Ignore the people who tell you, "No," and keep seeking a, "Yes."

"No" means absolutely nothing! If you're hearing the word "No," it either means you're talking to the wrong person, the wrong company, or your credit scores are not yet high enough to qualify for the specific loan or credit you want.

One powerful example of this principle in action was when I decided to start a small business shortly after bankruptcy. It was a home-based mail-order business that would depend heavily on customers giving their credit card numbers over the telephone. It was vital to this business to obtain what's called "merchant status." All this means is that my company would have the ability to accept customers' credit card numbers from people as a form of payment, just like at restaurants and stores.

I called every bank in the city. I immediately determined that banks frowned on three major issues:

(1) mail-order businesses,

(2) home-based businesses, and

(3) start-up businesses.

Rest assured, a previous bankruptcy did not help things. I was up for the challenge. I decided to meet with the bank that had the best program (in retrospect, I should have met with them last). Before I began filling out the credit application I asked the bank representative if a previous bankruptcy would be a problem. The woman froze. It was an awkward moment. I still wasn't completely over the fact that I had filed bankruptcy. I still felt like a financial leper. Her first words were something like, "We can't help you..." The meeting was over. I was told, "No."

Before I left the bank, I asked two very important questions. I asked, "Where would you go if you were me?" She didn't know.

My second question was, "May I speak with your supervisor?" She agreed, and proceeded to give me his telephone number.

I scheduled an appointment, and with my best suit on I met with the supervisor a few days later. It was a brief meeting. Maybe five minutes. I gave him my business plan and a two-minute sound bite, answered a few questions, then left. A few days later he called to request proof that I had obtained a small-business micro-loan a few weeks earlier. I faxed the loan agreement to him. Later that day I was given pre-approval for merchant status over the telephone from the sales representative who told me, "No." The final approval by committee took a few weeks. I was approved.

It was a great thing. My prayer was answered. I was excited—especially since I knew another business owner with good credit who couldn't get merchant status.

Years later I asked the bank supervisor what made him decide to grant me merchant status. He said it was my business plan and the new small-business micro-loan. By the way, the small business loan was for a whopping $2,000.

I could tell you so many more stories. They all have the same theme. And they all boil down to ignoring the word "No." You have to keep at it until you figure it out, which usually involves ignoring the wrong people and finding the right people to listen to.

What does "no" mean? Absolutely nothing.

NUMBER 13: UNDERSTAND HOW TO USE INDIVIDUAL AND JOINT ACCOUNTS TO YOUR ADVANTAGE

It's important that if you're married you make the extra effort to reestablish credit both as individuals and together.

I've witnessed many wives rely on their husband's credit. Everything is in their husband's name. I personally do not think it is a good strategy.

When we were first recovering, we realized how important it was to be sure that if one of us ever died, the surviving spouse would have reestablished credit as well. It also makes your credit applications much stronger when two credit-active borrowers are responsible for the loan. And let's face it, we need every advantage we can get.

We put our first car after bankruptcy in my wife's name with me as a co-applicant. Our second car was just the opposite. Our third car was in her name. Our fourth car was in my name. We have individual and joint bank loans, checking accounts, and savings accounts. Our home mortgages are in both names. We each have separate and joint credit cards.

If both of you are contributing to the household income, each of you should have individual accounts as well as joint credit accounts.

NUMBER 14: KNOW WHERE TO OBTAIN A COPY OF YOUR CRED-IT REPORTS

It's important to know the condition of your credit. There are three different credit reporting agencies. Ask around to find out which credit reporting agency is more commonly used in your area. The main telephone numbers to the three major credit reporting agencies are:

Equifax® *(800) 685-1111*

TransUnion™ *(800) 888-4213*

Experian® (formerly TRW) *(888) 397-3742*

You're allowed to get one free copy of your credit report from each of the three major credit reporting agencies on an annual basis (Georgia, Colorado, Massachusetts, New Jersey, Maine, Maryland, and Vermont get additional free reports). To get more information about ordering your free credit reports, go to: *www.annualcredit-report.com* or call: *(877) 322-8228*. However, the best way to obtain your free copy of each of your credit reports is by mail. You can go to: *https://www.annualcreditreport.com/cra/requestformfinal.pdf* and download the mail-in form.

If you've already accessed your free annual credit reports, you may want to purchase them directly from each of the three credit reporting agencies. To do this, contact the After Bankruptcy Foundation. They have created a free brochure called *How to Get Your Credit Reports* that will help you understand how much your credit reports cost, and where to purchase them. The brochure contains some useful information on other ways to qualify for free credit reports and also explains the different types of credit inquiries. You can email your request to: *maryann@afterbankruptcy.com.*

NUMBER 15: NEGATIVE PEOPLE HAVE FLEAS

Surround yourself with people who make you feel good when you're around them. People who make you grow. Who encourage and support you.

Mark Twain once said, "Keep away from people who try to belittle your ambitions. Small people always do that, but the really great make you feel that you, too, can become great."

People who live mediocre lives expect you to join them in their misery. Have no part of it. Negative people have fleas. If you get too close or stay too long, the fleas will jump out on you.

There are plenty of negative people in this world. Even your family can be a source of negativity. But there is a point where you must draw the line. It's okay to be around negative people for a brief time, but limit this time for your own benefit. In our case, we needed to distance ourselves from any type of negativity to enable us to move on with our lives.

When we first moved to Indianapolis there was a couple who befriended us. A nice young couple with a beautiful little girl just turning two. We had to limit the amount of time we spent with them because of what they said, their actions, and how they thought.

The man of the house was a real-life "Homer J. Simpson" who was barely making a living. Conversations with him were intolerable at best. He was always making negative remarks, justifying his own mediocrity. It was too much for me to handle. So we made a decision to severely limit the time we spent with them. It was hard at first. But our peace of mind was restored and our marriage improved.

NUMBER 16: UNDERSTAND THAT CASH IS QUEEN

The queen is the most powerful piece on the chessboard because she is the most versatile. That's what cash gives you, versatility.

You don't need a lot of cash to recover from bankruptcy. But you will need a little.

So if you're strapped for cash before you begin your recovery—it's best to start making some changes in your living expenses and daily spending habits, and focus on increasing your income.

You never know when you're going to need cash. You may need a deposit for a secured credit card...or a down payment on a new mortgage...or a new car loan. Even if you're able to qualify for no-money-down financing, it's always a good idea to have a cash reserve.

So if cash is queen, who is king? Your credit scores, of course!

NUMBER 17: MASTER THE "MULTIPLE USE" CONCEPT

Plan major projects around acquiring large sums of income or cash windfalls.

The idea is to figure out how many different things you can do with the money you have, with the intent to hopefully make it grow.

For instance, when our home equity loan closed recently, it triggered an entire series of events that we'd been planning for well over a year, including:

- Paying off one home equity line of credit (HELOC)
- Refinancing another HELOC into a home equity installment loan
- Paying off all revolving debt
- Buying a new home

We ended up with more money than we started with—and in the process, maintained credit scores that were nearly 800.

So before you spend your next tax refund check, inheritance, profit from the sale of your home, annual bonus, severance, home equity, or wedding cash...think about how you can strategically use the money for multiple projects at the same time.

NUMBER 18: THE POWER OF OPEN-ENDED QUESTIONS

Accept the fact that you don't know everything. Listen to what experienced people have to say. Save time by asking questions. It will help you accomplish your goals a lot faster.

Learn to ask open-ended questions. Let the curiosity of your childhood come back to life. It's a good thing. For example you can use open-ended questions such as, "What would you do if you were me?" or, "Do you know anyone who could possibly help me?"

That's how I first learned about Ford Motor Credit. My wife and I were turned down by Toyota Motor Credit for a new 1993 Toyota Corolla. As we were getting ready to leave I asked, "What would you do if you were me?" The lease finance manager said, "Visit the dealership across the street." He proceeded to tell us, "Ford Motor Credit has the best leasing program in the country. If anyone will take you, it will be Ford." (This isn't necessarily true in every city anymore.)

We couldn't believe our ears. That question led us to where we needed to be. We weren't excited about driving an American-made car, but remember—you're buying the financing. Ford leased us two new cars at very low interest rates that year.

By the way, we leased our fourth car after bankruptcy from the Toyota dealer that had told us about Ford. They just didn't want to be the first lender to extend credit to us after our bankruptcy.

You see, when a lender initially says, "No," it's just the beginning, not the end. You need to ask open-ended questions. If you ask enough people...eventually one of them will introduce you to exactly who and what you need. You just need to be persistent.

NUMBER 19: THE MAGIC NUMBER 24

Believe it or not, it can be easier to qualify for a mortgage than it is to get an unsecured credit card. I know it sounds weird, but it's true.

In fact, it's possible to get approved for a mortgage after bankruptcy even when your bankruptcy still appears on your credit reports.

After a bankruptcy, the three most important things in qualifying for a mortgage are usually your middle FICO® credit score, the length of time you've been discharged, and your ability to pay.

The easiest mortgage to qualify for after bankruptcy is called an FHA mortgage. An FHA loan is a home mortgage that allows for a purchase or refinance with a low down payment and is insured by the Federal Housing Administration.

FHA doesn't use credit scoring to make a loan decision. So as long as you have two years after discharge you usually get the same interest rate as everyone else. However, some FHA lenders are now using FICO credit scores to determine interest rates.

Other than the common-sense things you need to qualify for an FHA mortgage (like being able to afford the payments) the major credit qualification after bankruptcy is that you've been discharged for 24 months. If you've had a foreclosure, you'll need an additional 12 months with most lenders. And if you filed Chapter 13 and you're still making payments to your trustee, FHA/VA are the only mortgage programs that will allow you to purchase a home during the bankruptcy. After you're discharged, you'll have more options.

But be careful. Mortgage brokers don't earn nearly as much money getting you approved for an FHA loan. They'd much rather get you approved for a sub-prime mortgage. They make more money that way, and a sub-prime mortgage requires much less paperwork than an FHA government loan. This is one reason why it's critical to work with a mortgage lender that has your best interest in mind.

That's why I make sure there's always a good mortgage lender at the free Credit After Bankruptcy® seminar.

One last thing about FHA mortgages—in some cities they just don't make sense...like parts of California where the average priced home exceeds the FHA loan limit. In cases like this, a sub-prime loan is usually the best alternative. To determine the FHA loan limit in your area go online to: *https://entp.hud.gov/idapp/html/hicostlook.cfm*

The key to using the magic number "24" is to find an innovative lender. The fact is you're looking for a creative person, not a company. You don't do business with a company. You do business with a person.

NUMBER 20: KEEP THE FAITH

To understand the meaning of the word, "faith" let's first define it. According to the New Living Translation of the Bible...

> FAITH is the confidence that what we hope for will actually happen; it gives us assurance about things we cannot see.

So if you have to wait to see it...you don't have faith.

For example, in 2006 Michele and I purchased a new property. It was the most creative real estate deal we've made since we started investing. So creative, that it spooked the seller and his agent.

We had to educate them on how and why this deal made sense for both of us. There came a point where they said, "No." We pressed on. Even after they said, "No," and negotiations began breaking down, our faith in making the win/win deal a reality was strong enough to carry us through.

Faith gives you the power to believe that your dream will come true, but knowledge and perseverance are what turn that belief into reality. Sometimes that means you have to educate those around you.

NUMBER 21: TRANSFORM YOUR ATTITUDE

A friend of mine obtained a secured bank card with a low limit. He was shopping one day and saw a really nice coat he wanted to purchase. He realized that he was very close to his credit limit. He was declined authorization, since the purchase would put him a few dollars over his credit limit. He told me later that he planned to cancel that account because he felt their policy "sucked."

He had the wrong attitude. Closing an account could lower his credit scores.

Be thankful for the opportunity to reestablish credit. Lighten up. Maintain an attitude of thankfulness. You haven't had time to prove yourself financially responsible. That time will come. Be patient.

I can't tell you enough how your attitude affects other people. Just for fun, try this. Call a car dealership that you know you will never patronize. Ask to speak with the finance manager. Tell him your situation. Tell him you want a new car. Tell him what type of car you want. Tell him when you want it. Tell him what interest rate you expect. Tell him as much as you can. Then, ask if he can help you.

Now, call another car dealership. Ask to talk with the finance manager. Before he gets on the line, make a decision that this person knows more than you about cars and that you intend to listen more than you talk. Use his first name throughout the conversation. Explain your situation within 30 seconds. Ask him if this is a good time to talk. Ask him if he thinks he could help you. Ask him what he thinks you should do. Allow him to lead the discussion. Say things like, "That's interesting," or, "I never thought of that," or, "Good idea."

Lenders deal with difficult people all the time. A nice person who cares what they have to say is like a breath of fresh air. Don't give lenders an excuse not to go the extra mile for you. Be kind to everyone, and it will return to you multiplied.

NUMBER 22: THE POWER OF AGREEMENT

My wife and I are more powerful when we work as a team than we are individually. We each have our own strengths and weaknesses that compliment the other.

One of the most powerful commitments we have made in our marriage is to be in agreement on any major purchase or decision. And if we don't agree, we don't proceed. It's been challenging at times—especially anytime I want to buy anything that goes fast—but it's served us well.

And if you're not married...I'd encourage you to find someone to balance you. Find a good friend or someone you trust.

NUMBER 23: ACKNOWLEDGE YOUR WEAKNESSES—ACT ON YOUR STRENGTHS

Knowing your strengths and weaknesses is the key to personal growth.

I don't dwell on my weaknesses. I surround myself with people who make up for my weaknesses. I'm very clear on my unique abilities and try to limit myself to those tasks. Don't fool yourself into thinking you're good at everything—this will only slow your recovery. To learn about your strengths, go to: *www.kolbe.com* and take the Kolbe A Index.

NUMBER 24: RESPECT WOMEN AND THEIR SIXTH SENSE

Women are born with a "sixth sense." My wife told me many times, after meeting someone I intended to do business with, not to do business with them. She said, "There's just something I FEEL about them..."

If I had listened to her in the early years it would have saved a lot of grief. Men can learn this sixth sense, but women have it as standard equipment. Respect your wife's sixth sense. It can help you select people to help you recover faster from your bankruptcy.

NUMBER 25: MONITOR YOUR CREDIT REPORTS AND CREDIT SCORES

Monitoring your credit reports and credit scores are two different things requiring two different services.

A good credit report monitoring service notifies you when any of these changes are detected in your credit reports...

- Inquiries
- New accounts opened
- New public records
- Address changes
- Changes to public records
- Changes to account information

By monitoring changes on your three credit reports you minimize the risk of becoming a victim of identity theft, while becoming more informed about what is happening to your credit—when it's happening.

Monitoring your credit scores is a much different animal. A credit score monitoring service allows you to quickly see the relationship between how you manage your credit and its affect on your credit scores. Any time your credit score changes you would receive an email or text message.

A good credit score monitoring service tells you the reason for the change and allows you to log on to see how your score changed. It can be quite enlightening.

In a perfect world all three national credit reporting agencies would offer a service that monitors their version of your FICO® credit scores.

They don't. Only Equifax® does.

For more information on what I believe to be the best credit score monitoring service go to: *www.afterbankruptcy.org/scoremonitor*.

NUMBER 27: CREATE A VISION

A friend of mine named John Assaraf (you might recognize him from being involved with *The Secret*, which took the country by storm in 2007) passed on a very helpful strategy to me in the early stages of my bankruptcy.

He programs his mind with pictures. He got the idea from Olympic athletes who were trained to visualize their entire performance in their mind over and over again before their events.

For instance, if he wanted a new car he'd find the best picture he could and place it on a bulletin board. If he wanted a new watch or to meet a certain VIP, he'd do the same thing. Anything he desired he'd place on that board. He called it his visualization board (or vision board).

He placed his vision board where he would see it every day...on his home office wall. Every time he would place a picture on the board he would visualize himself already enjoying or achieving the thing.

One picture he placed on his vision board was a beautiful home he saw in *Dream Homes* magazine. When he moved to Southern California he began house shopping. He quickly found a home that seemed perfect. He made an offer and it was accepted.

It wasn't until a year later, after he moved into the home and found his old visualization board in some unpacked boxes that he realized...the home he purchased was the exact home from the picture on his vision board. True story.

Amazing isn't it?

That's the power of your mind. So many people focus on what they can't do. All my friend did was set a visual goal...envision the end result...look at it every day...and move toward the goal. What a great example of the power of goal setting.

Without a vision people perish. Make sure you have a vision. Write it down. Assign a date to accomplish it. If you don't do that, you're only wishing.

NUMBER 27: PLUG IN TO A LOCAL CHURCH

People ask Michele and me all the time how we stayed together during our bankruptcy. Our answer has remained the same. We got plugged in to a local church, began happily tithing, read our Bibles, and put into practice what we learned.

Of course, we've had setbacks, and in some cases major detours. That's life. We're not perfect. All we can do is learn from our mistakes and move on in faith.

There is a big difference between knowing about God and knowing God. Finding a place of worship is important to your spiritual growth. Think of yourself as a tree looking for fertile ground to bury your roots into. This fertile soil will help sustain you during difficult times in the transition into becoming financially responsible.

If you're like most people, walking into a large church can be an unnerving proposition. In fact, most people come out the same way they came in. This doesn't have to be.

Most churches now have what are called home groups. These are small groups of people within the church that meet on a regular basis. It's an opportunity to meet with other believers, share experiences, and pray for each other. It's like church all over again, just in a smaller, more personal setting. These groups usually meet in church members' homes.

I would encourage you to find a place of worship and get plugged in. If you have a friend who attends church, ask if you could go with him or her. Start there. Visit a few churches and prayerfully consider where God wants you to be. But don't take too long. There is no such thing on Earth as a perfect church. The sooner you get plugged in, the sooner you'll experience the rewards.

NUMBER 28: GIVING

Giving starts the receiving process.

If you don't have enough money, I bet I can guess how much you're giving away every paycheck...zero.

There was a time we weren't giving either.

But everything changed the day we made a commitment to give 10% of our money away each and every paycheck to our local church. We initially had enough faith to only give from our net income. We quickly switched to giving from our gross income and haven't looked back.

Do you happily give 10% of your income away every paycheck? If not...why not? And if you don't give...are you where you want to be financially?

If the habits you're currently committed to aren't working... maybe it's time to consider a different plan.

NUMBER 29: UNDERSTAND THAT RECOVERING FROM BANKRUPTCY IS MORE THAN JUST BEING ABLE TO BE APPROVED FOR CREDIT

I hear it a lot...

"...I don't need any help. I've already recovered from bankruptcy..."

After a few questions, it's clear these folks haven't recovered at all. Sure, they can get financed for a used car. But it's at 22% from AmeriCredit® and they needed to put $2,000 down...or they financed their home mortgage through a finance company with 10% down... or their credit cards have a whopping $200 limit, $170 in "set up fees," and a 29% interest rate.

That's not recovering.

Recovering properly from bankruptcy means you can qualify for credit on similar terms as people who've never filed for bankruptcy. It's all a matter of knowing where to go and how to structure the deal.

NUMBER 30: HOW MUCH CREDIT IS ENOUGH?

Recovering from bankruptcy and achieving a credit score of over 750 is not about how many credit accounts you can acquire—it's about having enough accounts, from the right lenders, and managing them well over time.

Overall I encourage people to rebuild their credit after bankruptcy by establishing these types of accounts:

- Start with a checking and savings account at a bank or credit union.

- Once you establish the basic accounts to deposit your money, you can get two secured Visas or MasterCards from two different lenders.

- Next, you may want to apply for one or two retail credit cards (just don't go crazy).

- When you demonstrate that you can handle your bank accounts without any problems, in most cities you can use the money in your savings account to get a secured bank loan.

- Depending on your needs, your next step may be to get a car financed through a captive lender, bank, or credit union (that reports to all three national credit reporting agencies).

- When you are ready, a home mortgage should be your next step. Mortgages have all kinds of benefits...they help your FICO® credit scores...they may give you a tax break...they are often an appreciating asset...they are usually cheaper than renting...and you can play your music as loud as you want.

■ When your credit scores surpass 700 it may be time to apply for a few unsecured credit cards. Just make sure you find out what their credit guidelines are first. You may have more success with your local banks than the big faceless national lenders.

■ A home equity loan can give you cash to increase the value in your current home...invest in more real estate...or provide seed money for your business (just be careful about the type of home equity loan you get...and it's still tax deductible).

When you go through all these steps, you'll have more than enough credit.

Of course, you're not going to run out and get all those accounts in one day. What I've listed here is a blueprint. It may take you a year or two (maybe longer). But, along the way, if you start to get these different forms of credit, your credit scores will increase (assuming you manage your credit well).

Once you have these accounts, it now becomes a waiting game while you properly manage your credit, pay all your bills and loans early (worst case on time), and allow enough time to pass to establish a stellar credit history.

Remember, it's not just about how much credit you've established, but how long you've had the credit that will help you increase your credit scores.

After analyzing thousands of credit reports, what I've seen first-hand is people with FICO® credit scores over 800 have a few things in common.

(1) They manage a few accounts from mainstream lenders.

(2) They manage these accounts well over a long period of time.

(3) They don't allow negative information to appear on their credit reports.

NUMBER 31: DON'T ALLOW EMOTIONS TO INFLUENCE YOUR DECISION MAKING

People tell me all the time that they filed bankruptcy to save their homes. These are homes that they have two or three mortgages on... have no equity in...or owe more on than the appraised value. They are too emotionally invested.

Allowing emotions to creep into your credit or financial decisions is dangerous at best.

When Michele and I bought our first home after bankruptcy it wasn't our dream home. We looked at it as an investment. Before every spending decision we made with that home we asked the question, "Will this increase the resale value of the home?"

We did the same thing when we purchased our first commercial building. Most of our decisions were based on whether it would increase the value of the building.

It's easy to get caught up in the emotion of the moment and start doing things to a house or car to make it special just for you.

If you want to make something special become a guest on *Pimp My Ride* or *Extreme Makeover: Home Edition*. At least you won't be spending your money! Bottom line: if you want to improve your investment for a higher resell value, don't customize to your special tastes. Think resell.

NUMBER 32: DON'T DELAY YOUR RE-ENTRY INTO THE CREDIT WORLD

There are a lot of "experts" with good intentions telling you how to manage your credit. Their advice is all over the board. They say things like:

"Avoid using credit at all costs."

"Pay cash for a used car."

"Pay off your home mortgage."

"Live debt-free."

"Debt is evil."

"Money is the root of all evil."

"Close all your credit card accounts."

The suggestions are well-intended, but wrong.

If the person offering you guidance hasn't experienced bankruptcy themselves—in my opinion they're not qualified to give you advice.

You may, in fact, need a brief cooling off period after filing bankruptcy...a time when you live on a cash-only basis. No credit. No credit cards. Nothing. But keep this period as brief as possible.

You need new credit to reestablish credit.

So start rebuilding your credit reports and FICO® scores as soon as possible. In fact, the "system" is set up to reward the bankrupt consumer who gets back in the game more than the consumer who sits on the sidelines and does nothing.

The longer you delay getting back into the credit world—the longer your credit scores will suffer.

Even if you don't use your credit cards that much—it's better to get them as soon as possible.

Why?

One of the key characteristics that make up your FICO credit scores is how long you've had established credit accounts. So the longer you have credit accounts—the better your scores.

It's surprising to me that I still meet people who filed bankruptcy years ago and never attempted to reestablish their credit. They pay cash for everything.

And they wonder why buying a new car or house seems next to impossible.

How can a lender extend credit to someone who hasn't proven they're creditworthy?

They can't.

Think about it. If someone came to you wanting to borrow money and they had filed a bankruptcy years ago, wouldn't you want to see that they've proven that they can now manage their credit better?

If I was a lender I certainly would.

The tough part about all this is that most people who file bankruptcy are good people. They earn more now than ever before.

But in today's world—where everything from insurance to student loans to employment to instant credit is based on a score—you just can't avoid rebuilding your credit.

Lenders and everyone else need to see that you've reestablished credit after your bankruptcy and that you can pay your bills on time. That's why reestablishing credit after bankruptcy is serious business.

So if you choose to be a cash-only person and wait 10 years to apply for credit, assuming your credit will magically sort itself out—you'll find out that your strategy is flawed.

NUMBER 33: A PERSONAL LOAN IS NOT THE ANSWER

"I need a personal loan for $3,000 fast to get my head above water. My bankruptcy was discharged last month. Help!"

I get this type of question too frequently on my: *www.askstephen. com* website. The only difference is the amount needed.

What you need to ask yourself is...

"Do I really need a loan?"

In almost every case where someone asks how he or she can pay off their bills and get back on their feet—getting a loan is not the answer.

In fact, I think just the opposite. A loan will usually do more harm than good because it will put you further into debt.

I almost always recommend either finding a way to make more money, raise cash, or cut expenses—not popular advice I'm sure, but the truth.

I encourage you to get creative in solving your cash crisis. Sure, you can ask for help—but try to rely on yourself, or you can easily get caught in a never-ending circle of always needing a loan for something.

The point I want to stress is this: you have to think outside the box and find creative ways to either earn or raise the money you need.

Had I not thought outside the box when I first filed bankruptcy, I would have never been able to recover as quickly as I did. Instead, I would probably be paying back loans right now. Similar to people that depend on student loans to pay for college without realizing they are signing up for a huge burden that stays with them for most of their adult lives.

I cannot tell you how many times Michele and I sacrificed short-term for a long-term pay-off (even when it hurt).

Keep working at increasing your scores, and when your FICO® credit scores surpass the 700 mark you should be able to confidently use more traditional sources that you may not have access to right now.

NUMBER 34: THE TRUTH ABOUT PUBLIC RECORDS AND COLLECTION ACCOUNTS

The public records section of your credit reports is where your bankruptcy will appear as well as judgments, tax liens and collections (although collections aren't public records, this is where the credit reporting agencies have chosen to put them).

Anything that appears in the public records section of your credit reports is bad. You simply cannot have anything good there. And while there are many different types of public records, only those that relate to how you've previously handled your credit will be reported to the credit reporting agencies.

For example, let's assume you have a collection account for $500. You decide to use your tax refund this year to pay off the collection item so it will show a $0 balance.

Don't do it just because you think paying it off will increase your credit scores. Paying off the $500 collection account will not increase your credit scores.

Why not? Because the balance on the collection account isn't what's lowering your scores. The collection account itself is what's lowering your scores. Just the fact the collection account appears on your credit reports lowers your scores.

It has nothing to do with the amount of the collection account. It could be for $5, $500, $50,000, or $500,000...it doesn't matter. What does matter is the fact that you have a collection—period.

So the only way for your credit scores to increase in this situation is to have the collection account completely removed from your credit reports.

"I have to tell you that since the seminar I have paid off my car note ($9,200), [and] I have gotten a $2,500 secured credit card..."

"Thank you SO much! I have to tell you that since the seminar I have paid off my car note ($9,200), [and] I have gotten a $2,500 secured credit card which I pay off 100% upon receipt of the bill. I have gotten a $6,500 secured loan through a credit union which reports to all three credit bureaus, I have formulated a reasonable budget which includes savings, investment and giving, and I have started tracking all expenses to monitor against my budget. My goal is to buy a house in two years with a good interest rate. Also, by paying off my car I was able to reconfigure my auto insurance and received an $800 refund. I used the $6,500 secured loan to (anonymously) lend my sister money for a house to start a day care and have received a promissory note from her. The installments I receive from her will fund my mortgage down payment. She will be paying me 10% interest while the bank I deposit it into will pay me 1.2% interest. I have figured out a way to double my 401k loan payments and should be free and clear this time next year. I also managed to be promoted, which increases my ability to save money and further rebuild my credit. I am so grateful for all of the information you have provided me—in your seminar, your book and in the research you did. Thank you. Thank you. Thank you. I hope the information I provided in the paragraph above will help you see just how powerful your book, seminar, and personal belief in this information really is!"

Lauren Heideman
East Palo Alto, California

Put Your Financial House in Order

It first seemed odd for me to be writing on the topic of putting your financial house in order. Then again, who else is more qualified to advise you than someone who has filed bankruptcy and fully recovered?

The majority of the principles expressed in this chapter originate from my friends Jim Rohn and Glenn Bland. Their books and audio programs helped me beyond measure. I recommend purchasing anything these men publish.

IT ALL STARTS WITH HOW YOU THINK ABOUT YOUR MONEY

The philosophy of the rich versus the poor is this: The rich invest their money and spend what is left; the poor spend their money and invest what is left.

Read the previous paragraph again. It's the key to understanding how to put your financial house in order. Ignoring it will always leave you in want. Practicing it will propel you as far away from your current situation as you can possibly imagine.

Warren Buffett, the third richest man in the world, is a living example of this principle. Even after he made his millions, he continued to drive around town in an old VW Beatle (when he could afford a Maserati). When his friends would tease him about not buying a new car he explained that the $25,000 extra he would need to pay for a new car would cost him $958,439 in lost wealth over 20 years.

Now, let's talk about reducing your cost of living, increasing your income, and learning how the rich handle their money.

STEP ONE: CUT LIVING EXPENSES

The first step anyone can take in an unstable financial situation is to immediately cut your living expenses. Take this very seriously. Most of us need to stage an all-out assault on everything that takes away from our income. Stop throwing away money on useless things.

Have you ever noticed that people in dire financial straits seem to have everything? Large-screen HD TVs, iPods, satellite dishes, cable television, fancy cell phones, etc. Here are some ideas for lowering your monthly expenses *(presented with a humorous tone)*:

1. Cancel all newspaper subscriptions

The news is almost all negative anyway. You'll be much happier without worrying about all the death, depression and destruction in the world. And if you really want to get in-depth news, go to the library. Not only will you find your local newspapers, but a bunch of national papers as well.

2. Cancel all magazine subscriptions—even your "special" magazines

Once again, a good library will have tons of magazines. And if the library doesn't, mega-bookstores like Barnes and Noble™, Borders® and Books-a-Million™ certainly will. Plus, by canceling all your subscriptions, you won't have to worry about hiding your "special magazines" from the wife anymore—she knows you get them anyway.

3. Cancel cable television (or get only minimum service)

Did you know some people pay up to $100 month for cable television?! That's crazy! If you're complaining about not having enough money and you're paying for cable television, you have no right to gripe. In fact, many highly successful people advise to not even have a television in the house. Remember, "Poor people have large TVs. Wealthy people have large libraries."

4. Find your pets a new home

Taking care of a pet is like taking care of a baby, and nowadays, just as expensive.

5. Move to a smaller home or live with friends or family members short-term

If you're struggling to make your mortgage payments, you may want to consider moving. You may even make money by switching homes.

6. Cook at home instead of eating out

Not only will you save money on the food, you won't have to go through the hassle of driving to a restaurant, getting a snooty waiter, and feeling guilty for not leaving a tip.

7. When you do eat out, share meals (and remember, breakfast food is cheaper than dinner food)

Pick your restaurants carefully and see if you can split one big meal between two people. And, if you're out for a romantic night, see if you can bring your own bottle of wine. Many restaurants will charge you a "corking" fee for your wine, but it's still much cheaper than buying one of their bottles.

8. Rent DVDs instead of going to the theater

By doing this you'll also avoid all the hassles of theaters these days...people talking during the movie...kids crying...food and soda on the floor...popcorn chompers who were never taught to chew. A cheaper alternative is: *www.redbox.com*. Through their kiosks you can rent a new release for $1 a night.

9. Cancel all telephone add-ons (caller ID, call waiting, etc.)

Caller ID? Why the heck do you need that? You know the only people calling you are collection agencies and people you owe money to. Save yourself the grief and get rid of all the phone extras.

10. Cancel your home telephone and just use a cell phone

Shop for the best family cell plan—or just use a voicemail box like we did. I've met a lot of people who have completely gotten rid of their home phones, and things work out perfectly for them. If you're having trouble getting approved for a cell plan because of your bankruptcy, try a pre-paid phone for a while. Having one number to give out will also simplify your life. And, best of all, there will be one less bill you'll have to pay.

11. Don't call long distance if it costs money

Send emails instead, or wait for others to call you. Of course, with national cell phone plans, long distance has really become a thing of the past.

12. Live closer to where you work

This is going to save you time and lots of money on gas. Maybe you can even kill two birds with one stone by walking to work so you lose some weight on the way. No one's forcing you to work or live where you are.

13. Sell items you no longer use through eBay® or a garage sale

You should sell anything you don't want or need. The advantage eBay has over a garage sale is that you're reaching a whole lot more people. I read one article where someone sold EVERY SINGLE ITEM in his home, one item at a time, on eBay! Everything! Even the food in his refrigerator! And people bought it!

14. Avoid ATMs (automatic teller machines) unless the transaction is free

Don't do business with a bank that charges you to access your own money.

15. Visit the public library instead of bookstores

If you want to make more money, the best advice I can give you is to begin reading. The most cost effective way to start doing this is to visit your local public library. Public libraries will actually allow you to borrow books free of charge! Imagine that. The only cost involved is taking the time to apply for a library card. Another advantage of libraries is that many of them now loan

DVDs. In fact, one of the local libraries here has a better collection than some of the video stores in town!

16. Bring your lunch to work

Most companies today offer some sort of lunch area where you can eat. And most have microwaves and other kitchen facilities... so brown-bag it for a while.

17. Try to eliminate day care expenses

If you're married and you have kids in day care, see if you and your spouse can work different shifts so you can each take turns at home. One of my valued employees saved $900 a month by doing this. That's a mortgage payment in some states!

18. No more Starbucks

Starbucks should change its name to FiveBucks! Seriously, you can't walk into the place without dropping at least $5. Instead, buy yourself a coffee machine and a bag of their coffee beans.

19. Think of "no-money" or "low-money" ways of entertaining

Instead of going to a movie or out to dinner, catch a free concert in the park, go to a museum (some are free, others charge very little), watch a free movie at the park, etc.

20. Eliminate fast food from your diet

Not only is fast food bad for you and expensive, you can fix much tastier and healthier meals at home for less money.

21. Refinance your mortgage

This is a biggie. Shop around for a lower mortgage rate. Just make sure that your FICO® credit scores are high enough to qualify for the rate you want before you apply. Purchase your credit scores and ask a qualified mortgage lender that you trust if it makes sense to refinance.

22. Raise the deductible on your insurance

Raising your deductible can greatly decrease your insurance payments.

23. Increase the number of allowances on your tax forms
If you receive a tax return each year, claim more allowances. That way, instead of waiting until the end of the year to receive your money, you'll be getting less taken out of every paycheck. This can be a HUGE temporary boost to your income. Just don't take so many allowances that you end up paying when tax time rolls around. Talk to someone in human resources where you work or your accountant about what will work best for you. You basically want the largest check possible each pay period without owing taxes at the end of the year.

24. Rent out spare rooms in your house
This is a great way to add a little extra income. If you have a spare room (or rooms), rent it out. We did this when we were first starting out after our bankruptcy and were able to make enough money to cover nearly 90% of our house payment.

25. If you own a home, verify your mortgage exemption was filed
On our first home after bankruptcy, Michele checked to see if our mortgage exemption was filed. Turns out it wasn't. Following up and making sure it was done resulted in a $2,000 check back to us...and more important, it lowered our monthly payment by $200. If you want more details about how this works, talk to your mortgage lender or another mortgage professional that you trust.

These are just 25 of the strategies you can use to improve your cash flow and help you recover from bankruptcy. Go to: *www.afterbankruptcy.org/72strategies* for the complete list of all 72 strategies.

STEP TWO: INCREASE INCOME
Now that you have eliminated some of your monthly expenses, let's look at your income. It could be as simple as getting a higher-paying job. If you're married, and both of you are self-employed, someone needs to generate enough stable income to support the whole family while the other works on meeting future goals and dreams. If you're single, it's all up to you.

A friend of ours was becoming frustrated with her husband. After talking with her, I discovered that they made the same mistake Michele and I made years ago. Her husband did not have a full-time job, and she did not make enough to support the whole family on her own, which made their income unstable. It put pressure on her to be the major breadwinner for the family while he pursued a dream of owning a restaurant. After one too many potential investors didn't work out, I made a recommendation. If his dream was to own a restaurant, he needed experience in running one—not just being a bartender. A management position within a restaurant would accomplish two goals: (1) provide experience and a work history of managing a restaurant which would look better to investors; and (2) provide a stable income to help support his family. She took my advice and convinced her husband to go to plan B. Within weeks their entire life changed. The husband accepted a position managing a restaurant. They bought a new house and a new car, and now have baby number two. Their dream to own a successful restaurant is still alive and well as he learns the skills that will transform their dream to a reality, while at the same time providing for his growing family.

If you are married, at least one of you needs a stable income that will support the family. If you ignore this simple principle, it could spell disaster.

How do you get a higher-paying job? The first step is to believe you can get one. The second step is to commit to "going the extra mile" for your employer. People who work hard, stay late, arrive early, and always ask for more to do will get noticed very quickly. For information on this principle, pick up the book *Think and Grow Rich* by Napoleon Hill.

Today you have so many options in finding employment. Here are a few places to start:

- *www.monster.com*
- *www.hotjobs.yahoo.com*
- *www.careerbuilder.com*

The problem we face at our company when we advertise for new employees is that many don't follow the instructions in the ad. Those people who don't follow directions exactly don't even get a chance—no matter how qualified they are.

If the ad says don't send a résumé...don't send a résumé! If it says send a one-page cover letter...make sure your letter is only one page.

Many employers use their ads to test candidates. They figure if someone can't follow the simple directions in an ad, they won't follow directions on the job.

In addition, don't just send a generic résumé. Personalize your résumé for each different position.

Will this take some extra time and effort on your part? Of course it will. But it could be the difference between your résumé sitting in a pile looking like everyone else's and your résumé standing head and shoulders above the rest.

And make sure you write a cover letter explaining why you think you're best qualified for the position. When you're writing the cover letter, it would be smart to visit the company's website and learn something about them. Then tailor your skills to their needs. The more in-tune you are with the company's needs—the better.

And if you really want to make an impression—send your résumé by FedEx and add something lumpy with it. One of our recent hires sent her résumé with a bouquet of cookies shaped like flowers. One of the flowers had her name on it. She included a note that said, "Pick the right one." That was memorable. Get creative to stand out above the clutter.

Also, let all your family and friends know you're looking for a new job. You would be amazed at what opportunities can develop. It helps if you're a good worker and a likable person.

Last but not least, read Chapter 5 in *Think and Grow Rich* by Napoleon Hill. Then read it again.

PUTTING YOUR BEST FOOT FORWARD

Step 1. Depend on the résumé to open the door, not do the work for you. So what's the best way to write a résumé? From scratch. Go to your library and check out a book entitled *The New Quick Job-Hunting Map* (ISBN: 0-89815-151-1) by Richard Nelson Bolles. This little $2.95 book contains an incredible skills inventory list anyone can use as the foundation for writing a successful résumé. Find the skills inventory list exercise and begin highlighting and writing down on a separate piece of paper all the skills that relate to you—word for word. What you're looking for are words and phrases that best describe your skills. Write them down in no particular order. Just keep writing.

Step 2. Once your skills inventory list is complete, move on to the next step. Have a separate piece of paper for each previous job position that will appear on your completed résumé. Now transfer each word or phrase to each previous job. When you're finished, most of the skills should be transferred to the job where you learned the skill.

Step 3. Now the more demanding task is at hand. Take your skills for each position and make them flow into a concise paragraph that informs the reader of what you can do. This is easy and fun for me, although it might be a nightmare for you. Give it a try! Or maybe you have a family member or friend who is gifted with words? If not, consider calling a nearby college journalism or English department. This effort may turn up talented students or an instructor who is willing to give you a helping hand for a nominal fee or nothing at all.

Step 4. At this point, your résumé should be formatted in a page lay-out program like Adobe InDesign. Try your library first. Most libraries have computers you can use. If not, Kinko's has a wonderful assortment of computers that you can rent by the minute. Or enlist a friend, family member, or college student who has a computer to help you. It will be important to have a copy of your résumé in digital form. For the more important positions you will need to slant your résumé toward that position.

Step 5. A good résumé needs a good cover letter. Keep it short and to the point. Before you put that first-class stamp on the envelope, consider using Priority Mail or FedEx. It will attract attention. For more information about résumés and cover letters, ask your librarian for recommendations or visit your local bookstore. Ask what books on the subject are popular.

INCREASE YOUR VALUE IN THE MARKETPLACE

If you desire higher wages you will need to increase your value in the marketplace. You get paid for the value you bring to the marketplace. You don't get paid for putting in time; you get paid for your value.

Is it possible to become twice as valuable to the marketplace and make twice as much money per hour? Yes. Three times as much? Yes. Ten times? Yes.

Why would someone make only $5 an hour? They're not very valuable to the marketplace. Valuable in the eyes of God, yes. Valuable to others, yes. Valuable as a person, yes. But to the marketplace, that person is not very valuable. Where you start is not where you have to stay. It's a ladder, not a bed—you're expected to climb.

Why do some people earn $50 an hour? Evidently these people must be more valuable to the marketplace. Why do some people earn $500 an hour? Evidently they must be far more valuable to the marketplace.

Why would a company pay one person $1 million a year to run a company? If you helped a company make a billion dollars, $1 million is chicken feed.

You can go as far up this ladder as you want to. Here's how: Work harder on yourself than you do on your job. If you work on your job you'll make a living; if you work on yourself you'll make a fortune. There is plenty of room at the top of the ladder. It's the bottom that gets crowded.

THE SECRET OF THE WEALTHY

Have you ever wondered how wealthy people get wealthy? Have you ever asked yourself why poor people stay poor? Think about it.

Wealthy people have 24 hours in each day. Poor people have the same 24 hours each day. The secret of the wealthy is how they manage their time. A better plan for how you will use your time will result in more money. Better plan—more money. Not, more money—better plan.

STEP THREE: HOW TO SPEND A DOLLAR

If you want your financial situation to change, you must change. One of the best lessons I ever received was from my friend Jim Rohn. Jim was broke at the age of 25, but within 6 years of applying the following principles he became a millionaire. When he was young, a millionaire friend of his asked him, "How much money have you saved in the last six years?" He answered, "None." His wise friend was astonished, and said, "Who sold you on that plan? You've bought into the wrong plan." Learn to invest first and spend what is left. If you continue to live the way you're living, the next six years will be exactly the same as the previous six. It's time you put someone else's philosophy to work for you.

So how does a wise person spend a dollar? The very first thing you do is give 10% of your earnings away each pay period. You decide whether you give from your gross or your net income. If you want to be "grossly" blessed, give from your gross income. If you want to be "netly" blessed, give from your net income. Enlightened people know that giving starts the receiving process.

My wife and I chose to plant our first 10% into our home church. It's the first check she writes each pay period. If you don't have a home church, find a worthwhile charity.

The next 10% is set aside for what we call our active capital account. It's the fund established for saving for a down payment on a house, new car, secured bank card, secured bank loan, etc. Once we get beyond that, the money is saved until we have at least six months of earnings. Wouldn't it be comforting to know if you lost your job today that you would have six months to find a new one?

The next 10% you pay to yourself. We call it our passive investment account. It's the account we never touch while it continues to accrue compound interest.

So there it is. We call this the 10-10-10 philosophy. It's the right way to spend a dollar. Consider the goal of living off 70% of your income. Less, if you have bigger dreams.

Some of you are staring into space right now. Okay, this is the ideal scenario. We didn't start off by living on 70% of what we made. We started by giving 10%. The second 10% was a challenge. It took us over two years to reach that point. It took us a little over 5 years to master the third 10% to the point of living off 70% of our income. Could we have done it sooner? Probably. The most important thing is to get started.

Begin to teach your kids these principles. The time to begin teaching them is now. A lot of the bad financial habits I grew up with I received from my parents. Children do what they see their parents doing. Our goal now is to live off 50% of our income by the time I turn 50.

One way to start giving, saving and investing is to make these the first three checks you write. The amount you save and invest is not the important thing in the beginning; it's the habit you're trying to develop. The amounts will get larger as time goes on. Focus on developing the habit.

This was very difficult for me. I never saved any money when I was growing up. I would always spend it. Years later, my wife and I had to literally trick ourselves into starting our passive and active capital accounts. Here's what we did. Our banker gave us two secured loans, each with a monthly payment that equaled 10% of our monthly income. We now had a payment book and the chance of spoiling our perfect credit history if the payments were late. It worked. The monthly loan payments were made on time, and in two years not only did we get the amount of the loan back with interest, but we also reestablished credit with a bank, and both loans appeared on our credit reports.

This may seem drastic. But we were so caught up in making excuses for why we couldn't save or invest that we had to figure out a way to develop the habit. We knew that once we created the habit it would come easy. We discovered things have a way of working out when they must work out.

BEATING THE CASH POOR ARGUMENT

"But, Stephen, there is no way we can give 10% of our income each pay period..." Then the next six years of your life will be just like the previous six years. "But, Stephen, there is no way we can build up to paying ourselves 10% out of each paycheck each pay period..." Then the next six years of your life will be just like the previous six years. "But, Stephen, there is no way we can invest 10% of our income each pay period..." Then the next six years of your life will be just like the previous six years. Get the idea?

You cannot afford not to.

PROPER TIMING (ALSO KNOWN AS THE MULTIPLE-USE TECHNIQUE)

Proper timing played an important role in each of our financial decisions. What about you? Any big cash bonuses coming up? Tax refund? Commission check? Birthday money? Christmas money? Can you sell anything you no longer need? Can you return things you bought within the last few months for credit?

With our first bank card, we needed $500 to begin the account. I verified with the company that they guaranteed to put a card in my hands in two weeks. With that in mind, we sacrificed $500 to begin the account, and the card arrived in exactly 14 days.

Sure, we had to eat spaghetti for two weeks straight. But the sacrifice was worth it.

Our first car after bankruptcy was acquired with $500 cash and two postdated checks for $1,300 total. We didn't have the $1,300, but we knew that if we didn't work hard to get it the car would be taken away. We came up with the money by saving everything we could and earning as much as we could. We did it.

We created situations where we *had to*.

Our second unsecured bank card is an excellent example of proper timing. With this bank the maximum credit limit on their card was $5,000. After 12 months of excellent payment history, the credit limit on your secured account automatically became your unsecured account limit. So the game was to raise the secured credit limit as high as possible. We decided to use the proceeds from our home equity loan to increase our secured credit limit before asking to be reviewed for unsecured status.

Our home equity loan closed the same month we were eligible to apply for unsecured status. We forwarded a cashier's check for $4,500 via FedEx to the bank. We gave them a few days to process the deposit, and called to verify that the account was paid off with a new secured credit limit of $5,000. We then placed a call to request being reviewed for unsecured status. In less than 10 days we had our $5,000 back and an unsecured bankcard with a limit of $5,000 at 9.9%. Proper timing can mean everything. So play smart.

"We were able to refinance our mortgage and take our rate from 8.5% to 7.125%."

"I saw the book, 'Credit After Bankruptcy' and read a little bit of it at the book store and decided to buy it. WOW, it was a really powerful book. We were able to refinance our mortgage and take our rate from 8.5% to 7.125%. We also paid off the credit debt we had accumulated from the past two years and now we are just left with my student loan, our one car and our mortgage payment. I finally feel that we can take a breath and start to make good money decisions."

Kathy Forringer
Lumberton, North Carolina

"Buying a home after one year of bankruptcy is really unbelievable to me. I'm still pinching myself."

"Buying a home after one year of bankruptcy is really unbelievable to me. I'm still pinching myself. Stephen you are an angel sent from heaven, it's really true that the Lord will bless you through other people. I've been kicking back waiting to send my success story, and now I'm ready. I thank you for all of your information. We filed for bankruptcy in September, we were discharged in February. Since then we have incurred two credit cards each, the ones that report to all three credit reports. All three of my credit scores were running around 447, ouch. My credit scores now are running around 618 to 647, and with about six payments of my house note, I'm looking forward to hitting the 700 club, boy I feel like I have a score of 1000, even when I know that they don't go that high. Well more good news, my husband's scores are running higher than mine. We were looking for a place to rent, and the rent was just so ridiculous, we knew that our scores had changed and we were one year discharged. We contacted a lender just to see if we would be approved for a loan, and wow, we could purchase a home. We started home searching, which we found one, and we know that we're getting a little beat up on the interest rate, but there's not too much to say with the loan amount and the 1 year discharge, and the credit score still ranking low, but good. With your material, we knew what to ask, what to look for, and we also learned how to say NO. Without you, we will still be lost, we are very well trained to tear up all the advertising that comes in the mail, with the high interest rates and high fees. Well back to the house, escrow will be closing around or about May 15th, we are purchasing with no money down, and the seller is paying all the closing cost! We even fussed about the appraisal fee, but felt like we had to give something, ha ha. With learning and studying your material, we have learn how to live in the world, and not let the world live in us."

Tina Cooper
Fairview, New Jersey

How to Interview
a Credit Lender

Why even bother interviewing credit lenders? It seems like a waste of time. Shouldn't they be interviewing me?

There are three main reasons to interview credit lenders.

■ The first is to avoid unnecessary credit inquiries, which lower your credit scores.

■ The second is to determine a lender's credit guidelines before filling out an application to avoid being denied.

■ The third is to evaluate all your options before you make a purchase decision to ensure you get the best deal.

As soon as we made the decision to file bankruptcy, I obtained a copy of the Sunday newspaper from the largest city closest to us. I wanted to talk with real estate agents and car dealers to see what our options were.

It was comforting to know what my worst-case scenarios were before I actually filed. You can use this method to determine what your options are after bankruptcy as well. It's good to have plans A, B, C, and D. Chance favors a prepared mind.

Save yourself time and effort by always using the telephone to interview lenders first. Take the time to visit the lender only when you're sure they can help you.

CREDIT INQUIRIES

You have an enemy. It's called the "credit inquiry." Every time you give someone permission to look at your credit report(s), it is recorded on your credit report(s) for everyone to see for up to two years.

Some lenders do not like credit inquiries. They get nervous when they see too many of them. In fact, having too many credit inquiries can lower your credit scores and be the cause of denial if you're applying for credit.

Avoid credit inquiries unless you are 99 percent convinced the lender will approve you. This can be difficult, especially when lenders cannot give you a definite answer until they review your credit reports. Ask a lot of questions to several lenders, then go with your gut instinct.

Don't give out your Social Security number or sign a credit application with anyone unless you are convinced they can help you. When you give out your SSN you give them permission to review your credit reports.

BEFORE YOU CALL

Before you begin calling lenders there are a few things you must do. First, your call must go to the person making the credit decision. With that in mind, you must rehearse a 30-second "sound bite" of what you want. Read *How to Get Your Point Across in 30 Seconds or Less* by Milo O. Frank. A phone call to the new-car finance manager at a car dealership might go like this:

"Could I speak to the new-car finance manager, please? Thank you. Hello, Ms. Dorsey. My name is Stephen Snyder. I filed bankruptcy six months ago and am interested in leasing a car. Do you provide financing for people with a previous bankruptcy?"

Or: "My name is Stephen Snyder. I filed bankruptcy six months ago and am interested in a car. I would prefer leasing a new car, but am open to your advice. I have reestablished credit since the bankruptcy and have never been late since. The credit I have reestablished is a Visa bank card and a bank loan. I have up to $500 I can put down, and can come up with more within 30 days. I have been employed for one year as a computer analyst and gross $2,000 a month. Can you help me?"

One of the questions they might ask you is why you filed bankruptcy. It's important how you answer this question. The best thing to say is the truth, but don't ramble unless they ask for more detail.

Rehearse a 30-second "sound bite" as to the reason you filed bankruptcy. A good response might be:

"I simply spent more money than I made. The bankruptcy was my wake-up call. And as you can tell by my timely payments, I've made a commitment to pay my bills early or on time."

The last thing a lender wants to hear is your "long story." Everyone likes to tell their story. But guess what? No one cares. All they want to know is whether your reason for filing bankruptcy will help them get what you need. Be short, concise, and to the point. Speak in 30-second sound bites!

The most lender-friendly reason for bankruptcy is medical. This reason, if substantiated, will provide you more credibility. Just be sure you can support what you say. Remember, it's very easy to spot someone who isn't telling the truth. Your credit reports tell all.

CREDIT GUIDELINES

Ask what the lender's credit guidelines are. Why go through the process of filling out an application, waiting for an answer, and risking a credit inquiry, if the probability of being turned down exists?

Some lenders will not tell you what their guidelines are. If they don't tell you, move on. It's not worth risking a credit inquiry. I have found it beneficial to be very direct. I like to say something like, "Do your credit guidelines permit extending credit to people with a previous bankruptcy?"

Usually, if their response is, "How long has it been since the bankruptcy?" I know I am talking with someone who knows what they are talking about.

Ninety-nine percent of the salespeople you talk to will not know what they are talking about. They are paid a certain minimum wage per hour to follow a telephone script. Any deviation from the script will activate their, "I better say something to sound intelligent," mode. Most of the time, what they say is wrong. It is best in this case to kindly ask to speak with a supervisor, the credit department, or someone who can answer specific questions concerning obtaining credit with that company.

Most of the time they will forward you to their "credit department." What you need to convey is that you are trying to avoid any unnecessary credit inquiries. You need to know what the chances are of getting an application approved with a previous bankruptcy. Back this statement up by affirming any new credit you have reestablished since the bankruptcy.

What you don't want to hear is this, "You must fill out an application, we will pull a credit report, and then be able to give you an answer." Be prepared; you will hear this a lot. I have a four-letter word for these people: N-E-X-T. If you are unable to convince the supervisor or credit department of your mission, move on to the next lender; this lender is not for you.

NEVER GIVE YOUR SOCIAL SECURITY NUMBER

By giving a lender your Social Security number, you give them permission to review your credit report(s). Do not give out your Social Security number until you are convinced the lender can do what you ask. Let me repeat, do not give out your Social Security number until you are convinced the lender can do what you ask.

Too many people freely give out their Social Security number and end up with a lot of credit inquiries. Don't be fooled. When they ask for your SSN, say something like, "It's not necessary to give that to you yet. I don't want to risk a credit inquiry. When it's time, I will gladly give it to you. Next question?"

Some slick salespeople will say, "I will not pull your credit report until it's necessary." Experience tells me not to believe them. Repeat your previous statement or blame it on a third party. One of my favorite lines in dealing with salespeople is, "My wife won't let me do that." It works.

TAKE NOTES

If you plan to interview several lenders, take good notes. After you talk with a few lenders you tend to forget exactly what each has told you. Take notes on things like the person's name, title, lender's name, telephone, fax, hours of operation, work schedule, comments he/she made during your conversation, and any answers to your questions.

I also suggest that you grade each conversation. I use the "smiley face" method. If the conversation did not impress me I draw a face with a frown. If the conversation was neutral I make a straight line for his mouth. If the discussion was productive, insightful, and I felt I could trust the lender, I make a smiley face with a big smile. Some even earn two smiley faces. In the end, those are the ones I usually do business with.

THE MOST IMPORTANT QUESTIONS TO ASK LENDERS BEFORE YOU APPLY FOR CREDIT

Now that you know the, "how," and the, "who," it's time to focus on the, "what." The following is a list of questions to ask a lender when you are trying to establish credit after a bankruptcy. By asking these questions, you'll ensure that you will get the best possible treatment from your lenders, and avoid the risk of an unnecessary credit inquiry that could hurt your credit.

1. Do you review credit reports when someone applies for credit with you? (The answer will almost always be, "Yes.")

2. Since I live in [enter your home state here], which credit reporting agency do you use as your primary source for credit reports? (This answer will vary depending on where you live. The point is that you want to know which of your three credit reports a lender is planning on reviewing before you complete your application. And once you know the answer, you'll know to only apply for credit with lenders that use your highest FICO® credit scores.)

3. Do you use a FICO score to make a lending decision? (Again, the answer will almost always be, "Yes.")

4. How does a previous bankruptcy affect your lending decision? (This is where you will find out if the lender will automatically turn you down because of the bankruptcy, or if they will consider it if a certain amount of time has lapsed.)

Once you get the answers to all of these questions, it's time to move to phase two, which is all about the type of offer you're going to get.

5. I have the highest FICO® scores possible, what is the best rate you can offer me? (Now you've just set your target rate. Anything less than that will cost you more in interest.)

6. What is the minimum FICO score needed to get the best rate? (This will tell you right away if you are going to be able to get the best rate or if you'll have to settle on a higher rate.)

7. What is the minimum FICO score needed for approval? (This question is really reserved for people who have very low scores and need to see if they would even qualify. Remember, it's important to avoid a credit inquiry if at all possible. Asking this question will help.)

8. If I have a FICO score of [enter your FICO score here], what kind of deal will I get? (This should give you enough of the specifics of the loan that you can decide if you want to officially apply. The lender will probably have some questions for you about your income, etc. That's fine. Just don't give out your Social Security number. A two-way dialogue is your goal.)

9. If you are talking to a lender that doesn't know the answers to these questions, or if they refuse to answer them, then you need to move on to another lender. Trust me, there are plenty of lenders out there that will work with you. You don't need to waste time with the ones that don't want to help you.

IN SUMMARY

1. Prepare rehearsed "sound bites."
2. Call each lender to ask about their credit guidelines.
3. Take notes.
4. Grade each conversation, using the "smiley face" method.
5. Decide which lender to start with.
6. Ask how many inquiries will show on your credit report.
7. Guard your Social Security number.
8. Don't give up.

"Thank you so much for the knowledge and power to know how to make it happen!"

"I attended your seminar in October and my bankruptcy was discharged in November. In January I bought a new van and a new truck! I called the mortgage company you recommended in March, and with their help, I closed on my first home at just 8.58%. MY DREAMS HAVE COME TRUE! Thank you so much for the knowledge and power to know how to make it happen!"

Christine Fraunfelter
San Diego, California

"We were approved for a $150,000 loan at 5.5%. We just closed on our brand new home in January."

"My wife, Theresa, and I would like to take a moment of your time to say thanks for caring enough to invite us to your bankruptcy seminar. We secured a bank card and a credit card for both of us. Then Theresa and I decided to move our family. I walked into the office of our lender and introduced myself and said my sound bite. We were approved for a $150,000 loan at 5.5%. We just closed on our brand new home in January. Shortly after the house closed we determined it was time to buy a new car. Walking into the car dealer I presented the same open to the FINANCE manager. (I added the mortgage we secured.) He said he appreciated us being so prepared and diligent in rebuilding our credit. I almost fell over when he came back to me and said with a puzzled look on his face: 'Theresa's score is 780 and yours is almost 700!! How many times would you like my help!!??' We left the dealer that evening with the new model car that Theresa wanted. We received the price we wanted and get this...the interest rate was lower than what we were expecting!!! Your name is a common subject in our house. It is possible that we might still be in the same situation we were in or worse if Theresa had not made me go to this seminar. Those are the reasons I felt it was so necessary to thank you. Good luck to you in all of your ventures."

Tim England
Little Rock, Arkansas

The Art of Filling Out a Credit Application

Just as a handwritten thank-you note is a lost art these days...so is knowing how to properly complete a credit application.

It's not as simple as just filling in the blanks.

In order to be approved for credit after bankruptcy at low interest rates and good terms, you're going to have to be properly prepared to complete a credit application.

You'd be shocked if you knew how many people are denied credit simply because they didn't fill out their application properly.

Here are a few rules to follow...

- Create a "credit folder"

- Always complete every question on a credit application

- Always skip over the, "Have you ever filed bankruptcy?" question

- Don't raise red flags with lenders

- Always complete the credit application at home

RULE 1: CREATE A "CREDIT FOLDER"

The first step to properly completing any credit application begins with assembling all of your information in one place. I keep all my information in something I call my "credit folder."

A credit folder is simply a file that contains the following:

1. Your bankruptcy discharge letter

2. Your most recent credit reports from each of the three national credit reporting agencies

3. A copy of your complete bankruptcy petition

4. Copies of all previous credit applications after your bankruptcy

5. Facts about you, your spouse (if applicable), and your nearest relative (e.g., dates of birth, Social Security numbers, addresses, telephone numbers, salaries)

6. A summary of all newly established credit since your bankruptcy

7. A one-page letter of explanation about why you filed bankruptcy (preferably edited by a mortgage lender you trust)

8. Your three most recent FICO® credit scores

I decided to create a credit folder because every time I filled out a credit application I could never remember my parents' address, my nearest relative's telephone number, my wife's Social Security number, bank account numbers, previous addresses, employers' addresses, dates of employment, birthdays, drivers' license numbers or any of the other information I don't usually use on a daily basis.

Seriously, how much of that information can you rattle off the top of your head?

By having all the vital information you need in one place it will allow you to complete each credit application completely and consistently.

Just make sure you put the credit folder in a safe and secure place. If someone else gets their grubby little hands on it, they could commit some serious identity theft.

One of the most important pieces of information in your new credit folder is the summary of any credit established since you filed bankruptcy. This will become an important sales tool for you to use when you are applying for more credit. At first there won't be much on your summary, but over time it will grow.

Every time you establish a new account, I recommend you keep track of the:

- Name of the lender
- Address of the lender
- Contact telephone numbers
- Account numbers
- Type of account
- Date opened
- Original balance
- Monthly payment—if it's an installment account
- Credit limit—if it's a credit card account

In a separate folder consider keeping the following on each individual account:

- A copy of your contract or lending agreement
- All of your monthly invoices or bills

RULE 2: ALWAYS COMPLETE EVERY QUESTION ON A CREDIT APPLICATION

Unanswered questions on credit applications plant seeds of doubt in lenders' minds. It's best to answer each and every question. And if a particular question doesn't pertain to you, just write "not applicable" or "N/A."

It's always better to write something rather than leaving a blank space. You don't want the lender to assume you meant to say something that you didn't.

It will be important to be accurate. If you come across as being accurate in your application, lenders may assume you're as precise in everything else.

Write legibly. It does you no good if a lender has to struggle to figure out what you have written. And, even worse, they may think you've written something that you haven't.

Having a bankruptcy on your credit reports means you need to do everything in your power to make it easy for people to work with you. And that includes making sure they can read your writing.

And don't think that this is coming from someone who dots every "i" and crosses every "t." My penmanship has been compared to that of a chicken having a seizure during an earthquake...

...but when I'm filling out an application, I make sure I'm as precise and clear as a third grade elementary school teacher. It's just that important.

You have to do everything better, cleaner and more accurately than all of your non-bankrupt brethren. Amen.

RULE 3: ALWAYS SKIP OVER THE, "HAVE YOU EVER FILED BANKRUPTCY?" QUESTION

"What!?"

"Wait a minute Stephen! You just told us to answer EVERY question or put 'not applicable.' Now you're telling us to ignore a question. What gives?"

Here's what gives...

I'm not asking you to lie. Au contraire! I'm telling you to ignore the question. This is the only time it's OK to violate rule number 2.

You see, when you check the "bankruptcy box," or admit you've filed bankruptcy, it's quite possible the salesperson will enter your credit application verbatim into their computer system. Once the system sees you've checked that box, there's a high probability you will be turned down on the spot. Done! End of story...

What I suggest is simply communicating with a lender such as a car salesperson or mortgage lender. Tell them you've had a bankruptcy in the past. But admit this only if your bankruptcy appears on the credit report they review. No need to alert them to your bankruptcy if they wouldn't see it otherwise. It's not your job to analyze your credit report—it's theirs.

So if they don't question you about it there's no reason for you to tell them. Heck, some lenders don't even have a bankruptcy box on their credit applications.

THE ART OF FILLING OUT A CREDIT APPLICATION

However, if they do ask you why you didn't check the box, then it is your responsibility to be honest with them and tell them you filed bankruptcy. This way you have a chance to talk to them and explain your situation, rather than letting some machine make an automatic decision without hearing your side of the story.

Applying for credit after bankruptcy is kind of like playing poker. I've seen people talk themselves out of a loan because they didn't know when to shut up. Some people think that the more you tell a lender the better off you'll be. That's not true. In fact, the opposite is true.

RULE 4: DON'T RAISE RED FLAGS WITH LENDERS

There are factors that can weaken your opportunity to get approved for new credit when completing an application. Here are a few of them:

- A previous bankruptcy
- Multiple bankruptcies
- An open Chapter 13
- A tax lien
- Outstanding collection accounts
- Credit counseling narratives
- A high-debt-to income ratio
- A high revolving credit balance to credit limit ratio
- A post office box as a mailing address
- Frequent changes in employment (not in the same line of work)
- Being self-employed without two years of verifiable income
- No telephone number verifiable in directory assistance
- Employment as an unskilled laborer in an industry where there is local instability
- Excessive number of revolving credit cards if you have a modest income

- Being an illegal alien without permanent resident status
- Having employers with unverifiable telephone numbers
- No checking account
- No savings account
- No newly established credit

Be sure to avoid any of these red flags as you prepare your credit application.

And if you're self-employed, there's a whole other set of red flags to avoid. But don't be discouraged...you can do it, and it's easier than you think...with a little planning. Visit: *www.lifeafterbankruptcy. com/feedback/businessseminar* for more information about building a business after bankruptcy.

RULE 5: ALWAYS COMPLETE THE CREDIT APPLICATION AT HOME

As long as your bankruptcy appears on your credit reports... never...and I mean never...apply for credit online or in any other automated way.

You're asking for an automatic denial, not to mention a needless credit inquiry that can lower your credit scores.

Almost all the online or automated credit application processing systems look for bankruptcies on your credit reports. Once they see one, you're probably going to be automatically denied. Here's why...

Most lenders don't have the time to deal with your individual situation. So, most lenders have determined that it's just easier to deny anyone who has a bankruptcy on their credit reports when they apply over the internet. That's why you should never apply online... because you're just a number at that point, not an individual with a story.

Don't be rushed or intimidated into filling out a credit application on the spot. Take the application with you. Fill it out in its entirety at your leisure. Then fax, mail or drop it off at a later time.

As long as you have a bankruptcy on your credit reports, "instant credit" (such as retail store credit cards you apply for at the counter) should not be in your vocabulary. Take your time to strategically fill out your applications.

This way you can ensure your application is complete. You are also sending a signal to the salesperson that you're not desperate. Of course, the salesperson will always say something like, "If you complete the application now you can..." Don't worry about what they say, it's just your typical sales pressure. Just take the application home with you.

However, there is one exception to this rule...

Some lenders base their decisions solely on your FICO® credit scores. So if you're 100 percent sure the lender is basing their decision only on your FICO scores, then it may be safe to apply...assuming, of course, your credit scores are high enough to get you approved.

HOW LENDERS USE YOUR APPLICATION

Some lenders use all of the information from your credit application and feed it into their own proprietary scoring model. The score they come up with is called an "application score." They use this score to either approve or deny your credit application.

The application score takes many things into consideration such as:

- Years of employment with the same company
- Years of employment in the same industry
- Income
- FICO score(s)
- Length at present address
- The existence of an open and valid savings account
- The existence of an open and valid checking account
- The total amount of checks you've had returned
- Previous history with the lender

CHAPTER 13

- Credit references

- Obligations—past due or not

- Debt-to-income ratio

- The existence of a previous savings or checking account

- Whether you own or rent

- Whether the telephone bill is in your name or someone else's

Fortunately, the majority of lenders use a FICO® credit score as a major part of their lending decision, so you don't need to be overly concerned about an application score. You just need to know how to make your application as strong as possible. By not raising any red flags and focusing on the steps mentioned in this chapter you can accomplish that.

WHAT TO DO IF YOU'RE TURNED DOWN

Sometimes lenders pigeon-hole people with a previous bankruptcy. The first "no" doesn't always mean "no." It's just how their system works.

If you call back and they still will not approve you, ask questions. Try to learn as much from the experience as you can. This will benefit you in the days, weeks, and months to come.

Ask the person what they feel would increase your chances of obtaining credit the next time around. Ask what they would do if they were you. Ask for a referral of someone who may be able to help you. Thank them for their time, and move on.

"I remember staying up until 4:30 am reading and taking notes. Then the next day I called the lawyer who did my bankruptcy, with fire in my belly..."

"I wanted to send a personal thank you note for the magnificent work you and your darling wife have done creating and delivering this priceless information...I remember going to Barnes & Noble looking for books on finance that could offer some assistance in helping me upgrade my knowledge on managing my finances. Low and behold I came across your book, and after sorting through several books and scanning the table of contents yours was the clear unquestionable winner. I remember staying up until 4:30 am reading and taking notes. Then the next day I called the lawyer who did my bankruptcy, with fire in my belly, I told him about your book and suggested that he have many copies available to his clients as part of his service or at least have it available for them... an invaluable tool. My new lease on life went up 10 notches... I did start applying some of the things you suggested and now have two credit cards with $3000 and $4000 credit limits. I was patient and did what you said in the book and it paid off."

Ramona Henry
Newport, Kentucky

"Our mortgage broker said he had never seen anything like it. I'm sure you hear it all the time, but thank you for giving us our life back."

"I don't know if we can ever thank you enough. We lost our company due to a data theft two weeks after our honeymoon/ wedding. All of our clients' data of three years was lost. To make matters worse, the incredible pressures of the loss forced me into hospitalization. We were devastated. We were over $300,000 in company debt secured by us, and bankruptcy was our only option. My wife lost her engagement ring and her trust fund that her father had left her when he passed away. We received your invitation in the mail about a month after filing. We attended the seminar and also opened a credit card within a few weeks of the seminar. We read your book, negotiated with some creditors for 10 cents on the dollar settlements, and began saving 10% gross, investing 10% gross and giving away 10% gross through our church and other charities. The first year was tough on us both professionally and personally. We managed to survive however. About two months ago, Lori and I started shopping for homes knowing interest rates were heading up. We found a home. The mortgage broker pulled our credit. My wife had gone from a 550 credit score to a 730 credit score (in 18 months). I was at 684 and climbing. Through the exception department of our mortgage company, we were eligible for a Jumbo, interest only loan at a very good interest rate. We now receive pre-approved credit card applications (don't touch them) and I'm on a mission to be to 750-775 24 months out of bankruptcy. Our mortgage broker said he had never seen anything like it. I'm sure you hear it all the time, but thank you for giving us our life back. It wasn't easy. It took a lot of hard work, saving, spending some money to make it right, but we feel normal again. If you ever are in our area for a seminar again, please let us know so we can stop by and thank you in person. And if you ever need someone to speak as a testimonial, I would be happy to."

Christian Scherf
Eloy, Arizona

Personal Development 101

The following few pages are a summary of the audiobook Success! The Glenn Bland Method *by Glenn Bland. It is, in my opinion, the best book available on personal development, and applies so closely to my message that I decided to purchase the rights to the audiobook version and reprint it here. It's my gift to you. If you prefer the unabridged version of the book it is available at:* www.amazon.com *or your local bookstore. Enjoy.*

If I drew a line and told you that simply stepping over it would guarantee inner peace, riches, enlightenment and physical well-being, would you take that step? Stepping across the line does work. I've seen derelicts changed into decent people. Debt-ridden individuals into financial successes. Misguided souls into persons who possess the wisdom of the ages. Mentally and physically ill weaklings into healthy and productive citizens.

Years of thought, study and planning preceded the development of the Bland method of goal-setting and planning. The heart of these teachings can direct you to a life of happiness and success. The principles in my method are not unique. They've been responsible for the making of kings, the building of empires and the creation of vast fortunes.

My method of goal-setting and planning had its beginning many years ago when I first became success-conscious. At that time in my life I was doing my work well. But only because it was something I had to do. I was drifting, I had no direction, no goals, no plans. I didn't understand the one basic principle: Men who have goals and plans dictate to others, while men who have no goals or plans are dictated to. I read this principle in a book called *Think and Grow Rich* by Napoleon Hill. As I read I said to myself, "He has found the key that can unlock the door to happiness and success in my life. This is what I've been looking for."

Success consciousness is the place where all achievement begins. It's when you first realize that there is a happy and successful way to live. You suddenly know you can change your life for the better. I read many books, spent many hours listening to records and tapes with only one goal: to program my mind for happiness and success. As I studied, I hit upon a basic truth. Techniques and methods change, but principles never do. I knew at that moment where to find the information I had been searching for. Everything you and I need to know about happiness and success is contained within the Bible. The Bible contains the answers to all of life's opportunities and problems. From the wellspring of the Creator, stimulating wisdom will never run dry. We are limited in our understanding only by our willingness to abide by the principles and to grow.

Mankind faces great problems today because people have become so self-sufficient that they sometimes forget there is a God. We forget that there is an omnipresent power bigger and more powerful than you or me. God created everything that exists, and He certainly can create happiness and success for a man if that man will play the game according to the rules. The Bible is no mere book, for through its message the secret of happiness and success will become a reality in your life. You'll be asked to do only one thing as these principles are unfolded for you: believe.

History reveals that there have always been those individuals who spend their lives in a negative world where "can't" is the most frequently used word in their vocabulary. But one of the most important and basic natural laws of the universe is: Anything you can think of and believe in, you can achieve. Jesus made the same point. If you can believe, all things are possible to him that believes. Jesus didn't eliminate anything; He said, "All things." Belief is a powerful force, and when properly used it can move man to accomplish great things. Our Creator gave us the choice of living in two worlds, positive or negative. A world where you can accomplish your lifetime dreams or a world where you can't do anything because a million trivial excuses hold you back. Decide that you are going to be a member of that select group of successful people who live in a positive world. Take the "can't" out of your life by believing. Mankind has always been aware of God's creative force.

The evidence of this great force is found in the birth of an infant, in the roar of an ocean wave, in the unparalleled beauty of a flower and in the magnificent design of a single snowflake. Each of us has the opportunity to use this creative force to accomplish our goals, but few do so. This creative force has been given to us free. To receive its full power we must only believe. The statement, "The best things in life are free," is true. They are the things that are responsible for putting happiness in your life.

To take advantage of the natural laws of the universe, we must understand the essence of the Creator who governs all life and creation.

Sovereign: The Creator is the ruler of all things.

Righteous: It is impossible for the Creator to be wrong.
He is perfect in every way.

Just: The Creator knows everything.
Therefore, it's impossible for Him to be unfair.

Eternal: The Creator has always existed;
He is everlasting.

Omnipotent: The Creator knows everything.

Omnipresent: The Creator is everywhere at all times.

Immutable: The Creator never changes.
He is the same yesterday, today and forever.

Truthful: The Creator is absolutely true.
It is impossible for Him to lie.

The Creator established the rules, and simply playing the game with all of your heart will produce fantastic rewards. Before going on, take these two steps:

- Convince yourself that there is a happier and more successful way of living than your present way of life; and

- Accept the fact that God is a tremendous guiding force in this universe and that He is wiser and more powerful than you.

How would you define success? There are probably as many different definitions as there are people in the world. A businessman might say that being successful means earning a lot of money. A football coach may believe that the pinnacle of success is winning the national championship. To a salesman, success means becoming the number one producer with his company. To the architect, success would probably be beautiful creations on his city's skyline.

Everyone may have a personal definition for success, but success is more than any of the preceding definitions. True success avoids extremes. It's a gradual process. Through balanced living you'll find happiness and success. Our Creator intends for you and me to lead happy and successful lives by applying the natural laws established by Him to keep us in tune with the universe. If I were to choose one word to define our Creator, it would be balance.

Consider the perfect balance between the plant and animal worlds, each complementing the other, so that both will survive. Our Creator provided for everything. He is aware of all of our opportunities, as well as all of our problems. Great people lead balanced lives, which are made meaningful by belief. William B. Walton, president of Holiday Inn, spoke of his four great loves. They were: love of God, love of family, love of country and love of work. His idea of success was woven with the threads of direction, balance and belief. Coach Vince Lombardi guided his players with the following statement, "There are only three things that are important in your life: your God, your family and the Green Bay Packers." Again, you should see the threads of direction, balance and belief woven throughout this statement. Any definition of success must contain these threads of truth.

Direction is setting your sights on things that are worthwhile and then establishing a plan to work toward their fulfillment and accomplishment. Balance is keeping the proper perspective about every area of your life. Staying in harmony with nature's laws produces a perfect balance. Balance in all things brings about happiness, and no man will become successful who does not possess belief. The greater his belief, the greater his degree of success. With these three ingredients as a foundation, we can define success. *"Success is the progressive realization of predetermined worthwhile goals stabilized with balance and purified by belief."*

Here are seven dynamic rules to help you put this definition to work immediately:

1. Let God guide you. Get yourself out of the way and let the great creative mind of God give you direction. Have faith.

2. Establish a faith period. Set aside 30 minutes each morning to engage in meditation and planning.

3. Crystallize your goals. Decide on specific goals you want to achieve, and keep them before you each day.

4. Make a plan of action. Develop a blueprint for achieving your goals and a target date for their accomplishment.

5. Develop a burning desire. Desire for the things you want in life will motivate you to action.

6. Believe in yourself. You can accomplish anything if you believe you can.

7. Never give up. Success cannot elude a will that stays in existence in spite of the pressures of adversity. Success comes to persistent people. It may require changing your entire way of life to apply the dynamic success plan, but remember, successful men do things that failures never get around to doing.

Carefully protected by your cranium, you carry with you the most intricate and baffling computer ever conceived—your mind. This fantastic computer of yours was created by God's infinite intelligence. It's capable of conceiving any idea you'll ever need. Despite its wealth-giving potential, the mind is used by most people at about 10 percent of its potential. We occupy our minds with insignificant things, instead of letting them soar to accomplish big and important things. Your mind is the computer and you are the computer programmer. If you put positive information in, the results will be positive and worthwhile. If you feed your mind negative information, the results will be directed toward failure. In the Bible we find, "As a man thinks in his heart, so is he." You're guided by your mind, and you must live upon the fruits of your thoughts. Since we become what we think about, then it's most important that we carefully regard our thought patterns. Developing right thinking is not easy, because it involves establishing new habits, which take days, weeks, months, often years before they become an integral part of your life.

New habits are not easily formed, especially when they must replace entrenched bad habits—but it can be done. If you strive to be happy and successful, establish good habits, because while in the beginning you make your habits, in the end your habits make you.

Each of us has bad habits and negative thoughts that hold us back and keep us from becoming the dynamic person that lives within. Now is the time to put away the cloak of failure, worn in the negative life, and replace it with a shiny new suit of armor, called success doctrine. How can you get your suit of armor? Well, the first step to acquiring success doctrine is deciding that you want to become happy, successful, and to possess great wisdom. You may need to reprogram your thinking so that you can truly hold the key to happiness in your hand. You will not gain this wisdom overnight. Your negative thoughts will not suddenly disappear. It takes time to replace negativism with positiveness. It's a gradual process.

Now that we've established that thoughts have power, that thoughts become reality, and that by programming your mind with positive thoughts you can become a positive person, let me explain how to build a success complex in your life. A success complex has six steps, which are backwards:

6. Mastery of the details of life
5. Capacity to love
4. Relaxed mental attitude
3. Inner happiness
2. Success orientation
1. Success doctrine or wisdom

Step 1. Imagine for a moment that you are a master builder and that you've been hired to construct a six-story building. You select the strongest supports and the best materials in designing the foundation. Without a firm foundation the structure cannot stand. It would crumble and fall. The full weight of the other five stories will rest upon this firm foundation. Success doctrine is a firm foundation on which your future can be built. The Bible says, "*Wisdom gives a long good life, riches, honor, pleasure and peace.*" (Proverbs 3:16-17) "*He who loves wisdom loves his own best interest and will be a success.*" That's Proverbs 19:8. You gain wisdom by becoming a student. You read, you study, you listen, and you must do these things each day on a planned and organized basis. It must become part of your life. You must eat, sleep and drink success doctrine. "*I, Wisdom, will make the hours of your day more profitable and the years of your life more fruitful.*" That's Proverbs 9:11.

Step 2. You'll be success-oriented when you understand yourself, and you can then begin to understand others. The world will truly be your oyster, for you will be a wise person. One who possesses the wisdom of the ages, a man who believes.

Step 3. Everyone in the world seems to be searching for inner happiness. You find inner happiness as soon as you possess success doctrine and become success-oriented. Because you understand the Creator and His natural laws, your life will be in complete harmony with the world around you. This generates inner peace and happiness.

Step 4. Once you have success doctrine in the front of your mind and it becomes success-oriented and possesses inner happiness, you will develop a relaxed mental attitude. You'll then have everything under control. The Bible says *a relaxed attitude lengthens a man's life.* That's Proverbs 14:30. Belief fosters a relaxed mind.

Step 5. The next important step in the success complex is acquiring the capacity to love. Don't confuse this with the selfish humanistic love found so often in society today. This is the true, complete and unselfish love the Apostle Paul talked about in 1 Corinthians. *If I gave everything I had to poor people and were burned alive for preaching the Gospel, but did not love others, it would be of no value whatsoever.* Even as great a man as the Apostle Paul, readily admitted that without the capacity to love, everything else is meaningless. With success doctrine you will have a deeper and more meaningful feeling for your family and your fellow men.

Step 6. The pinnacle of the success doctrine is the mastery of the details of life. Most people find it difficult to meet the daily trials and tribulations, but those who possess success doctrine know how to organize themselves through goals, plans and priorities to handle anything that comes up. The individual with success doctrine learns to solve what he can and to live with what he can't without destroying his peace of mind.

Most people want to be success-oriented, have inner happiness, display a relaxed mental attitude, possess the capacity to love, and want to be able to master the details of life. Few are willing to pay the price, however, of gaining the success doctrine.

Imagine that you are an internationally known architect commissioned to supervise the construction of the world's tallest and most beautiful building. The materials are piled high. The contractors are surrounded by their workmen. You give the command, "Build me a building." The first question on the lips of every craftsman and contractor would be, "Where's the blueprint?" A master craftsman must have a plan. He can't effectively use his talents unless he has guidelines to direct his genius. You are the architect of your own life. You can construct happiness and success, or a life filled with misery and failure. The blueprint is the key. People with goals and plans succeed in life, while people without them fail. We are living at a point in world history when people wander restlessly about looking for something that can't be explained. They're confused, frustrated and filled with anxiety, and they can't understand why. There's only one solution. Man must go back to the basic fundamentals of skillful living given to him by the Creator, the great natural laws of the universe. Ecclesiastes 7:13 reads, *"See the way the Creator does things and fall into line. Don't fight the facts of nature. You can't beat Him, so you might as well join Him and let His natural laws work for you and not against you."*

One of the best-known natural laws of the universe is the law of gravity. If you climb to the top of a tall building and jump off, you'll fall down. You never fall up. You can't see, smell or touch the law of gravity, but you know it's there. So it is with the natural laws of happiness and success. You can't see, smell, or touch them, but they are there. Operate within the framework of these laws, and happiness and success will be yours for the taking. The Holy Bible is the Creator's plan for the ages. Goals and plans are the magic keys to happiness and success. Goals and plans made within the framework of natural law take the worry out of living. Conformity to God's laws frees your mind so that you may get on with your opportunities.

There are four reasons most people don't set goals and establish plans. They are:

1. They don't know why.

2. It's too much trouble.

3. They don't have faith in their goals and plans after they're developed.

4. They begin on a long-range basis, and this prevents them from seeing immediate results, so they become discouraged.

If one of these reasons is holding you back, the Bland method of goal-setting and planning will solve your problem.

My method teaches the principles of short-range and long-range planning, enabling you to discover immediately that planning really works. My method is based on natural law, which will give you the confidence and faith you need to stick with the program. Take time to establish definite goals and plans for yourself. You will find that the most difficult part of the process is carrying out your plans once they've been committed to writing. You'll encounter temporary defeats many times, but by sticking with the program you'll charge through adverse situations like an all-pro running back on his way to the goal line. Remember, out of every adversity comes an equal or greater opportunity.

In Houston, Texas, several years ago a great sports arena was planned, the first of its kind. A glass roof would cover the arena so that sporting events could be conducted under perfect climactic conditions despite Mother Nature. But when the magnificent structure was completed, grass wouldn't grow on the playing field. The developers had a multi-million-dollar sports complex that had become worthless. This adversity resulted in the discovery of an artificial playing surface, even better than grass. Today, artificial turf covers many outdoor stadiums across the nation. Out of adversity comes opportunity. Welcome adversity; it's your springboard to great achievement.

As you begin to formulate goals in your mind, dare to think big. For example, let's say that my income for the past year was $15,000. I set a goal for the coming year of $35,000. After working hard to attain my new objective I found that I had earned only $28,483. Did I fail? Certainly not. I didn't reach my goal of $35,000 in income, but look at the fantastic progress that was made. Dare to aim high, as long as you sincerely believe that you can reach your goal at some time in the future.

It's wise to use the counsel of other qualified people when you set goals and make plans. Proverbs 15:22 says, "*Plans go wrong with too few counselors; many counselors bring success.*" I suggest that you choose one or two individuals whose judgment and ability you greatly respect, and form a success council for the purpose of exchanging ideas regarding each individual's goals and plans. The Bible says, *"The intelligent man is always open to new ideas. In fact, he looks for them."* That's Proverbs 18:15. And in Ecclesiastes, *"Two can accomplish more than twice as much as one. For the results can be much better. If one falls, the other pulls him up. Three is even better, for a triple-braided cord is not easily broken."* (Ecclesiastes 4:9 and 12) *"Be with wise men and become wise."* (Proverbs 13:20)

For your success council to function properly, there must be complete harmony among the members. There can be no negativism, or the group will destroy each individual involved. Stay away from negative people, because they'll program you for failure. Guide group thinking by establishing positive guidelines, and schedule regular meetings with time for each member to make a personal progress report. This provides the follow-through necessary for individual goals and plans to become reality. Just setting a goal and making your plans to attain it are not enough. You must also set a date when you wish to attain the goal. It could be as short as an hour, or it could be five years or 65 years.

In 1960 President John F. Kennedy addressed the nation, announcing the beginning of a 10-year space program designed to put a man on the moon. Let's analyze why this effort was such a huge success.

- First, a definite goal was selected. A man on the moon.
- Second, there was a basic plan.
- Third, there was a target date, 10 years.

There was a fourth procedure employed on this project. After the first three steps—a goal, a plan and a target date—it was necessary to constantly keep the goal before them each day. There were many unknowns, but the men and women engaged in the moon shot project kept their goal constantly before them. They used group thinking and maintained their faith through temporary defeat. Because they believed their goal would be accomplished, the

United States successfully landed a man on the moon with one year to spare.

Let me repeat the steps the space project took.

- First, a goal was set.
- Second, a plan was made.
- Third, a firm target date was established.
- Fourth, group thinking was employed.
- Fifth, everyone kept the goal constantly in mind.
- Sixth, action was applied.
- And seventh, they fervently kept the faith.

It was impossible for them to fail.

Now, we reach the most important phase of the goal-setting and planning process. The principles already presented will bring material success into your life, but they will not bring happiness. True happiness can only be achieved by living a balanced life. Balance is the key for us. All the natural laws brought into being by the Creator are based on the natural law of balance. Each of us needs to learn to live within the boundaries of this great natural law. If you're in balance with the world around you, you'll be happy. If you're out of balance with the world around you, you'll be unhappy. Your life is made up of four major areas: spiritual, financial, educational and recreational. Without proper blend and emphasis upon these four areas, your life will be out of balance, and you'll be unhappy.

Area One—Spiritual Balance. Do you know someone who's spiritually out of balance? Perhaps you know someone who is so obsessed with things of the spiritual nature that he's a fanatic and people avoid him. He's overbalanced in one area. Or perhaps you know someone who has no spiritual life at all. These examples are two extremes, but each illustrates spiritual imbalance. Man's very nature embodies an innate drive to worship something, and the Bible says *there should be only one object of worship, the Creator.* Make definite spiritual plans for you and your family to enjoy the balanced fullness and meaningfulness of life. You'll never be sorry.

Area Two—Financial Balance. Perhaps you have a friend who is financially out of balance. This individual is driven by money alone. The pursuit of it has caused a complete collapse of his personal life and family harmony. In Ecclesiastes 5:10 we find, "*He who loves money shall never have enough. The foolishness of thinking that wealth brings happiness.*" At the opposite extreme, an individual to whom money means nothing fails to provide for his own and lives in poverty. This individual has just as serious a financial imbalance as the person who is money-mad. Somewhere between these two extremes is a place of perfect balance. In almost every case the single biggest problem people face is the handling of money. Most people simply don't understand that they can't have both money and things. At least in the beginning. To accumulate money you must give up things. But if you accumulate things, you will never have money. If you sincerely want to accumulate money there are seven things you must do.

1. Don't charge. Charge accounts and credit cards get people into financial trouble. Remember what Proverbs 22:7 says, "*Just as the rich rule the poor, so the borrower is the servant to the lender.*"

2. Don't consolidate your bills. This is popular, but it doesn't always work. You may consolidate bills into one monthly payment at extreme high interest rates and end up with the consolidated debt to pay, plus many new ones if the old, bad money-management habits haven't been changed.

3. Don't buy impulsively. When you desire to purchase anything of consequence, write it down. Wait one month, then, if you still want it, consider working it into your budget. You'll often discover that your desire was only a passing fancy.

4. Establish a budget. Keep records of your income and expenses. Decide exactly what you will spend for necessities and luxuries each month and then stick with it. Watch every penny.

5. Pay yourself first. Every time you receive your paycheck, put something aside for yourself. At first the amount may be small, but this will grow because you are forming a good habit. A habit of saving. Proverbs 21:20 says, *"The wise man saves for the future, but the foolish man spends whatever he gets."*

6. How to pay monthly bills. When you write checks each month, write them in this order: church or some worthwhile charity, savings, insurance for security, food, shelter, and then finally all other things. This procedure will help you provide for the necessary things first and let other things take care of themselves.

7. Investing. There are five steps to good money management. Putting these five steps to work will provide financial security in your life.

   a. Basic needs. You must provide food, clothing and shelter before investing in other things. For those who progress beyond providing these basic needs for their families, the next step is...

   b. Insurance. Protect yourself from possible financial disasters with life, health and casualty insurance. For those who manage to provide basic needs and insurance, the next step is...

   c. Cash fund. Build a cash fund for emergencies and opportunities that come along. Build a savings account until it equals six months of your income. For those who build this cash fund, the next step is...

   d. Unimproved land. Investing in unimproved land is a relatively safe investment with a very high return. The value of land should never decrease, so at this point in your accumulation of wealth, buy unimproved land. Some people can provide for basic needs, insurance, cash fund, and unimproved land and never proceed farther. For those who do, the next step is...

e. Stocks and bonds. This is properly the last step because it's speculative investment. This step can prove to be risky, and caution should always be exercised when engaging in this type of investment.

These are the five steps to good money management. Normally, the only problem arises if you decide that the five steps are too slow. You decide that you want to make it quick and jump all the way to step five. When you do so, look out. You're headed for financial disaster. Stick with the five steps. They work.

Remember, the Bible does not say that money is evil. The Bible does say, "*The love of money is the root of all evil.*" That's 1 Timothy 6:10. When you begin to accumulate money in large amounts, many good and evil opportunities, never available to you before, will tempt you. Jesus said, "*It's easier for a camel to go through the eye of a needle than for a rich man to enter the Kingdom of Heaven.*" The temptation to do evil is great when you have an abundance of money, and if you become a slave to money it will destroy your peace of mind and your relationship with the Creator, but this need not happen if you have firmly entrenched sound goals and plans to guide you. Many rich men have entered into the Kingdom of perfect peace and harmony that the Creator planned for them. It can be done through goals and plans that keep the pathway to happiness and success open.

The way in which you regard money is extremely important. When you love money, you have financial imbalance. Money has become the master, rather than the slave. No one can attain riches unless they enrich others. The Bible tells us that *God loves a cheerful giver and will return his gifts many times over if the gifts are given with the right attitude.* You can't give with the expectation of getting. When gifts are given unselfishly, with nothing expected in return, they'll be returned many times over.

Just where are you going to get the money so that you can start giving some away? Well, there's only one source: the money you earn. That must come from some beneficial service you can render to your fellow man. Do you need to find some service to render? Probably not; most people can render a beneficial service in their present work. You probably have a virtual gold mine right where you are. Don't overlook the obvious. Establish your goals and make your plans to render the best possible service in your present work. Money will come to you on a sound basis in only one way. The formula: service, success, then money.

There is a price to be paid for success. In addition to the long years of preparation, there must be dedication to service. The price is no different, no matter what your occupation may be. If you sincerely want to earn money, you must be prepared to pay the price: service.

We have already discussed the importance of the first two areas for true happiness—spiritual and financial. To attain true balance, two additional areas are essential.

Area three is educational, and if this is not in harmony with the other principles, your journey toward happiness will be erratic, if not impossible. The fourth area, recreational, meets the needs expressed in the old saying, "All work and no play makes Jack a dull boy." Without relaxation and satisfactory balance, Jack is headed for a breakdown.

Area Three—Educational Balance. Have you ever known an individual who was educationally out of balance? He has become so obsessed with gaining knowledge that he becomes an educated fool. He's so technical in his thinking that he forgets how to apply his knowledge in practical situations. He never seems to find a way to use knowledge to benefit himself and his family. Then there is the individual who possesses little or no education. He and his family must suffer the consequences of insufficient education throughout their lives. Both extremes illustrate educational imbalance. Somewhere between these two extremes is a place of perfect educational balance. You arrive at this point through goal-setting and planning in the educational area.

There are two kinds of knowledge: generalized and specialized. Generalized knowledge can help you become a more well-rounded person, but it doesn't necessarily help you earn your living. The knowledge that will guide you in your work and form the foundation for setting goals and establishing plans is called specialized knowledge. Specialized knowledge is knowing your business through experience and study. Engage in at least one organized educational activity a year. This educational experience will prevent your mind from becoming stagnant and unproductive and will keep you mentally alert so that you may perform at peak efficiency. You can do this in several different ways: through formal classroom programs, correspondence courses or individual study. Do it on a planned basis and for the purpose of gaining specialized knowledge. If you are a person of normal intelligence and have the willingness to work and the desire to obtain specialized knowledge, you can succeed.

Area Four—Recreational Balance. Have you ever known someone with a recreational imbalance? There are two types. The first recreates himself right into financial disaster. He wants to play all the time, never giving enough attention to the spiritual, financial and educational areas of his life. The man with the second type of recreational imbalance enjoys no recreational pleasures at all. He keeps his nose to the grindstone, never having enough time for such, as he calls them, foolish things as physical exercise and relaxation. These two extreme cases point out the need for balance. Planned recreation is important to our physical and mental well-being. A strong body and a sound mind must function in harmony for success. The Bible says, *"Any enterprise is built by wise planning, becomes strong through common sense, and profits wonderfully by keeping abreast of the facts."* That's Proverbs 24:3 and 4.

Definite goals and plans are important to you as an individual, but they are equally important to your entire family. Setting family goals and establishing definite plans for their fulfillment is a tremendous positive force. Choose a worthwhile goal and then release yourself from your old self and go to that goal. No one can stop a man with a plan.

We live in a very complex world. Our modern environment does not automatically create a wholesome atmosphere for slowing down. Consequently, we miss the miraculous blessings that are ours for the taking. Get the most out of your life by setting aside 30 minutes each morning when you can be completely alone for what I call the faith period. The faith period is an important part of the total goal-setting and planning procedure. Without faith, no goal or plan would ever become reality. The Bible defines faith as, "*The confident assurance that something we want is going to happen. It's the certainty that what we hope for is waiting for us even though we cannot see it up ahead.*" That's Hebrews 11:1.

Faith is what you have left after everything else has been lost. It's the most powerful motivating force in the world. Millions of people are looking to the future with great expectancy because of their faith. Wishes and hope devoid of faith and belief are fruitless. The faith period's sole purpose is to help you grow in faith, which in turn will enable you to do outstanding things. Let's get into the actual mechanics of how to conduct your own personal faith period.

The faith period should be very personal. Its purpose is to put you in tune with the great infinite, intelligent God of the universe. First, form the habit of becoming an early riser. There was a time in my life when I would set my alarm clock to sound just 30 minutes before I was required to be on my job. I would awaken, rush, rush, rush and arrive at my work totally and mentally unprepared to meet the opportunities and frustrations of the day. The early-morning hours set the stage for the activities of the day. If they are pleasant, the entire day will be pleasant. Today I arise each morning at 5:30 and slowly prepare myself for the day. I look forward to the day with the greatest expectancy that good things are going to happen. I drive to the office, arriving at 6:30. Going to the office at this hour of the day creates a tremendous feeling of power and authority. At that time of day you are probably the only person going to work because you want to. The others you see are going to work because they have to. You feel you are out in front of everyone else, and you are. You feel the world is yours for the taking. It is. You feel you can conquer any obstacle standing between you and your goal. You will. The Bible says, "*If you love sleep, you will end in poverty. Stay awake, work hard and there will be plenty to eat.*" That's Proverbs 20:13.

I've also formed the habit of complimenting those with whom I come in contact in the early-morning hours. The compliments give others a tremendous boost for the day, but I benefit most of all, because giving compliments gives me inner happiness.

Resolve now to arise early, take your time and be a cheerful friend, and as a result you will have many friends. You're probably thinking there's no way you can rise early and be a cheerful friend. I'm a late sleeper. I once felt the same way. There's a price to be paid in the beginning. But once you form the habit, you will discover that your early-morning time and your faith period will be the most enjoyable and important time of the day. In the morning your mind is rested; it's not crammed with the thousand trivial details that fill it at the end of the day. You can do your most productive thinking in the morning. Become an early riser no matter what your present sleep habits may be.

When I arrive at my office, I begin my faith period. I sit in a comfortable chair and totally relax my entire body. Relaxation of the physical body frees the mind for deep meditation. I continue my faith period by reading the 91st Psalm, which includes these words, "*For the Lord says, because he loves me I will rescue him. I will make him great because he trusts in My name. When he calls on Me, I will answer. I will be with him in trouble and rescue him and honor him. I will satisfy him with a full life and give him My salvation. You should not put your faith in a man. Put faith in God and His promises and you will have the strength to withstand any adversity.*" Ralph Waldo Emerson once said, "Alone, a man is sincere." The faith period is a time when you have the opportunity to be sincere with yourself. Everyone needs time alone with God daily. It helps you keep a proper perspective about life.

As I continue my faith period, I communicate with God. I imagine He is sitting in a chair in the room with me, and then I talk to Him through my thoughts. I imagine that He is not only the best and most loyal friend I've ever had, but also the wisest. He has all the answers. God is the one who forgives. If I have committed any sins I discuss them with Him, ask Him to forgive me. Next, I give thanks for all the good things that happened to me on the previous day. Then I express my concern for those I love, those in need, the sick, and those I resent. Next, my thoughts turn to my own personal needs, both problems and opportunities. Through my thoughts I petition for answers and results, claiming the promise that is mine in Mark 11:24, *"Listen to me, you can pray for anything and if you believe you have it it's yours."* We're also given the promise, *"Ask and you will be given what you ask for, seek and you will find, knock and the door will be opened."* That's Matthew 7:7 and 8.

After the meditation portion of the faith period has ended, program your mind by repeating your goals and plans. If you'll keep your goals before you each day, they are certain to become a reality. Repeating orders from your thinking mind to your subconscious mind will convert thoughts into reality. At this point, glance through your monthly and weekly activity planners to be sure that top-priority items and details have been written down. Transfer plans from your weekly planner to your daily planner and then take action. Make it happen. Design a faith period for yourself. Take 30 minutes to be alone each morning and follow an established procedure. If you do, your life will immediately change for the better, and within a 10- to 30-day period you will experience some remarkably good things. *"I will instruct you, says the Lord, and guide you along the best pathway for your life. I will advise you and watch your progress."* That's Psalm 32:8. You can do it if you have faith.

The man who is a master of human relations is priceless. Industry and business will richly reward the individual who can expertly achieve positive results through other people. In all my experience, I don't believe I've ever met more than a handful of men who were masters in the art of human relations. I've found, without exception, that men who possess this outstanding skill are men who are on their way to the top, or who have already reached the pinnacle of success. Why are men who master human relations so successful? Because they have learned and accepted a simple principle called the Golden Rule: Do for others what you want them to do for you. By enthusiastically applying the Golden Rule in your own life, you will enrich the lives of many others, but by far the greater reward will come to you. Good will radiated from you will be returned to you in the form of happiness and prosperity. The people you come in contact with will suddenly become members of your fan club. Treating others as you like them to treat you will cause them to do everything within their power to help you achieve your goals in life. You may meet someone who will not respond to this rule. If so, go the extra mile. Show them patience and understanding. Treat them exactly like the person you want them to be and they will do their best to become that person.

Now let's examine the portrait of a master of human relations:

1. He will seem simple, but is wise. The French author Modisque said, "I've always observed that to succeed in the world a man must seem simple, but be wise." If you appear to be a simple man, others will tend to underestimate your ability and will present you the opportunity to deal with them when their guard is down. By seeming simple, but being wise, you can accomplish your objectives before anyone actually realizes what has happened and yet everyone will be happy. Psalm 37:35 through 38 says, *"For the good man, the blameless, the upright, the man of peace, he has a wonderful future ahead of him. For him, there is a happy ending."*

2. He will be humble; he will be able to accept his achievements for their true worth and not as something that makes him better than others. He will possess control over his temper, because a quick temper affects his judgment and relations with others. The good shepherd said, *"For everyone who tries to honor himself shall be humbled. And he who humbles himself shall be honored."* That's Luke 14:11.

3. He will be genuinely interested in others. He will treat everyone with respect regardless of their social status, because he knows that everyone is a child of God and has a useful service to render to humanity. He is a man you can talk with. He will take time to listen, and he is able to offer you sound advice. He has the capacity to sincerely love his brother. Don't just pretend that you love others. Really love them. Hate what is wrong. Stand on the side of good. *"Love each other with brotherly affection and take delight in honoring each other."* That's Romans 12:9 and 10.

4. He'll be honest in business dealings and in his personal life. To succeed in working with people, you must be honest in every aspect of your life. In Romans 12:17 we find this statement, *"Do things in such a way that everyone can see that you are honest clear through."* Leave no room for any doubt. If your friends and business associates consider you an honest man, they'll entrust to you the big responsibilities regarding business and financial matters.

5. He'll not involve himself in gossip and slander. He realizes that malicious gossip is spread by people with small minds. *"Any story sounds true until someone tells the other side and sets the record straight."* That's Proverbs 18:17. Idle gossip destroys others, and it will destroy you if you clutter your mind with it. If you can't say something good about a person, don't say anything.

6. He'll give credit and praise to others. One of the easiest ways to lose the loyalty and support of others is by taking credit for the accomplishment of objectives yourself. *"Don't praise yourself; let others do it."* That's Proverbs 27:2. This is difficult, but praise will come to you in abundance if you truly deserve it.

7. He will be patient and kind. The inexperienced don't understand the great power of having patience. They tend to want everything to happen yesterday. Benjamin

Disraeli said, "Everything comes if a man will only wait. A human being with a settled purpose must accomplish it, and nothing can resist a will that will stay in existence for its fulfillment." Another important virtue is kindness. This characteristic will create an inner peace that can be found no other way. *"Your own soul is nourished when you are kind. It's destroyed when you are cruel."* That's Proverbs 11:17.

8. He will be fair and just. Your associates and friends can accept almost anything you do if they feel they are being treated fairly. Present each individual an equal opportunity and then let their own efforts determine how happy and successful they'll become. A master of all human relations must also be just. He must gather all the facts, consider all the solutions, then make the best decision based on the facts and stick with it. If you treat others with justice, they will hold you in high regard. *"The Lord demands fairness in every business deal."* That's Proverbs 16:11.

9. He will give and accept constructive criticism. Constructive criticism has only one purpose: to help others. It should never be administered as a rebuke, but only as a means to arrive at solutions for adverse situations that occur to everyone who takes action. The only people who do not create problems are those who do nothing. The rest, the doers, must continually face problems each day. The master of human relations must be willing to listen to complaints, weigh them carefully in his thoughts, extract the truth and profit by them. *"Don't refuse to accept criticism. Get all the help you can."* That's Proverbs 23:12.

10. He will be a decent person. He must strive every day to live within the boundaries of the laws of God. You will fail from time to time, but when you do, get back on track. King David, one of God's most beloved, was continually getting off the right track, but he was aware of his human

weakness, and by admitting his mistakes put himself on the correct course. If others know that you are basically a sound person, they'll focus their attention upon the many good things you stand for. *"The Lord blesses good men."* That's Proverbs 12:2.

11. He will be generous with others. We're not referring to the word "generous" in the material sense. We refer to his generosity in offering himself to others. He cannot allow self to stand in the way. Others come first. Simply forget about getting. *"Be generous, and give of yourself and all goes well for the generous man who conducts his business fairly."* That's Psalm 112:5.

12. He will possess a positive mental attitude. This is a powerful magnet that will attract others. Learn to live in the expectation that good things are going to happen if you are to be a master of human relations. A positive mental attitude rubs off on others. Maintain a positive mental attitude and you'll go far in dealing with people.

One who possesses all 12 qualities will rise to great heights during his life and will be long remembered after he returns to the grave.

There are several other topics that should be discussed before leaving the topic of human relations.

First, if you sincerely want to accomplish outstanding things, you must surround yourself with capable helpers. You will be no better or no more effective than the people around you. A head football coach is no better than his assistant coaches, and the president of a corporation is no better than his staff.

Another principle is that as you go to the top there will always be inequalities. There will always be the corporate president who promotes his 23-year-old son to vice president after only six months of service. There will always be the guy who receives the same raise you do when you've been doing all the work. There will always be unfairness to face as long as there are people. Don't get involved. Keep working toward your own personal goal. Free yourself from all pettiness and prejudice, set your sights on your personal goals and let no one stand in your way. It takes character to keep forging ahead.

If you master the art of human relations, you can achieve anything your heart desires, just by working through people. Take time to find out what other people want, and spend your time helping them to get it, and you will be successful. Remember, *do to others what you want them to do to you.* You can be a master of human relations if you believe you can.

You possess talents that are possessed by no other living creature. You need only to develop your talents and you will be well on your way to a lifetime of happiness and success. You possess these talents because you are a unique creation, the only one of your kind. It was planned that way by the Creator from the beginning. The useful services you can render are unique to you. You must search inside yourself to find those talents. Your talents will coordinate perfectly with your wants and desires once you discover them. Once you discover your talents and put them to work as a useful service for others, you'll be happy and successful because you will be doing the things you want to do and those are the things you do best. The apostle Paul said, *"Don't copy the behavior and customs of this world, but be a new and different person with a fresh newness in all you do and think."* That's Romans 12:2.

Paul is saying, don't conform. Dare to be different and operate within the bounds of the great natural laws of the universe that were established by God. You have a spirit that will lead you to greatness and can mold your life so you will truly achieve your maximum potential. This spirit is available only to those who seek it. It is the spirit of the Creator. Regardless of your present circumstances, you can be happy and successful by taking complete control of your thoughts, and you can rise above your negative circumstances.

Throughout history few people have suffered greater adversity than Helen Keller. A serious illness destroyed her sight, hearing, and speech before she was two years old. She was entirely shut off from the world, living as a blind deaf mute. Her teacher, Ann Sullivan, made contact with the girl's mind through the sense of touch. Within three years Helen knew the alphabet and could read and write in Braille. In 1904 she graduated from Radcliffe with honors. She became a noted lecturer and author. Her best-selling books have been translated into more than 50 languages. It would have been very easy for Helen Keller to lose her faith and give up hope many times during her life. But she didn't, because she had realized that she was a child of God, a unique creation possessing an important service to render to mankind. Her love and concern for others gained her worldwide fame. She became a legend in her lifetime.

You probably don't have to overcome as great a degree of adversity as Helen Keller did to secure a happy and successful life. Your circumstances can be altered at any time you choose so that you may begin your journey toward inner peace, riches, enlightenment and physical well-being. Are you allowing your present circumstances to keep you from achieving your full potential as a person? If you are, you are wasting your God-given talents. If you have a genuine thirst for opportunity, then launch out confidently, leaving the details of providing for the necessities of life to the spirit within you. Jesus said, *"Your heavenly Father already knows perfectly well that you need them, and He will give them to you if you give Him first place in your life and live as He wants you to."* That's in Matthew 6:33.

If you have worthwhile goals and are going in the right direction, your needs will be provided for. If you are living within the boundaries of God's guidelines for mankind, He will meet all your needs. Too many people today feel unloved and unwanted. They are wrong. God cares for each of us with a perfect love, which is beyond human understanding. To Him you are very important. The psalmist instructs, *"It is better to trust the Lord than to put confidence in men."* That's Psalm 118:8.

Human love is imperfect, but the love of God is perfect. In Him you have a true friend. If you are His child, His spirit is within you. When you call upon Him He will be there. If you think you are not loved, forget it. You are so loved that Jesus gave His life for you.

You need no other love than the one true love offered in great abundance by the one who really cares the most about you, the Creator of all. Fully realizing that you are a unique being with talents and services to offer and that you are deeply loved, it's time to explore the unlimited opportunities available to you.

Some people believe that opportunity knocks only for the rich and powerful. Some believe there is a fickle finger of fate that taps certain individuals on the shoulder and points them in the direction of wealth and power. Some believe that opportunity has passed them by. They don't believe that an individual is rewarded in direct proportion to the thought and effort he puts forth.

Just after graduation, two young friends asked a multi-millionaire about the chance of earning a million dollars. The old gentleman had little formal education, but he possessed a lot of common sense. My friends thought it more difficult to earn one million dollars today than ever before, and they gave many reasons to prove their point. Finally they asked the old man his opinion. "I think it is easier to earn a million dollars today than ever before," he said. "You boys have a problem, though. You went to college. College doesn't teach you how to strike out on your own, as I did when I was your age."

We must break the bonds of conformity and then use all our mental and physical resources to produce a lifetime of happiness and success. Observe the tremendous abundance all around you. Nature blossoms with unending beauty. Our Creator has provided for all the needs of nature. Drive through your city and consider the fantastic ingenuity and wealth required to construct skyscrapers and freeway systems.

As you observe the tremendous abundance around you, remember that you have as much right to that abundance as any other person. But it will not be given to you, it must be earned. Opportunity comes to those who seek it. Webster's Dictionary defines opportunity as a time or occasion that is right for doing something. The time or occasion will appear when you have mentally prepared yourself to recognize and receive it. To bring this opportunity to fruition requires doing something. Opportunity is everywhere. Most people don't recognize it for what it is, or they allow fear to cripple their thoughts of success.

An elderly man had been earning a meager living from a grocery business for more than 35 years and had reached retirement age. Because of inadequate retirement income, he was forced to enter life insurance sales as a new career. He was an immediate success. He repeatedly told me of the tremendous fulfillment he received from his work. His annual income was considerably more during retirement than during his peak earning years in the grocery business. He said he wished this opportunity had been available to him when he was younger. He never stopped to realize that this opportunity had been available when he was younger, but he had not taken time to discover it.

Francis Bacon, the English philosopher, wrote, "A wise man will make more opportunities than he finds." You must make your opportunities if you want to enjoy a happy and successful life. God has provided everything you need to live a good life. You are exposed to exciting opportunities each day. To capitalize on them you must grasp only those opportunities that are in harmony with your ability to take advantage of them. You possess the spirit to be happy and successful, and you live in a world that provides you with unlimited opportunity. You are important, you are loved, you are a unique creation, and you have unlimited opportunity available because you live in a world governed by a God who knows no limitations. In God's world you can be great if you believe you can.

If you were going to live to be 800 years old, you could afford to waste three to four hundred years of your life doing unimportant things. But this is not the case. From the moment you draw your first breath you begin a personal race against time. Time is a precious jewel that must be guarded well and worn with discretion or you will suddenly realize that it has been stolen. If you use your time wisely and with respect, your life will be one of abundance.

But if you neglect time, it will neglect you. You might have wasted yesterday, you may even be wasting today, but tomorrow is kept fresh and waiting for you. You can turn over a new leaf with each dawning day, if you choose. But don't delay. The proper use of time in your life will guarantee you happiness and success. Proverbs 10:4 tells us, "*Lazy men are soon poor, hard workers get rich.*"

We live in an age of gross materialism. Increasing physical wealth is accompanied by a decline in spiritual values. There is a feeling that something is wrong. People express a feeling of emptiness and unrest. They want more leisure time. They want to work less and play more. Because so many are interested in getting more money for doing less, think how great the opportunity is for someone who is interested in giving more and providing better service to the people he serves, spending his time and energy and equipping himself to do a better job, learning to enjoy life fully as a thoroughly balanced individual and adding to his share of happiness.

Avoid materialism, and don't rest on your laurels once they are won. To continue prosperity, engage in worthwhile work and efficiently use your time. You can do this by having personal goals and plans. God said, "*Six days shalt thou labor and do all thy work.*" By totally committing yourself to work you will be able to enjoy your leisure. In Ecclesiastes 11:4 we find another important key to becoming happy and successful, "*If you wait for perfect conditions you will never get anything done. Perfect circumstances will never come. Get on with your opportunity.*"

Many people resemble the little-known painter who planned a masterpiece. He described it in detail to friends many times as the years passed, but he never found the right time or conditions to begin painting. He took his masterpiece to the grave with him, for it lived only within him.

Don't reach the sunset of life having accomplished nothing worthwhile. Forget about your age, status, nationality or race. Decide what you really want from life and go after it. Action makes dreams become a reality. The vital elements of a happy and successful life are time, work and action. Time control combined with hard work and action, built on the firm foundation of belief, create a potent force.

The line has been drawn. If you step over it, you will have inner peace, riches, enlightenment and physical well-being. Taking that step means that you accept these principles. It also means you must put them to work in your life today.

Decide to take that step. As you begin to live in this happy and successful way, you will find that the floodgates of balanced living will open for you. Your view of your opportunities and the future will be overwhelming, and you will feel better than you have in many years. You will be among an exclusive minority who lead wonderfully happy and successful lives. Begin today; you have nothing to lose. But you have a happy and successful life to gain.

Almost 2,000 years ago Jesus showed us the secret of success. Let His life be an example by which you will achieve happiness and success, and you cannot possibly fail. May the Creator bless you as He has me.

"We attended your seminar three months after our discharge and I'm absolutely convinced that we wouldn't be where we are today if we hadn't. Thank you!"

"Our bankruptcy was discharged three years ago. Since then, we've rented two townhouses, gotten a credit card from our credit union, bought a car, and now have been approved for a $400,000+ mortgage at a competitive rate. Our FICO scores are 725+ and we've stayed debt-free. We have more money and a better quality of life than before our filing. We attended your seminar three months after our discharge and I'm absolutely convinced that we wouldn't be where we are today if we hadn't. Thank you!"

Cami Cacciatore
Nogales, Arizona

"Now I can shop with confidence & without fear."

"I just want to thank you for writing your book. I filed for bankruptcy & I walked away from my lawyer's office feeling bad about myself & my life. I was in a bookstore and was in the financial book section because I was determined to not make the same money mistakes again. Yours was the only book that caught my eye. First of all (I know this will sound sappy) but the bookshelf was right by the window & the sunshine highlighted the book. It was as if something/someone was saying look stupid here it is. I was so glad to hear that I wasn't the only person who had filed bankruptcy. I started using your book's advice from day one. As soon as my bankruptcy was discharged I got an unsecured credit card. I paid all of my bills early or on time & within a year's period I was being offered credit with better interest rates. My credit score shot up 75 points. Now my credit score is in the upper 600s & I should have it over 700 within 3 months. I will be moving soon & am thinking about buying my first home. Now I can shop with confidence & without fear."

LaShawn Hill
Lynwood, California

Personal Development Game Plan

Income seldom exceeds personal development. There is a reason why homes that cost over $750,000 have libraries. If you cannot afford to purchase books, you're in luck. Public libraries will actually allow you to borrow books free of charge! Imagine that. The only cost involved is taking the time to apply for a library card.

It's sad that only a small percentage of Americans use their library cards regularly. If you don't have one, run out and get one today. It's one of your keys to personal development if you're short on cash. The best advice I can give you is to begin reading, listening, and participating in seminars that will stimulate your personal development on a regular basis. Begin a new reading or listening habit today. Turn your car into a mobile classroom!

RECOMMENDED READING

- *Success! The Glenn Bland Method*
  ISBN-10: 084236689X
  By Glenn Bland

  This book will show you how to set goals and make plans that really work. Glenn Bland's ingredients for success include spiritual, financial, educational, and recreational balances.

- *Financial Freedom*
  ISBN-10: 0802426042
  By Larry Burkett

  This little booklet really helped me get over filing bankruptcy. Don't let the size fool you. It gave me peace of mind. Priceless.

- *Legend of the Golden Scrolls: Ageless Secrets for Building Wealth*
  ISBN-10: 1559587059
  By Glenn Bland

This book is in a story format where the hero finds knowledge on how to build wealth. The chapter about how to increase your income is worth the price of the entire book.

- *Rich Dad, Poor Dad: What the Rich Teach Their Kids About Money—That the Poor and Middle Class Do Not!*
  ISBN-10: 0446677450
  By Robert T. Kiyosaki and Sharon L. Lechter

This is a story about how a child learned about wealth from two people, his father (who was poor, financially) and his best friend's father (who was a wealthy businessman). This book will really open your eyes as to the difference between working hard and working smart. After reading this book, you'll never look at a "job" the same way again.

- *1 Minute Bible 4 Students: With 366 Devotions for Daily Living*
  ISBN-10: 0613889606
  By Doug Fields, John R., III Kohlenberger (Editor)

This book is a great way to learn the Bible as it moves you through the entire Bible—from Genesis to Revelation—in just one year.

- *Think and Grow Rich*
  ISBN-10: 1585424331
  By Napoleon Hill

If you were to ask the most successful people on Earth which one book they would recommend, I would put my money on almost all of them recommending this one. I haven't met anyone successful who has NOT read this book. What more of a recommendation do you need? Best of all, it's well stocked at your library. You have no excuse not to read this book.

- *Law of Success*
  ISBN-10: 1932429247
  By Napoleon Hill

First written in 1928, this book teaches the life-changing philosophy upon which *Think and Grow Rich* and most modern motivational books are based. Don't let the date of when it was published discourage you from reading it. It was way ahead of its time, and the advice in it is still as valid today as it was then.

- *The Templeton Plan: 21 Steps to Personal Success and Real Happiness*
  ISBN-10: 0062502867
  By John Marks Templeton

John Marks Templeton is regarded as one of the world's wisest investors and he believes that his financial accomplishments are directly related to his strong convictions. In this book, he shares the secrets of his phenomenal success in 21 principles that provide solid guidelines for prosperity and happiness.

- *The Richest Man in Babylon*
  ISBN-10: 0451205367
  By George S. Clason

This book will show you the importance of investing to get wealthy. It makes the point that you can live off of your income, but you'll never attain true wealth from income alone.

- *The Life Application Study Bible—New Living Translation*
  ISBN-10: 0842384936

This study guide makes the Bible easy to understand and helps people see how the Scriptures are relevant to today's issues. Now with the New Living Translation, the *Life Application Study Bible* makes God's Word even more accessible to those who need it. I turn to it often.

CHAPTER 15

- *The Tao of Warren Buffett*
  ISBN-10: 1416541322
  By Mary Buffett

Quotes and philosophy from Warren Buffett, the third richest man in the world. This simple and powerful book is the ultimate introduction to the way of the world's most successful investor.

- *The Power of Thought: Ageless Secrets of Great Achievement*
  ISBN-10: 0761503412
  By Glenn Bland

Glenn Bland studied examples of successful people to understand the common traits they share, despite their diverse beginnings and paths to success. His findings indicate that there are special human qualities such as character, trust, dreams, purpose, and effort that guarantee success when cultivated and applied.

- *The Five Rituals of Wealth*
  ISBN-10: 0887307841
  By Tod Barnhart

In this book you'll learn the straightforward techniques one of the nation's premier investment counselors used to become a top performer in the brokerage industry. This is information everyone can and should know.

- *The Strangest Secret: How to Live the Life You Desire*
  ISBN-10: 9562912671
  By Earl Nightingale

One of the first and greatest books of its kind, this simple book walks you through the powerful "secret" that has propelled men to greatness for centuries.

RECOMMENDED LISTENING

- *Success: The Glenn Bland Method* audio CD

- *Think and Grow Rich* audio series

- *The Strangest Secret* on audio CD

- *Credit After Bankruptcy* on audio CD

- Jim Rohn's *The Weekend Seminar*
Recorded live in 1999, Jim Rohn shares the ideas, strategies and proven principles that have helped him achieve mega success in both business and in life over the past 39 years.

- Jim Rohn's *The Day That Turns Your Life Around*
This six CD course shows you that one critical day is all you need to turn any "what if" in your life into what IS. Some people wait years, decades, even an entire lifetime for that day to arrive. YOU don't have to. You can make that magical, transformational day—the day "That Turns Your Life Around"—be today!

- Jim Rohn's *Cultivating an Unshakable Character*
This program is an inspirational look at the 12 pillars of character, the inner resources that support and sustain you on your journey through life. These pillars form the foundation of personal and professional success, and without them, achievements are fleeting and far less satisfying.

- Jim Rohn's *The Power of Ambition*
Ambition is at the very core of success and extraordinary achievement. Harness the power of your own personal ambition by mastering these six simple steps.

- Jim Rohn's *The Art of Exceptional Living*
A guide for making your life a masterpiece. Includes four major lessons you must master to become successful and to overcome self-imposed restrictions. Also includes a detailed, step-by-step goal-setting workshop to help design the next 10 years.

- Jim Rohn's *The Challenge to Succeed*

  Discover through these five inspirational topics a guide to help you through self-evaluation and commitment. Topics include the five major pieces, personal development, the fundamentals for prosperity and success, attitude, change, and more.

- Jim Rohn's *Take Charge of Your Life*

  Learn how to develop the power of persuasion, control your emotions, work on team-building, and develop techniques for being a great communicator.

- Jim Rohn's *How to Use a Journal*

  Jim's insights and guidance show you how to use a major tool he has used over the past 39 years for gathering and collecting ideas and experiences.

- Jim Rohn's *Three Keys to Greatness*

  A guide for teenagers to achieve financial independence and success! Learn the places to begin for any teenager (or adult) in the quest for success, happiness and wealth.

RECOMMENDED PARTICIPATION

- Bible Study Fellowship
  (877) 273-3228
  www.bsfinternational.org

- *Credit After Bankruptcy*® internet or live seminar
  www.afterbankruptcy.org

Most of the books and audio products listed in this chapter you will want to read and listen to over and over again. These are not just books you read once and put back on the shelf. Renewing your mind takes time.

"For the record, know that your weekly newsletters are the best I have read on the subject—forthright, concise, succinct and extremely informative."

Wil Stakes
Swarthmore, Pennsylvania

"Thanks to your books and newsletters...all three of my scores from MyFICO came back over 700 the highest being 763 and the middle score being 728."

"I am getting ready to go out and celebrate, so I thought I'd drop you a line to thank you for all your help and share my story with you. In February 2002 my Chapter 7 bankruptcy was discharged and from that point on I was on a mission. That mission was to reestablish my credit and never make any of those mistakes again. About 6 months or so after that I came across your book and signed up for your newsletter. Shortly there after I received my first unsecured card and finally found a bank to open an account for me. Then I set some long term goals. Well guess what? Thanks to your books and newsletters...all three of my scores from MyFICO came back over 700 the highest being 763 and the middle score being 728. All this in about 5 years instead of 10, that needs a Wooooo Hooooo! I own a small construction company and plan on getting into the real estate business, mainly buying, fixing up, and reselling houses now that my scores are in the premium range. Wish me luck! I also have my sites set on the big 800 ;o) Again thank you Stephen for all your help and your hard work in putting all this great info together for us, I couldn't have done it without ya."

Richard Puleo Jr.
Hapeville, Georgia

CHAPTER **16**

How to Establish a New Bank Relationship

If you're like me, you've really never met a banker you truly liked. It started very young with me. I was an entrepreneur as a teenager.

I wanted to be a professional photographer, and needed money to purchase photography equipment. No bank would consider loaning money to me. Bank after bank sent me a decline letter. Ever since then I have always felt that bankers "didn't have a clue."

Well, when you meet the right banker it makes a world of difference. They're out there; just hard to find. There are bankers who really want to help you get reestablished, and will do everything in their power to help you. Let's get started.

BANK VS. CREDIT UNION

The biggest problem I have with credit unions is that they usually do not report your timely loan payments to all three of the credit reporting agencies.

So when you establish new credit with your credit union it may not be helping you since no other lender will see your timely payments! The account won't help your FICO® credit scores, either. If you're using a credit union now, call the branch manager and ask which of the three credit reporting agencies they report to. If they don't report to all three, my advice would be to find one that does.

CHECK VERIFICATION SYSTEMS

When I first moved to Indianapolis I was quickly turned down while attempting to open a checking account with a certain bank. It irritated me, even though I had a previous habit of writing checks that bounced. The history of my rubber checks showed up on various check verification services. So how do you get around check verification services? There are two ways.

The easiest way is to let your fingers do the walking in the Yellow Pages. Call each bank branch closest to you and ask some simple, yet direct, questions about opening a new account.

I found something really surprising: Not all banks subscribe to a check verification system—Especially the smaller banks. What's more, there are different check verification systems! So find a bank that doesn't use the check verification system you're listed with.

I called and asked for the person in charge of opening new accounts. Once that person was on the phone I introduced myself and said I was interested in opening checking and savings accounts. I asked the person to explain the most cost-effective account fees and minimum deposit requirements. It was also important to me to have a debit bank card, so I asked how I could obtain one and what the requirements were.

If everything seemed okay, I asked which check verification system they used to open new accounts. If the person hesitated even slightly, I quickly responded that I had a few returned checks that might prevent me from opening an account.

After reviewing the notes I had taken on each call, I would then decide which bank I felt offered the most services for the money, and would visit the branch to open new accounts.

The second way is more fun. It involves paying attention to new bank branches in the area. New bank branches are eager to sign up new bank accounts, and they sometimes waive standard procedure in verifying accounts.

After my first attempt to establish a bank account failed, I tried again. While waiting for my wife at a job interview, I noticed three brand new bank branches on the same corner of a fairly new part of town. I knew something special was going to happen.

I went into one of the banks and asked to speak to the person in charge of opening new accounts. As I was sitting down in his office, I told him I would like to open checking and savings accounts.

I then proceeded to tell him that I might have a few returned checks on his bank's check verification system and I was not sure whether they would accept me as a client.

His answer was, "No problem." Within 10 minutes I walked out of the bank with checking and savings accounts. No check verification system was used.

So, if you're in a situation where you don't think you could get a bank account, let my story be an encouragement to you. Make it happen.

At this point I was so elated that we had a checking account again that it didn't matter that this banker wasn't interested in helping me reestablish credit. The important thing now was that with an existing bank account I could be more selective in choosing a long-term bank partner. Once you have a checking account, few bankers use their check verification system to establish a new account. Bankers love it when you switch to their bank from a competitor. In fact, some banks give you a special bonus for being a new customer.

Remember to always pay any outstanding checks listed on the check verification system. This will help you if the banks in your area all subscribe to the same system.

FINDING A GOOD BANKER

How I found my good bankers was through referrals and by hard work on the telephone. In this case two referrals came from people working for organizations extending micro-loans to low-income people within the community. The other was a result of a telephone survey of bankers in the area.

My logic was that anyone dedicated to helping low-income people rehabilitate their lives would be connected to people who might be able to help me.

If you have the time and energy to locate your own good banker, the place to start is on the telephone.

1. Start with your existing bank branch.
2. Call your bankruptcy attorney and ask for a referral.
3. Call bank branch managers directly.

Finding your good banker is well worth the time and effort you put into it. Having a good banker will accelerate your ability to obtain mainstream credit.

GO WHERE THE GOOD BANKER IS

Our bankers were 30 minutes or more away from our house. In fact, I passed at least 19 other banks while driving to their location. Where your banker is located should not matter. You simply open accounts with your good banker and do your regular business with branches that are closest to you. Having a banker who is willing to help you is more important than how close the bank is to your home.

My friend David didn't see the importance of working with a banker who was willing to help him reestablish credit. He decided to ask the bank manager closest to him to do the same things my banker would do. Not only was the banker not willing to help, but she told my friend that it couldn't be done. What's interesting is that it was the same bank I used, just a different branch.

This happens time after time. Don't be discouraged if one branch manager says no. The next one you talk with may be very open to working with you. It's a matter of personality and experience.

WHAT MAKES A GOOD BANKER?

A good banker will provide several important things as you begin your journey back to financial stability:

1. A secured bank loan.

2. Free checking and savings accounts.

3. Minimum checking account activation deposit of $25.

4. Checks starting at a higher number instead of 001.

5. An automatic approval of a Visa debit bank card.

6. No charge to use their ATM.

7. The high probability of receiving overdraft protection within 6 to 12 months.

A good banker is usually someone in authority, like a branch manager. Someone without authority will not help you in the long term. Don't waste your time with anyone other than a manager.

Bob, one of my favorite bankers, is so good that he has managed four different branches since I've known him. I moved my accounts wherever he went. It pays to go where the good banker is. You are building a relationship with a person, not the bank.

One of my other bankers, Tom, was also very good. He was responsible for my first overdraft protection account of $2,500.

Sometimes one banker can't do it all. You may need a few of them. Bob couldn't get me an unsecured overdraft-protection account, but Tom could. Just go with the flow.

Today I deal with bankers on my terms. I don't go into the bank—the bankers come to me. Boy how quickly things can change.

WHAT TO EXPECT FROM A GOOD BANKER

The most important thing a good banker can do for you is help you reestablish your credit by means of a secured bank loan.

My good banker set me up with several secured bank loans. I decided to visit a few other banks and do the same thing. Most of them couldn't understand what I wanted to do.

Remember that these people are doing a specific job. To most of them it is just a job, that's all. They don't really care about your needs or special concerns. A good banker will do everything he or she can to help you.

This is how to approach your banker. Tell them you have a previous bankruptcy and want to reestablish credit. Tell them the best way for you to do that is by getting a secured bank loan. Ask them whether their bank approves secured loans. If you get a yes, ask whether they can use the loan proceeds as collateral so you will not have to put up your own money. You may have to repeat yourself slowly a few times. Uncreative bankers need to hear it more than once to understand it.

So how does a secured loan work? After you find a banker who is willing to do one, it's pretty simple. First you need to open checking and savings accounts. You can usually open these accounts with $25, depending on the individual bank. After you have bank accounts you need to fill out a loan application. The banker should know your credit history before you submit a credit application. Use the methods outlined in previous chapters to help you prepare. Once approved, it's a matter of signing paperwork. Some banks can approve the loan the same day, while others require you to come back the next day. It depends on that particular bank's policy. The bank then deposits the loan proceeds (or check) you sign over to them into a savings account, and places a hold on that account. This hold means you will be unable to withdraw funds put on hold. Other than that, it's a regular savings account. If you default, the loan is completely secured. Within a week or so you will receive a bank loan payment book in the mail. You start making monthly payments on your loan. When you pay off the loan, the money you've saved belongs to you.

Another hidden benefit of the secured bank loan is that it acts as a forced savings account. Now you can honestly write on any credit application that you have so many thousand dollars in a savings account in your bank. The lender can even call to verify that it is true.

Most banks will require you to put up the loan amount in cash. There are creative banks and credit unions, like the East Boston Savings Bank and Alternatives Federal Credit Union that have specific secured-loan programs. The secured-loan program is usually called "Credit Builder." It's a great program that more banks should have.

The second thing a good banker can do for you is provide no-fee bank checking and savings accounts. With the monthly fees on checking accounts averaging $10 a month, this becomes an important issue to someone trying to save money.

Most customer-oriented banks have a program whereby if you have a certain amount of money in savings with them they will waive all normal bank maintenance fees. This is the kind of bank you want to work with. Most banks have these programs. Having just received a bank loan should also qualify you to receive no-fee accounts. I recommend obtaining a secured loan amount that would qualify you to have all bank fees waived. At one bank, having

$1,000 secured in savings may qualify you for no-fee bank accounts. At another bank, you may need a $5,000 loan to qualify. Ask before you decide on the loan amount.

The third thing a good banker can do for you is allow you to open your new checking and savings accounts with a minimum amount. Every bank has a different policy, but most will allow you to start a new account with $25. The amount varies from state to state. The most I have ever opened an account with was $100 in Chicago. Simply ask what the minimum deposit is to open an account.

The fourth thing a good banker will do is allow you to start your checks at a number higher than 001. You will likely be hassled by merchants over a low check number wherever you go, so be sure to remember to ask for this when you're placing your check order. Some banks have a policy limiting the number for new accounts. If that's the case, open an account, but do not order checks from them. There are many companies you can purchase checks from that allow you to have any check number you want; in addition, the cost of the checks is usually half what the banks charge.

You can find many of these companies by using: *www.google. com* and searching for, "checks" or, "checks online."

Most of the check printing companies will allow you to place your first order through the mail or online. However, if you place your order online and the company can't verify with your bank that your name and address match your account information, they will need to request a copy of a check from your bank to make sure the information is correct.

The fifth thing a good banker will do for you is automatically approve you for a Visa or MasterCard debit card. This is good to have when you are just starting out. It works like a normal Visa or MasterCard, except—instead of accessing a line of credit, the money comes out of your checking account.

For several years these debit cards were just as hard to get as a normal bank card. Bankers have finally awakened to understand that they save money when their customers use electronic debit transactions to pay for things, versus writing checks. Now most of the larger banks have adopted new policies that push debit cards. Keep in mind, having a debit card does not help your credit rating since no line of credit is being extended and it doesn't report to the three credit reporting agencies.

The sixth thing a good banker provides is waiving the service fees for using their ATM. Those small fees add up to a small fortune over a period of time. My wife and I refused to pay ATM service fees. We either drove to use one of our bank's machines or visited our local grocery store, which cashed personal checks. Only in emergencies did we use an ATM that charged us a service fee. Most banks do not charge when you use their own ATM. Today we just don't have a need to use ATMs. We pretty much just use one credit card for everything.

The seventh thing a good banker will do is slowly trust you with unsecured lines of credit. It may start with overdraft protection consisting of a few hundred dollars connected to your checking account.

The important thing to remember is that it takes time to get to the place where you can get unsecured credit with banks, even if your salary has tripled since your bankruptcy. My wife and I worked on reestablishing credit for almost six years before we began to go after unsecured credit through traditional channels.

Do not expect to be able to qualify for unsecured credit immediately after you finish paying off your first secured bank loan. Just stay credit-active and pay your bills early or on time. Always be on the lookout for good bankers. Your patience will pay off. Keep a good attitude and your time will come. Besides, if you're doing everything right, you won't need the unsecured lines of credit, they will only be a convenience. Happy hunting.

"We have just been approved (OVERNIGHT with your recommended mortgage company) for a $230-$250,000 mortgage..."

"Wow! That's all we can say! We followed your advice and things started to happen right away. We did the things you discussed in your seminar about using and establishing new credit and we are very proud to say we have just been approved (OVERNIGHT with your recommended mortgage company) for a $230-$250,000 mortgage on a custom made, WHEELCHAIR ACCESSIBLE home only four months following our discharge!! Thanks for helping us to achieve true 'Life after Bankruptcy!'

P.S. Thanks for sharing your personal mortgage broker with us too!"

Dale and Cynthia Patterson
Guttenberg, New Jersey

"After only 2 months after discharge, I had to check my credit scores again (just addicting—really!) and my scores have gone to 698!! Only 2 more points and I'll get to my 6 month goal of the 700 club!!"

"I first found your website after filing for Chapter 7 by simply typing in *www.lifeafterbankruptcy.com* figuring—someone smart enough must have started up a website called this and there you were! I first started out by reading the success stories and then became a subscriber of your newsletter, which I read religiously EVERY WEEK! I since then have also bought your book and then the entire course on increasing my credit scores. After only 2 months after discharge, I had to check my credit scores again (just addicting—really!) and my scores have gone to 698!! Only 2 more points and I'll get to my 6 month goal of the 700 club!!"

Lisa Brown
Cleveland, Mississippi

How to Get Approved for a Major Credit Card

I s it really necessary to have a credit card? Yes. Major credit cards are an important ingredient in reestablishing credit after bankruptcy.

There are many valid reasons to carry a credit card. But most important is that lenders like to see a credit card on your credit reports, with a history of timely payments.

It's also a matter of convenience. When was the last time you tried to make hotel reservations without a credit card? Or rent a car while on vacation? Or purchase airline tickets? Or purchase something online? Or make a payment over the telephone?

The three lesser-known benefits of credit cards are liability, fraud protection, and purchase protection.

Liability is the most powerful reason to carry credit cards. Unlike its cousin, the debit card, a credit card offers protection to the consumer under the Fair Credit Reporting Act (FCRA) for any liability over $50. Not so with debit cards or business credit cards.

If you accidentally get involved with a company that defrauds you, the chances of getting your cash back with a debit card are pretty slim. But by using your credit card, a credit for the purchase is just a phone call away. The bank does everything for you!

Purchase protection is a value-added perk that is available on some cards which guarantees the items you purchase from theft, accidental breakage, etc.

UNSECURED CREDIT CARDS

So how do you qualify for unsecured credit cards? You don't, at least in the beginning when your credit scores are low.

Almost all of the unsecured credit cards you receive offers for will be high-interest, low limit cards. The worst offenders are Capital One, Household Bank, First PREMIER Bank, and Applied Bank.

I recommend you wait to apply for an unsecured credit card until your credit scores are above 680—or even better, over 700.

Here's an often overlooked problem with these high-interest, low limit credit card providers...low limits can hurt your FICO® credit scores.

Having a $200 credit limit can end up slowing your recovery. How? With such a small credit limit, chances are you will max out your card. In other words, you'll use 100% of your available balance, which will have a negative effect on your credit scores.

And since it's a relatively new card, it's not like you can just call for a credit limit increase. You need about 6 to 12 months of on-time payments before you will have established enough positive history with a lender to request a credit limit increase.

Remember: the higher your revolving credit balances—the lower your credit scores.

And be very skeptical of unsecured credit card schemes. My friend Steve told me about an advertisement he noticed in the local newspaper for an unsecured credit card. He wasn't interested in obtaining new credit with an unknown bank, but was curious as to what they were up to. This company advertises in newspapers, guaranteeing a low-limit unsecured credit card. All you need to do is participate in a local seminar in your area.

The bottom line was that they were more interested in selling you merchandise. Steve walked out halfway through the seminar after they began talking about their merchandise catalogs being linked to a "Platinum Credit Card." There is no free ride with credit card lenders. Stop wasting your time and energy looking for something that doesn't exist. Begin with a secured credit card.

SECURED CREDIT CARDS

There are many benefits to using secured credit cards. My four favorite reasons are:

1. You have control over your credit limit.

2. Secured cards turn into unsecured cards with a timely payment history.

3. If something happens and you can no longer make your payments, your deposit covers your balance.

4. No one will know it's a secured credit card except you.

Secured credit cards are the way to go. They work like any other major credit card. The only difference is that your deposit equals your line of credit. Some banks require as little as $250 to get started, others $300, and still others $500 or more. There's even a bank in Chicago that will let you deposit up to $25,000 for their Gold Secured Card.

The good news is that with an excellent payment history, many secured cards will turn into unsecured credit cards within 24 months. Each secured credit card company makes their own rules. That is why it's important to ask questions.

The major complaint from people about secured credit cards is that the credit limits are so low that it doesn't seem to be worth their time and effort. Nothing could be further from the truth. Be responsible over little, and you will be trusted with much. Remember, you have to prove that your bad money management habits have disappeared.

There are two drawbacks to having low limits on a credit card. If you max out your credit limit each month you end up doing more damage than good. You fix this by not carrying a balance each month and not coming close to your credit limit. And, if you have a secured card you also have the flexibility to raise your credit limit by making additional deposits to increase your limit.

Another drawback to having low limits is known as the authorization problem. Hotels are especially known for this. Let's say you check into a hotel in Manhattan with a room rate of $250 and you plan to stay for 2 days. The hotel may authorize your credit card for the entire $500, plus an additional $200 to cover dining, long-distance calls and snack bar purchases. This could be a problem if your limit is only $600. These situations can usually be worked out in advance. Call and ask their policy and be aware of this potential challenge.

Ignore most of the direct-mail solicitations you receive from credit card companies after bankruptcy. Read the fine print! The last thing you want is a credit card from a predatory lender. Find a shoe-box and "file" all credit solicitations there until a later date.

Having a secured card is nothing to be ashamed of. The waiter or cashier who takes your card doesn't know it's secured. Best of all, most secured card companies report to the credit reporting agencies the same as an unsecured card.

Our story in obtaining a secured credit card is interesting. I quickly found out that it was necessary for our bankruptcies to be discharged before applying, so I was ready the day we received our discharge letters in the mail. In fact, our first applications went out the same day we each received our discharge letters.

We really couldn't afford to deposit $500 to begin our first secured credit card only 3 months after filing bankruptcy. So to come up with the money, we each put in extra hours at work, sold unnecessary items around the house, returned things for credit, ate very light, and saved every dollar we could. My wife fought me every step of the way. I usually listen to her, but she couldn't see the big picture. She still saw credit as the enemy. My logic was, the longer we waited to reestablish credit, the longer it would take to recover. So don't wait six months before applying for credit; that six months of good payment history could be working for you. It's best to start as soon as possible.

The company we chose guaranteed that we would have our card within two weeks of mailing in the application. This was very important to us, since we would probably need to use it immediately after receiving it. Sure enough, in exactly 14 days we had our first major credit card. Unfortunately, the bank was recently bought out, and they no longer issue a good secured credit card.

WHAT TO LOOK FOR IN A SECURED CREDIT CARD

Before selecting a secured credit card provider, you need to ask a lot of questions. Every bank has its own standards. Here are some things to consider before you choose a credit card.

WHICH CREDIT REPORTING AGENCY DO THEY USE TO MAKE A LENDING DECISION?

Most lenders today use one of your FICO® credit scores to determine your rate, terms and approval. When you know which credit reporting agency the lender uses, you can pick the lender that uses your highest score. This greatly increases your opportunity to get approved at the best terms.

WILL THEY ACCEPT YOU WITH A PREVIOUS BANKRUPTCY?

This is a basic question. But guess what—some secured credit card programs do not accept people with a bankruptcy. Go figure. In addition, most require that your bankruptcy be discharged. You can easily prove you've been discharged by mailing a copy (not the original) of the discharge letter you received in the mail from the bankruptcy court. Only one bank I know will approve an application without a discharge.

IS THERE AN APPLICATION FEE?

Avoid any credit card provider with an application fee. The best credit cards do not require one. Companies that ask for an application fee are usually the companies that specialize in approving credit cards for non-creditworthy individuals. Do not waste your time, money, or effort with these companies. They are not your long-term players. You do not need to pay an application fee just because you filed bankruptcy.

WHAT IS THE MINIMUM INITIAL DEPOSIT REQUIRED TO OPEN AN ACCOUNT?

The minimum amount of your initial deposit varies from bank to bank. I've seen initial deposits as low as $250 and as high as $25,000. It is usually better to deposit as much as you can in the beginning, but if it's impossible for you to come up with the additional money, start immediately with what you can.

WHICH CREDIT REPORTING AGENCIES DO THEY REPORT TO?

This is a very important question. What good is it if they will not report your excellent payment history to all three of the credit reporting agencies? Credit card companies should report to the three major credit reporting agencies (Equifax®, TransUnion™, and Experian®), but there are many that choose not to or only report to one.

WILL THEY REPORT YOUR CREDIT LIMIT ACCURATELY?

A disturbing trend has started among some credit card lenders. Instead of reporting your actual credit limit to the credit reporting agencies, they report your highest balance ever, or worse, they don't report a limit at all. It is very important that your credit card lender report your actual limit because your credit balance-to-limit ratio is a part of the formula that determines your FICO® credit scores. If your credit limits are not reported correctly, there is no way for other lenders to get an accurate picture of how you are really managing your credit.

DO THEY ACCEPT OUT-OF-STATE CUSTOMERS?

Not all credit card providers accept out-of-state customers. Be sure to ask.

HOW QUICKLY DO THEY APPROVE?

The most common amount of time it takes to get an approval is three to four weeks. However, it is possible to receive one in 7 to 14 days. Our first secured credit card arrived in exactly 14 days. Our next credit card, with the help of FedEx, arrived the same week! If you're in a hurry, mention that you're planning a vacation and would really like the convenience of their credit card. (You can plan a vacation without ever going on one.) Ask if they have a different address to send applications via overnight mail. Priority Mail is inexpensive and usually arrives in two to three days. If a tracking number is important to you, FedEx three-day service is guaranteed and cost effective. It will put you on the top of the "normal" mail applications. Some may charge you for rush service; if you can afford the additional fee, it may be worth it for you.

HOW LONG UNTIL IT TURNS INTO AN UNSECURED CARD?

Choose a credit card provider that specifically states how long before it turns into an unsecured card. The best programs are 24 months or less. Anything beyond that is too long.

What sometimes happens is that you have the option to keep your deposit invested and have your credit limit increased, or request that your deposit funds be returned to you and retain the same credit limit, although unsecured.

Ask what factors, other than late payments, would negatively affect your credit standing with them. Each lender is different. One lender may perceive going over your limit as a negative mark; another may ignore it if it was paid before the next statement was issued. Just ask, and they will tell you.

If you do not establish an excellent payment history during the secured time period, the bank may delay or decline your credit card from converting into an unsecured card. So your question should be, "If I pay on a timely basis as agreed, when might I be considered for unsecured status?"

Some lenders issue a new credit card when your card converts into an unsecured card. All our credit card lenders issued us new cards. This is good. Another credit reference is added to your credit reports.

HOW MUCH OF YOUR DEPOSIT IS AVAILABLE?

Not all banks will allow you to use the full amount you send in as a security deposit. Just make a point of knowing what your credit limit is before you begin to use it.

Our first cards allowed us full benefit to the entire deposit amount. Our second card froze $100 of the security deposit. Within six months, however, they reapplied the amount to our limit after seeing a perfect payment history.

HOW MUCH OF MY CREDIT LIMIT IS AVAILABLE VIA CASH ADVANCE?

Some lenders severely restrict how much of your limit you have access to via a cash advance. One of our cards gave us access to only 25% of our limit in the form of a cash advance. Of course, we found that little policy out when we needed it the most! I would have closed the account right then and there if it wouldn't have hurt my scores.

IS TOLL-FREE OR ONLINE CUSTOMER SERVICE AVAILABLE?

This may not be important to you, but for us it was. We constantly called to hear our available limit and payments received.

At times we would call the automated information line several times a day, usually just before eating out or going to the movies. Nothing is more embarrassing than standing in front of a long line of people and having your credit card denied. We always called first before making a purchase when our balance was close to the limit. It was close to the limit a lot in the beginning. If each long-distance call had cost us 50 cents, we would have easily spent $30 a month on long distance.

Our first credit card gave us toll-free access to the customer assistance center and long-distance access to the automated information line. When our credit cards were purchased by a larger bank 18 months later, we gained toll-free access to everything.

Keep in mind that we opened our first secured credit card accounts before the internet was popular. Now, most credit card companies give you the option to check your balance and even make payments online.

WHAT IS YOUR INTEREST RATE?

Frankly, your interest rate isn't very important right now. More important are the benefits as a cardholder. Expect to pay 17% to 26% for any secured credit card. Over time this will go down as your credit scores increase.

A few months after our cards converted into unsecured cards, I called to tell customer service that I was considering switching banks. They responded by lowering my interest rate on the spot, and at the same time increased my credit limit.

Accept any interest rate, within reason. Ask when you might expect the interest rate to go down. The best times to ask are after you have had 12 months of perfect payment history, when your card converts to an unsecured card, or during the holidays. Most secured card lenders are having a tough time holding onto their customers after they turn unsecured. In fact, what a lot of lenders are doing is "selling" good accounts to larger banks that will allow lower interest rates, more benefits, and higher credit limits. This is good. The more positive credit references on your credit reports, the better.

WHAT IS THEIR MAXIMUM DEPOSIT AMOUNT?

Most secured cards will limit the amount of money you can put into them. The maximum is usually $5,000. Each bank makes their own rules.

CAN YOU FIND AN UNSECURED LIMIT LOOPHOLE?

This is exciting...a few banks are really interested in helping you reestablish credit. They do this by providing an opportunity. The opportunity is a higher unsecured line of credit. Timing is everything when taking advantage of this loophole. To best explain it I will again draw from personal experience.

It all started when the customer assistance center of our credit card company informed me of a neat way of getting a higher unsecured limit. If I paid as agreed for 12 months I could then call and request to be reviewed for an unsecured card. The best part about it was that the unsecured credit limit became whatever the security deposit was at the time on the secured card. So this meant that if my credit card's maximum deposit amount was $5,000, in theory, I could automatically qualify for a $5,000 unsecured credit card in 12 months. All I had to do was figure out a way to save an additional $4,500 in 12 months. The opportunity had presented itself!

We tried very hard to increase our credit limit by sending in additional deposit amounts over the 12-month period, but it was obvious we were not committed to do it. What we decided to do was apply for a home equity loan and use $4,500 of the loan proceeds to increase our secured credit card limit before we requested that they review the account for unsecured status.

We sent the bank a $4,500 cashier's check via FedEx. We waited four or five days, and then verified that the payment posted to the account using the automated information line. We then called to request that our secured credit card with a $5,000 secured line of credit be reviewed for unsecured status.

It worked. In less than 10 days:

1. We were approved for an unsecured credit card

2. We were approved for a $5,000 limit

3. We had the $5,000 security deposit plus interest returned to us in the form of a certified check

4. We were extended a new account number, which meant another positive reference on our credit reports

5. The bank lowered our interest rate to 9.9%

We started out with no clue how we were going to come up with the $4,500. We knew it might be tough. We were already saving close to 30% of our income. Our responsibility was to believe it would happen, and it did. We still have that account today, although the limit is now six figures.

So you're saying you don't want a $5,000 line of credit. Fine. What about $2,500? Decide what amount is comfortable for you and proceed.

It became a real convenience for us. We could decide to take a vacation and just go. We didn't need to call to see if there is enough credit available. When the bill came, we paid it off.

When I first learned about this trick I didn't believe it. I called back at least 10 to 15 times over 12 months just to be sure the person on the other end was telling the truth.

What they didn't tell me was to wait until the last minute and make a large deposit into my account, wait a few days, request a review for unsecured status, and look for my $5,000 back in less than

7 days. This we figured out on our own. In fact, I'm convinced my bank changed their policy because of me. They have since changed their program and closed that loophole.

Can you see that the benefits of the right credit card become more important than quibbling over an interest rate? Keep your eyes open and look for every opportunity. Sometimes all it takes is a friendly voice and a sincere interest in the other person.

DO THEY GRANT CREDIT LIMIT INCREASES?

It's easy to forget, since it's so simple. Most banks are on a six month credit limit increase cycle. This means that you can call every six months and expect a credit line increase if you have paid as agreed. But be warned, when you request a credit limit increase the inquiry lowers your FICO® credit scores.

As I began writing this section I called my bank and asked for my credit limit to be increased. They asked me a few basic questions, and within a few minutes my credit line doubled. I call it my $50,000 telephone call—all because I remembered to ask.

Why is it important to always increase your credit limits? Because other lenders make their credit decisions based on compensating balances. For example, if my highest credit limit were $500, and I asked for a $2,000 loan, the chances of getting it would be slim. This is because my other credit limits were not at the same level as my request.

It's sort of like wanting to lease a Mercedes Benz, but you can only afford a Yugo. So keep increasing those credit limits. It makes recovering from bankruptcy that much easier.

In addition, a higher limit will increase your credit scores, assuming your balances remain the same. For more information about increasing your credit scores, subscribe to the free *Life After Bankruptcy*® newsletter at: *www.lifeafterbankruptcy.com/subscribe.*

CREDIT CARD RECOMMENDATIONS

Currently there are nearly 50 banks that offer secured credit card programs. I monitor them all on an annual basis. Out of those secured programs, I recommend only one.

If you have attended the free Credit After Bankruptcy® seminar live or on the internet, you probably received an application from what I consider to be the best secured credit card company in the country. If you purchased our book in a bookstore, please contact the After Bankruptcy Foundation at: *(317) 578-7118* or email Mary Ann at: *maryann@afterbankruptcy.com* and ask her to mail the application to you.

So why don't I just list the best credit card programs in this book? Because they constantly change. In addition, there are different cards for different people.

For instance, most banks will not take people who have not been discharged; one will. Some banks offer business credit cards. Another has a program for people in the military. Some offer initial deposits as low as $250. There are even banks that offer credit cards to people with no income. There are many programs to choose from.

If you want to spend a few hours doing your own research, I recommend: *www.cardweb.com.*

"I was able to refinance my van from 21.95% to 8%, bought a new car for 2.9%, and got a new $10,000 credit card with 0% interest."

"Good news! Since I started following your advice four years ago after my bankruptcy, my credit scores are up to 728!! Thank you!! I was able to refinance my van from 21.95% to 8%, bought a new car for 2.9%, and got a new $10,000 credit card with 0% interest. I am applying for a mortgage now. So far, with my income, I am qualifying for up to $160,000. Thanks again for all your advice!"

Anita Emerson
Gatesville, Texas

"I just found out I am going to purchase my home with a no money down loan with 5.8% financing... my second home since my bankruptcy."

"Just recently wrote you...but wanted to add that I just checked my FICO scores from myfico.com/12 and I have scores of 644, 719, and 753!!!!! I could not believe my eyes, thanks to you guys. I just found out I am going to purchase my home with a no money down loan with 5.8% financing...my second home since my bankruptcy. I truly cannot believe how much you have changed my life. And an added note, my ex-husband who said your seminar was not worth going to did not go and his credit scores last time he checked were all below 550 and he has no house and no credit...not that I told him so...but I told him so. Thanks again so much for your seminar and your desire to help those of us that want to be helped!!!"

Cristi Chauncey
Bethel, Pennsylvania

Where to Apply for a Mortgage

I remember when I applied for my first mortgage after bankruptcy. It was pretty intimidating.

That was nearly 13 years ago. But it feels like it was just yesterday when I called a mortgage company and timidly asked about getting a mortgage.

I didn't know what to expect. Many questions ran through my mind...

> "What if I start this process and don't have enough money to finish?"

> "How do I know who to trust?"

> "Can I really get approved for a mortgage this quickly after my bankruptcy?"

> "How much money will I need?"

> "Are my credit scores high enough to qualify?"

> "Will they make me feel like a loser?"

All of those questions and more went through my mind. What I discovered startled me. I found out that I had options and that there are many different sources you can go to for a mortgage.

HOW TO BEST USE THE DIFFERENT MORTGAGE SOURCES AVAILABLE TO YOU

The mortgage industry offers several different types of sources to finance your home. The differences can get a little blurry at times, but here are the major categories...

- Banks

- Credit unions

- Finance companies

- Mortgage companies

- Mortgage brokers

- New homebuilder mortgage companies

- Mortgage bankers

BANKS

A bank can be a great place to get a mortgage—if you have at least two to four years after your discharge, outstanding credit since your bankruptcy, and high FICO® credit scores. A bank credit reference appearing on your credit reports is great to have. Another benefit to working with a bank is that your loan may cost less in up-front fees than other sources.

But here's the kicker...each bank has its own policy for how it deals with bankrupt people. Some welcome you while others will simply just not want to work with you. So the first item of business is to determine which banks will understand and accept the bankruptcy appearing on your credit reports.

Banks usually have the most strict credit guidelines. You see, the majority of banks originate mortgages and have them guaranteed by the Federal Home Loan Mortgage Corporation (Freddie Mac).

Freddie Mac doesn't like bankrupt people.

It's obvious because of their credit requirements to guarantee a loan. Your bankruptcy has a higher risk factor with Freddie Mac.

They prefer four years after your discharge. This is why your local bank may not be the most "bankruptcy friendly" place to go—even if you've been banking there since you were a young pup. Banks are usually the first place to turn you down—even if your credit scores are high enough—just because your bankruptcy appears on your credit reports.

Who is Freddie Mac? Freddie Mac buys mortgages from lenders on the "secondary mortgage market," bundles them together, and sells them as mortgage-backed securities to investors on Wall Street. This secondary mortgage market helps ensure that money continues to be available for new home purchases.

So stay away from banks that use Freddie Mac. Instead try to find banks that use Fannie Mae's conventional underwriting standards or offer FHA financing.

CREDIT UNIONS

Some credit unions are more lenient, some are more strict...it just depends on the credit union you're working with. But credit unions have a fatal flaw when it comes to helping you rebuild your credit standing. Many do not report your payment history to all three national credit reporting agencies.

So if you're planning to pay your mortgage on time every month to establish credit...forget about it. You're only really establishing good credit with the credit union...not the rest of the world. What good is paying your bills on time every month if you're not getting the full benefit from it?

Personally, I think that's their plan. To make it so they become your only choice in financing. Lenders should report to all three credit reporting agencies. Period.

So here's the lesson. If your credit union reports to all three credit reporting agencies, they're just as good as a bank. In fact, you should write the president of the credit union a letter and extend a thank you for reporting properly.

But if they don't report to all three...it's time to find a new place to keep your money and get your loans. You're spinning your wheels. And when the time comes when you don't like what your credit union offers you...you'll find yourself "starting over" yet again.

FINANCE COMPANIES

You shouldn't even consider working with a finance company. When a finance company credit reference appears on your credit reports...your FICO® credit scores go down quickly.

In addition, finance companies are known for their high interest rates, constant telemarketing campaigns to sell you more stuff you don't need, and rude collection departments that harass you if you're one day late.

Life's too short. Choose a different mortgage lender.

MORTGAGE COMPANIES

Years ago traditional mortgage companies focused on only one or two types of mortgages. For instance, Waterfield Mortgage was a traditional mortgage company. They gave Michele and me our first mortgage loan after bankruptcy.

Back then...they almost exclusively focused on providing one type of mortgage—FHA loans. They didn't have sub-prime lender relationships. They didn't broker deals they couldn't handle internally. FHA loans are what they did and you either fit into that mold or you didn't.

Traditional mortgage companies have become very rare. They're being bought up and merged with larger mortgage companies...or hybrid mortgage companies, as I like to call them.

These hybrid mortgage companies generally do their own mortgage underwriting, closing, funding, etc...but typically do not service the loans they originate. They sell them on the secondary market, which is why you end up making your payment to a different company within a short period of time after you close.

But because the average mortgage loan officer has such a wide variety of programs to deal with, they may not be familiar with the various credit guidelines pertaining to a bankruptcy.

Because they're not prepared, or knowledgeable, or flexible enough they could see "bankruptcy" and automatically regurgitate the word "DENIED," (making you feel discouraged) all because the loan officer wasn't familiar with each of their products' guidelines.

So for a bankrupt person it can be difficult to navigate the waters within a large mortgage company.

Too many choices...sales people with minimal bankruptcy experience...no empathy for a bankrupt person...and due to the amount of documentation required to obtain an approval, the average loan officer tends to shy away from doing the extra work required and may push you into a sub-prime mortgage because it's less work for them...even though there's a better solution for you that may require a little more effort.

MORTGAGE BROKERS

A mortgage brokerage is usually a small operation that has several lenders available to them, but do not underwrite, close, or fund their own loans.

They submit your application to a lender or investor for underwriting. The lender closes and funds the loan in their name. Then pays the mortgage broker a fee.

Most mortgage brokers concentrate on conventional (Fannie Mae or Freddie Mac) or sub-prime financing and may not be familiar with other mortgage program guidelines for bankrupt people.

Mortgage brokers were once a good alternative before credit scoring became prevalent. But that's not the case anymore.

Most conventional lenders have their own sub-prime mortgage programs that are usually less expensive than what smaller mortgage brokers can offer.

Mortgage brokers also have different personalities.

There's the mortgage broker who drives the Porsche and only cares about how much he can charge his buyers in fees so he can make his car payment. It's all about the "Benjamins" for him. There are too many of these types floating around...so steer clear.

Then there's the mortgage broker who only works with sub-prime lenders. So every customer who walks through their door, they try to figure out how to fit into sub-prime. It doesn't matter that the customer would be better off in an FHA mortgage or qualify for a conventional loan. These brokers don't work with FHA or get involved with conventional lenders.

Then there's, "Sally Smiles" mortgage broker. Looks like a nice mortgage broker. Acts like one. Smells like one. And you're a happy customer...until you want to refinance and you find out she forgot to mention the prepayment penalty. Which is huge. Not good.

I even know guys who train mortgage brokers to target us (bankrupt people) to squeeze as much money out of us as possible when obtaining a mortgage.

You have more options than this.

NEW HOMEBUILDER MORTGAGE COMPANIES

Another type of mortgage lender is the new homebuilder mortgage company. This is when new homebuilders create their own exclusive mortgage company to help finance more of their homes.

Just remember: all of the incentives the homebuilder offers are probably built into the price of the home or your interest rate. This isn't necessarily a good or bad thing. Just be aware, you're paying for these incentives one way or another.

This might be a good option...especially if you're cash poor.

But the only way you'll know for sure is if you compare what they can offer you with what the other lenders mentioned in this chapter can offer you.

If you do choose to use this type of lender, expect more—like down payment assistance or paid closing costs.

Remember, they're making money on selling you a home and financing it. So they may have a little more incentive to give you a good deal.

MORTGAGE BANKERS

I think your best mortgage source is a mortgage banker. A mortgage banker can be considered a mortgage company or bank. They're essentially a mortgage company that loans their own money. Many mortgage bankers also have the ability to broker loans.

In addition, they have the ability to keep their loans and not sell them to the secondary market. Therefore, exceptions to the guidelines are more of a possibility. You'll have the most options with mortgage bankers.

I use a mortgage banker.

How do you know you have a good mortgage banker?

- They can do FHA/VA loans

- They can do conventional loans

- They have access to the best sub-prime lenders (the ones that survived the crash in 2007)

- They can broker to other lenders

- They have access to bank programs

- And most important, they have the knowledge and experience (but this is irrelevant if they don't have access to the right mortgage programs)

Michele and I have a favorite mortgage banker we've used for nearly 12 years.

In fact, she got us approved for our first home equity loan after bankruptcy. She wouldn't give up on our deal. The underwriter kept coming back and asking for more information. She'd give it to them. This happened for weeks. We think the underwriter finally got tired and just gave us the loan to get us off his back!

In fact, after our deal closed the bank changed their mortgage guidelines pertaining to bankruptcy! Before the Snyders came along, they only required two years from discharge. After the Snyders, it became three years after discharge.

OK, so now you know the different types of mortgage lenders available to you. Here's how I would suggest you shop for a home.

First and foremost, purchase your FICO® credit scores.

Then interview one or two lenders in each of the different categories in this chapter (except for finance companies), and see who gives you the best offer.

Remember, only interview them...don't give them your Social Security number or allow them to review your credit. When you have some idea what you qualify for, start the pre-approval process to obtain a pre-approval letter from one of the lenders. You are now ready to shop for a home.

"Two years since my discharge, I'm debt free, [have a middle] FICO score of 680, and purchasing a house at 6.5%. I followed your advice religiously, and it worked. Thank you so much."

Kathy Seweryn
Trenton, New Jersey

"In 2006 I got my new SUV and now I have 2 investment condos at 6.875% fixed rates."

"My husband passed away in 2002 leaving behind a lot of debt. I filed for bankruptcy that year and attended your seminar also in 2002. Attending your seminar was a blessing for me. I followed your advice from the seminar and the newsletters and read your book. In 2004 I got an FHA loan at 5.875% fixed for 30 years by just putting 3% down for my primary residence. In 2006 I got my new SUV and now I have 2 investment condos at 6.875% fixed rates. From 540 FICO score in 2002, now my middle score is 697. I thank you very much, for without your help I would not have achieved all this. I am a single mom with 2 kids. If I could do so with your help so can others."

Rajini Verma
Easton, Pennsylvania

CHAPTER 19

The "Best Buys"
in Real Estate

You need to know where to find the "best buys" in real estate. I qualify a "best buy" as being a property that you can purchase at a price lower than what it's worth with a good chance of fast appreciation. There are four types of "best buys" to look for as you begin your search:

1. Builder "spec" homes

2. Independent new home builders

3. Old listings

4. "Don't wanters"

Why are these types of purchases considered the best buys? They hold the most promise for fast appreciation and the opportunity to purchase a home for less than appraised value.

BUILDER "SPEC" HOMES

New home builders sometimes get caught in a pinch and need to sell a home they are building just to break even, because their spec home didn't sell as soon as expected. Why didn't it sell? Who knows? It could be anything from the color of the carpet to the number of bedrooms on the upper level. How do you find these homes? Most top Realtors® know home builders that need to sell certain properties. All you need to do is tell them what you're looking for. Or simply get in your car on a Saturday and drive around neighborhoods. Our last six homes have been builder's spec homes.

INDEPENDENT NEW HOME BUILDERS

Not to be confused with the large new homebuilders, these small companies build less than 5 to 10 homes a year. They have many of the same issues as large home builders and can be even more aggressive in negotiating the best deal for you (i.e., best price, more equity at closing, smallest down payment, and possible cash at closing used for financing the home). The key here is to work with the builder directly or work with their preferred mortgage lender.

OLD LISTINGS

The home we bought had been on the market for over a year, and the owner was getting tired of making two house payments. The Realtor showed us 91 "showing slips." These are similar to telephone messages, but contain the response of the potential buyers after they have seen the property. Ninety-one showings is a lot of showings. The average seller is lucky to have 10 to 15 showings. Because of that we were in a really good position to negotiate the best price. In fact, the seller had to bring money to the closing. Usually the seller receives a check at closing.

It's important that you find out as much about the seller's situation as possible. Look for a seller's pain. A few signs of pain or a motivated seller are a divorce, making two house payments, pending foreclosure, bankruptcy, and moving.

Find their motivation for selling. It's a good indication of what may be possible. Are you beginning to see why the Realtor is an important resource for you? A good one will find out as much as possible. Especially a buyer's agent.

By the way, if you really get a good price on a home, do yourself and your neighbors a favor and request a "confidential sale" from the MLS. Everyone will benefit long-term. This keeps the sale price and other details confidential, and won't assist in lowering the value of your home.

"DON'T WANTERS"

You or your Realtor won't usually know what is possible with a "don't wanter" until you make an offer. These home sellers know they are in a compromising situation, and usually don't tell their realtor all the details until the last minute.

A good story about a "don't wanter" comes from our friends Bob and Patty. The house they wanted was listed at over $100,000. They told their Realtor to offer $85,000. A $15,000 discount off the top is unusual in real estate, as a general rule. By law a Realtor must present all offers.

The owners accepted the offer. The house was weeks away from being foreclosed on. The previous owner had cancer and was dying. They just wanted out of the mortgage. The mortgage company just wanted what was owed on the mortgage. It became a win/win situation for everyone involved.

Now, I am not advocating that you go out and drag a Realtor around with you to make lowball offers all the time. It depends on the property. The property I mentioned supported a lower offer based on the comps in the area and the condition of the home.

Don't be afraid to offer low when the situation warrants. You just might find a "don't wanter."

"[We received] a better rate than we received on our current home 3 years ago before we filed!"

"We were discharged from bankruptcy only 4 months ago. And the mortgage company from the seminar was able to get us pre-approved for a mortgage of $400,000 with 5% down at 6.99%. That is a better rate than we received on our current home 3 years ago before we filed! And we have only been discharged since December!"

Chris Minnich
Lamont, California

The Benefits of Being Pre-approved

There are several benefits to being pre-approved for a mortgage. Don't begin looking for a home until you speak with a mortgage lender, get pre-approved, and obtain a pre-approval letter to submit with your offer.

Most homebuyers don't take the time to be approved. They make an offer and then wait to see if they can get financed. If you want to present a strong offer, there is nothing stronger to prove to the seller you're already pre-approved.

How do you find a creative mortgage lender that has a track record of getting difficult loans approved? Through your Realtor®. When you find a Realtor you like, ask for a referral to a mortgage lender that is experienced in difficult mortgages. If your Realtor does not have any contacts, move on. Having no contacts is a sign of inexperience or ignorance. You don't have time to become someone's training ground.

Each mortgage lender is different. You could get really discouraged on one phone call with a lender that prefers dealing with borrowers with perfect credit, and start dancing after finishing the second phone call with a lender that knows all of the programs for bankrupt people.

Just keep calling until you find what you want. As long as you don't give permission to review your credit reports, you're okay. Call as many mortgage lenders as you have time for. Get a feel for what is going on in your local market. Take good notes. Write down their name, the date, telephone numbers and comments from the conversation. If a particular person cannot help you, ask for a referral to someone who can. Or simply ask the question, "What would you do if you were me?"

Once you find a mortgage lender, ask them how to go about becoming pre-approved for a mortgage. If it's just a few minutes on the telephone, it's not a real pre-approval...it's a prequalification. There's a difference.

Being prequalified means absolutely nothing. It's a complete waste of time. You're looking to submit proof of income, tax returns, a credit application, verify employment, and provide as much paperwork as possible. This is a real pre-approval.

Our friends Robert and Minna were tired of dealing with mortgage lenders that promised more than what they could deliver. They had given up on owning a home. They lost half of their earnest money due to the incompetence of an inexperienced Realtor.

They finally met a mortgage lender that got them pre-approved. That put Robert and Minna in a really strong position.

1. They knew exactly how much house they could afford.

2. When making an offer, their new Realtor could notify the seller that her buyers are pre-approved. This translates into a faster closing and a sure bet for the home seller. This is important when more than one offer is presented at the same time. Pre-approvals carry more weight because there is less risk to the seller.

3. The stress and pressure was relieved up front. Once they found the house, they could close within a few weeks.

4. They wouldn't miss out on the home they really wanted to a buyer who was more prepared.

5. It gave them leverage to negotiate concessions.

Pre-approval is the way to go. Ask your mortgage lender about it. One of the advantages to attending our free Credit After Bankruptcy® seminar is meeting local lenders. Visit our website at: *www.afterbankruptcy.org* to learn more about a seminar near you or one that is available on the internet.

"I honestly did not think I would ever be able to purchase my own home. Being from an Indian reservation, the thought of home-ownership was a very foreign concept."

"I attended your seminar nearly two years ago. I'm still grateful to have had the opportunity to hear what you had to say. I followed the steps you outlined, and just completed the purchase of my first home...a nice town home, in an older part of the city that sets itself apart from the cookie cutter, manufactured templates which are the trademark of the housing market where I live. It has charm, nice neighborhood, and has shown its stability through its homeowners association. I honestly did not think I would ever be able to purchase my own home. Being from an Indian reservation, the thought of homeownership was a very foreign concept. All the homes where I grew up were government subsidized—every one of them. They belonged to no family but the government. So it wasn't natural for us to think about ever owning a home on our own. I carried this mentality into my adult life. In any case, I never thought I would qualify for a home loan because of my bankruptcy, and never thought I would be able to get a fixed rate at nearly the average for the country. Thank you for introducing me to the mortgage company you recommend. Even my realtor commented that she had never dealt with such a friendly company that seemed to truly have the consumer in mind. Thank you Stephen. You have helped me to make one more step forward in piecing together my life."

Kyle Ethelbah
Somerton, Arizona

Mortgage Tips
You Can't Ignore

There are certain things you must know before you can decide whether you begin your search for a new home. The following list of important mortgage tips will help ease your home buying experience.

YOU'RE BUYING THE FINANCING

The most important thing is getting it through your head that you're buying the financing. If it weren't for the financing, you might not be buying a home right now. Forget your dream home for now. We liked to think of our first home after bankruptcy as a "short-term investment property."

We help friends buy homes all the time who have lists of "must-haves" for their new home. They must be in a certain area, must have a three-car garage, must have four bedrooms with a loft, must have a contemporary interior, must be close to work, must be this and must be that. Forget it. You're buying the financing. After you've been in the house 24 months you can sell it at a profit (if you bought it right), and then buy your dream home. You need to reestablish credit first. The dream home comes later.

BUY IN AN APPRECIATING AREA

Another service your Realtor can provide is comps. Comps, or comparables, compare your property with others like it in the neighborhood.

Since we nicknamed our home a "short-term investment property," it was easier to be more logical about the purchase. The emotion was tamed. We were more excited about being able to actually have a mortgage.

The comps will quickly tell you whether the home you are considering is priced right. Not only are you looking for a no-qualify assumption, but if possible, you're looking for one you can pick up inexpensively.

Ask for the statistics on how long a property takes to sell in that particular area. This is a good indication of value as well. It's common for homes in "hot" areas to sell in less than 30 days.

We figured our prospective home was undervalued by at least $20,000. The previous owner had moved before this property was sold and he was making two mortgage payments. He just wanted out. The home had 91 showings on the property, but no one had bought. The Realtor® said a lot of the comments from people were that it was small and dark.

Less than a year later, after putting new white carpet in the place and painting the wood and walls white, the house appraised for over $30,000 more than we paid for it. Now that's appreciation. If you buy smart, you will have more options down the road. We sold the home in 2005 for more than double what we paid for it.

AVOID THE MOST EXPENSIVE HOUSE

Never purchase the most expensive house in the area. And also never purchase the most inexpensive house in the area. You will receive more appreciation in a shorter amount of time by being in the middle.

When you go to sell you will have a much easier time than the person who has the most expensive house. This person will usually lose money.

LOOK FOR HOMES THAT NEED MINOR TENDER LOVING CARE (TLC)

When my wife took me to preview the home that later ended up being our home, I wouldn't even go in. It was "beneath me." The carpet was ugly brown. The walls were dark. And there was a lot of wood. This house needed some TLC.

Homes that need minor TLC represent the best possible chance for high appreciation. I am not talking about tearing out walls and adding onto the existing structure. More like new carpet, new paint, new countertops, remove wallpaper, etc.

Expect homes that need TLC.

FIRST IMPRESSIONS ARE REMEMBERED

It helps to dress appropriately when meeting the Realtor for the first time. First impressions count. Be nice, positive, have a firm handshake, and smile a lot. If you're with a spouse, do not argue. Be on your best behavior. Remember, you are selling yourself to someone who will represent you.

MAKE IT EASY ON THE REALTOR

The Realtor will need to put a little more effort into helping you find a home than he or she would with a normal buyer. So have the attitude of doing whatever it takes to save him or her time. One of the best things you can do is offer to do "drive-bys." Drive by the home to see if it's something you would consider. Showing homes takes time. The more homes you see, the more time the Realtor has invested. Time is money to a Realtor. Offer to do as much legwork as possible. Not only will you establish a better relationship with your Realtor, but you will increase your odds of finding something faster.

HOW MUCH SECURITY DEPOSIT IS NECESSARY?

In Indiana, where we used to live, it is common to put down $500 to $1,000 with your offer as your earnest money deposit. Put down as little as possible. Your money isn't earning any interest.

This will vary from city to city. Be sure to have a clause in your offer that if you are unable to obtain financing, your earnest money will be returned to you.

Five hundred dollars is all we had in our checking account the day we made our offer to purchase our first home after bankruptcy. We had less than 30 days to come up with the balance.

It's interesting—I never would have thought it was possible to save $2,000 in less than 30 days, but we did it. Well, actually we were $1,200 short on the day of closing. We worked out a deal with the Realtor who sold us the property that $100 a week would be directly taken out of my wife's check until it was paid in full. Anything is possible when you can see the reward.

TOTAL CASH NEEDED

The Realtor may be willing to let you borrow a portion of the commission, or delay the commission for a period of time.

And don't forget about owner financing. The owner may be in a position to "loan you the money" in the form of a second mortgage or even a side note. If he or she needs to sell it fast, it may be an option. This is one area where an experienced Realtor can negotiate on your behalf to help the homeowner see the benefits of giving you a second mortgage. However, if the owner needs to sell his or her existing house to qualify for a mortgage on their next house, the chances are bleak. Every situation is different. You find out by asking.

BE IN AGREEMENT WITH YOUR WIFE

My wife and I made a promise to be in agreement on the purchase of our home, no matter what. As we began our search, we quickly learned that we had different ideas on what we wanted in a house. The house I wanted (the first one we saw), she "didn't get a good feel about."

It took me a while to realize that women are born with this natural instinct to "feel" things. It's kind of like a sixth sense. Women are born with it, but men can learn it.

As it turned out, the house she thought we should buy was the one we ended up with. I hated it. It wasn't the palace I had envisioned, but it quickly became one. I have now learned to listen more to my wife.

We each brought important strengths to the table. I had faith that we could find a house and get a mortgage. She understood the local real estate market. We complemented each other. Look for each other's strengths, ignore the weaknesses.

WHAT TO EXPECT AT CLOSING

Closing is a term used in the real estate business that means the day the ownership is transferred. This happens once the appropriate documents are signed and certified funds are received.

The closing should be simply an exciting time where you sign legal documents. All your questions should be answered before the closing date.

Always ask for an end-of-month closing date so your first payment will be prorated to the lowest possible amount—that way you will have to come up with less money at closing.

A few days before the closing is scheduled, your Realtor should inform you of the exact amount in certified funds to bring to closing. Realtors normally do not know this exact figure until sometimes hours, but preferably days, before the closing. They rely on the title company to run the numbers.

Any problems with title work, ownership issues, legal problems, tax lien issues, etc., should be discovered weeks before you are scheduled to close.

In Indiana you usually meet at a title company in a small room with your Realtor and a representative from the title company who has prepared your paperwork.

The title company representative briefly describes what you're going to sign, then you sign where appropriate. The whole thing can take less than 45 minutes, depending on how many questions you have. Once you have finished signing all the documents, you provide the certified funds and the house is yours.

If you're one of those people who needs to read every line of legal jargon you sign, even though they are standard forms, tell your Realtor this in advance. If you don't, you may not close on that day.

Title companies have numerous closings scheduled throughout the day, and your Realtor has other homes to sell. Holding up the closing because you need to read everything is rude. It may result in the closing being rescheduled to another day, perhaps weeks away.

Your Realtor will gladly ask the title company to prepare a copy of the paperwork for your review before the closing date. You only need to ask.

My friend David was one of those people. He insisted that he read every document word for word before signing. His Realtor sensed that he was going to be difficult, and suggested reviewing the documents at the title company the day before the closing. So everyone was happy.

When I asked him whether he understood anything he read, he quietly replied, "No." It just made him feel better. This brings up a good point. It may be a good idea to engage the services of an attorney at a different title company to review the documents for you. Although I do not feel this is necessary, it may give you peace of mind. Ask your Realtor for a referral.

Most people don't realize all the services a title company can offer. In fact, all the paperwork in a mortgage transaction can be done at a title company. They even have attorneys on staff to review documents.

Another Realtor friend says home buyers who hire new lawyers are always the ones who delay closing. They feel they have something to prove to everyone. If you're a new attorney, ask to review the documents before closing. Be considerate of other people's time.

Another important thing to remember about closing is that the title company will accept only certified funds. Both buyer and seller need to present certified funds at closing.

A lot of people assume that certified funds means anything a bank will provide. This is not the case. Money orders may not be considered certified funds in your area. Ask your title company what qualifies as certified funds to be presented at closing. Avoid a last-minute dash to the bank.

Our first closing was close to a disaster. We were short of cash. I received the check we were expecting to allow us to close, but the bank put a seven-day hold on it, since it was for a large amount of money and it was out-of-state. Keep these things in mind before your closing date.

AFTER CLOSING

Three weeks after the closing, call your new mortgage company and ask a few questions:

1. When is my payment due?

2. When is the latest date I can pay before I am assessed a late fee?

3. Where or how else can I make a payment?

4. How long does a payment take to post?

5. Do you have a different mailing address to receive overnight payments?

6. Which credit reporting agencies do you report to? How often?

You may preface a few of these questions with, "Although I plan to always pay early or on time, it is good to know in an emergency."

We have never had the misfortune of being late on any revolving debt reported to the credit reporting agencies since the bankruptcy. My wife manages our accounts, keeps them up to date, and sends the payments on a timely basis.

Decide whose responsibility it will be to make sure the mortgage payment will be paid early or on time each month. Better yet, consider having your mortgage company automatically debit the mortgage payment from your checking account on a certain day each month. Although this may work for some people, I feel more comfortable in having the flexibility to pay when I want to.

Only after calling our mortgage company did we find out that we could make payments at a few bank branches they owned. We didn't know they were affiliated with the bank. This became very convenient in the early days. We could wait until the very last day before it was considered late to make the mortgage payment, in case we were short that month.

We learned that it took two days for the payment to post to our account. So we adjusted our payment schedule accordingly. Remember—early or on time!

Ask a lot of questions, even if you feel you know the answers. You will always learn something you did not know before.

CREATE A MORTGAGE FOLDER

You will refer to the closing documents from time to time. Create a mortgage folder and put it in a safe place. Make it a policy never to allow anyone to use the originals; only give copies of what is needed.

"We were able to get a loan from a bank to pur-
chase a used SUV and purchase our $350,000
dream home on a beautiful setting of 3-1/2 acres
with a fishing pond, huge workshop, and gorgeous
swimming pool...oh...and a barn."

"Your newsletters have been so helpful! I don't have time
now to tell you in detail, but the short version of our recovery
is...less than a year after it was final we were able to get a
loan from a bank to purchase a used SUV and purchase our
$350,000 dream home on a beautiful setting of 3-1/2 acres
with a fishing pond, huge workshop, and gorgeous swimming
pool...oh...and a barn. We attended your seminar...[It was]
extremely helpful and gave us tremendous confidence to forge
ahead! Thanks for your more than generous information!"

Dawn Burdine
Bloomington, Indiana

"We filed a Chapter 13. We made our monthly payments faithfully, all the while juggling to pay all of our other bills on time. My husband and I attended your seminar and I am happy to say, met the mortgage representative that sponsored the seminar. We refinanced our house, including two mortgages and our remaining BK balance and are now saving $1200 a month! We got a 6.9% interest rate. We are so relieved and happy now that we have gotten this taken care of. We owe it all to you! Thanks from both of us!"

Stephanie Cappello
Peoria Heights, Illinois

How to Refinance Your Existing Mortgage

The best place to start your search to refinance your existing mortgage is with your current mortgage company.

If you have an FHA mortgage, the government has provided another program that enables anyone to refinance their mortgage, regardless of credit history. It's called the FHA Streamline.

Here's how it works. You call a mortgage lender that offers an FHA Streamline program. They take a regular loan application and review your credit. The only thing they look at is if you've had 12 months of consecutive timely payments. You can even qualify without having to prove income. In fact, in most cases a new appraisal is not even required.

We knew about the FHA Streamline before we purchased our first home. Our strategy was to mortgage our first home after bankruptcy at 10.5% interest, then FHA Streamline it to 6% six months after we closed. And we did just that.

FHA guidelines stipulate that you must wait at least six months before you can refinance. During that six months we interviewed several lenders. Everyone had a different type of program. In the end, we called the existing mortgage company and asked what kind of program they had. Their program beat all others hands down.

The most difficult thing for us was to prepay the first month's payment at closing. In essence, this meant we had to make two mortgage payments in one month! We did it. Each of us lost body fat as we saved money from our food budget, held our first garage sale, and sold other things around the house. It was worth it. Our monthly house payment went from $661.50 to $441.32.

Within 45 days we had a lower house payment, a lower interest rate, and more cash in our pockets each month.

When you use the FHA Streamline you don't receive any of the equity in your home—just an adjusted interest rate, which translates into a lower mortgage payment. Our motive was clearly a lower house payment to increase our cash flow.

One of the nice things about the FHA Streamline is that we now have two positive credit references on our credit reports: the old mortgage and our new mortgage. Our positive references were beginning to outweigh the negatives.

Look for FHA mortgage lenders in the Yellow Pages. Call them and inquire as to the requirements for a Streamline loan in your situation. Or contact any mortgage lender that can do FHA financing.

Just be careful when you're researching. Mortgage lenders will do and say anything to get your Social Security number from you. Don't give it to them until you have interviewed several lenders and called your existing mortgage company.

Out of all of the people I worked with in reestablishing credit, mortgage lenders were the most unreliable. Of course, once you find the right one it makes all the difference in the world. But until then, expect to meet some interesting people. For example, one guy took my credit application, worked with me over a period of a week or so, and promised to call me with an answer in a few days. I still haven't heard from him.

QUESTIONS TO ASK AN FHA STREAMLINE LOAN OFFICER

Most of the questions revolve around how they do business. Start with the following questions:

1. Do you offer FHA Streamline mortgages?

2. Have you closed any?

3. Tell me how the FHA Streamline works.

4. Will the closing date affect how much money I bring to closing? If so, when is the best closing date?

5. What are the current interest rates?

6. I am paying x% now, how much would I save if I would Streamline now?

7. Do you need to review credit reports?

8. What are the credit qualifications?

9. How long does it take from start to finish?

10. Do you sell the mortgage to another company or hold it yourself?

11. If you sell my mortgage, who will most likely service it, and where would I make payments?

12. Does the loan have a grace period?

13. What credit reporting agencies does the mortgage company report to?

After you have finished asking these questions, if the person is in an authority position he or she may ask you whether you want a job. Lenders are not used to dealing with customers who know what they are talking about. That's the impression you give by asking questions, even if you don't know the answers.

In the end, I chose our original mortgage company to do our FHA Streamline, simply because they are a well-known name in the mortgage business and the total out-of-pocket expenses were lower than with the other companies.

"Thank God for your help! Now our FICO scores are all around 700! We have a house 4 blocks from the beach, with nearly $550K of equity, that we have a 30 year fixed mortgage on at 6.7%."

"I received my Chapter 7 discharge and had FICO scores hovering around the low 500s. After attending your seminar a few months later, I was given hope. Unfortunately, I didn't start taking action (other than changing my spending habits) for almost a year after that. But having subscribed to your weekly newsletter kept your advice in the forefront of every financial decision I had to make during that time. I own my own business and had to make several changes to increase my income rather than rely on incurring further debt. Thank God for your help! Now our FICO scores are all around 700! We have a house 4 blocks from the beach, with nearly $550K of equity, that we have a 30 year fixed mortgage on at 6.7%. All three of our cars are paid off, and I recently purchased an investment property using the equity from our primary residence. Your advice on using real estate investment is very important, especially here. I have close friends that are mortgage bankers, real estate company owners, and developers that share their knowledge of surrounding markets freely. The fact that I now volunteer my time for the local community comes directly from you. Giving back to others what you so freely gave me is truly one of my life's greatest rewards. Thanks again and God Bless you!"

Jon Bevington
Homestead, Florida

How to Get Approved for a Home Equity Loan

The big reason the home equity loan is so popular is that it is one of the last 100% tax deductions for the average homeowner. You used to be able to deduct bank card interest, but that was phased out several years ago. Home equity interest is completely deductible. This can save you a ton of money at tax time. That's a lot less money you have to pay the IRS on April 15.

THREE-YEAR RULE

The credit guidelines to get approved for a home equity loan have changed over the last several years.

Today you need three years after discharge without a foreclosure in the last seven years. If you have three years, no foreclosure, and a high enough credit score—you're approved. It's just that simple.

And there are still 100% programs available. This means if your home is valued at $250,000 and you owe $100,000 you could get approved for a home equity loan for as much as $150,000.

Most lenders max out at a $500,000 loan amount, although there are a few that will go to $1,000,000.

CASH-OUT REFINANCE

If you don't have three years after your discharge date or you have a foreclosure, you can still tap the equity in your home...but you need to do it with what is called a "cash-out refinance." With a cash-out refinance, you refinance your mortgage for more than you currently owe, and then pocket the difference.

Cash-out refinancing is different from a home equity loan in several ways.

First, a home equity loan is a separate loan on top of your first mortgage; a cash-out refinance replaces your first mortgage.

Second, the interest rate on a cash-out refinance sometimes (but not always) is lower than the interest rate on a home equity loan.

Another difference: You have to pay closing costs when you refinance your loan; you don't have to pay closing costs for a home equity loan. Closing costs can amount to hundreds or thousands of dollars.

Cash-out refinances have long been a favorite method when you have less than three years after discharge or a foreclosure. Talk to your mortgage lender and compare all of your options.

"In February 2007 I was able to mortgage a $250,000 home at 5.5% and my credit scores are really improving..."

"I want to thank you for all of the great information that you are sharing with us. I filed bankruptcy in July 2003 after divorce. I thought life was over for having good credit. Before bankruptcy my credit score was 730 and after filing, I was unable to finance furniture from a local department store. I attended your seminar in October 2004 and I can say it has made my life and credit produce a total turn around. In June 2005 I financed a new 2005 SUV and in February 2007 I was able to mortgage a $250,000 home at 5.5% and my credit scores are really improving: 646 EQ, 665 EX and 674 TU. I started with the 'crapitolone' for my first credit card and I have paid them and gotten a lower interest rate credit card. I applied all of the information I learned at the seminar and from the *Increase Your Credit Scores—Improve Your Lifestyle* course I purchased. I want to encourage you and your wife to continue the good deeds and I pray God's blessings upon your lives. I look forward to more information from you because it is priceless and very appreciated by many people."

Saralyn Purnell
Alva, Oklahoma

"Hi Stephen...I am so glad that I went to your Credit After Bankruptcy seminar. Before attending I felt that I was the only person to go through this. My business was failing, and I used my personal credit to try to shore it up. What a mistake. I let my emotions override my common sense. I used to have a credit score of 785. Then I fell down to about 580 with the bankruptcy. I attended your seminar and found HOPE! My biggest obstacle was that not only did I have to file BK, but I had also gotten divorced. All women should know that at some time during their married life they need to establish their own credit. All of the cars that my ex and I purchased were in his name (the credit union required that!) Once I tried to reestablish my credit, the biggest negative item was that I had never purchased an auto!!! Well, this January, a mere 8 months after my BK was discharged I got a brand new car. I did my homework, worked closely with the financial manager at the dealership and got a new car. He went the extra mile for me... and I am glad that I had the knowledge from your seminar to work with him. Within 30 days of purchasing the car, my credit score was up to 650! I am anxiously waiting to check it again this month! I am due to refinance my home (which I was able to retain through the BK), and am sure that all will go well. Thanks for all of your help and support."

Chery Daly
Truth or Consequences, New Mexico

Our First Cars
After Bankruptcy

Getting approved for a new car at a low interest rate is very easy. It can happen the very day you receive your discharge letter from the bankruptcy court. The problem is that most people think their only option is to purchase a used car at a high interest rate from a high-interest company. That's not the case.

THE CAR I HAD TO OWN

I had my heart set on a used red Mazda Miata within months after bankruptcy. I test drove that car two weekends in a row. It felt good driving it with the top down, wind in my hair, music playing, in the warm weather—I was hooked.

I found the car. I located the financing through a high-interest finance company. Still, no matter how hard I tried, the two could not be put together. Needless to say, I did not become the owner of the used red Mazda Miata. As I look back, it was the best thing that could have happened to me. It helped me see that I had more options.

EXPECTATIONS

If you truly want to reestablish credit after bankruptcy and quickly rid yourself of the stigma associated with bankruptcy, your expectations must be in order. Forget about the car you want—and focus on what you need.

What you should expect is a brand-new car at a normal interest rate through a reputable dealer. That's more than billionaire investor Warren Buffett drives. And he's the third wealthiest man in the world.

OUR FIRST CAR

After the failed Mazda Miata experience, all I wanted was a car to drive. I began calling car dealers to determine which ones could get me financed. Since I am not fond of car salespeople, I always asked for the new car finance manager. I figured that once I found someone who could get me financed, it wouldn't matter whether the salesman was an idiot.

I visited a lot of car dealerships, never test driving anything. Getting the financing was more important than becoming hooked emotionally to a certain car. After randomly visiting several car dealerships it was apparent that we needed a new game plan. No one could get us financed.

Then one day, after being turned down by Toyota Motor Credit, we became desperate. We needed a car. Something with four wheels. The "wish list" was thrown out the window, and we decided we wanted a new car we could afford. I asked the Toyota finance manager what he would do if he were me. What he said changed everything.

He told us that, "Ford Motor Credit has the best financing program in the country and if anyone can get you financed, they can." He went on to say that Ford usually approves loans he turns down. "We can't even come close to what they offer," he said.

I was silent.

My wife and I turned to each other with facial expressions that looked like we just ate a sour lemon. A Ford? Made in America? Will it fall apart? They got a kick out of our line of questioning. We were dead serious. We had never owned a Ford.

Knowing that Ford was our last chance to obtain mainstream credit for a new car, we decided to talk with them. The Toyota dealership recommended the Ford dealership across the street.

That evening, with recent credit report in hand, I visited the Ford dealership. I met the new-car finance manager, Bob Spalding. Not wasting any time, my first question to Bob was, "Can you finance people with a previous bankruptcy?" His reply was a confident, "Tell me more." I then sat down and proceeded to give him a "sound bite" of my accomplishments since the bankruptcy.

Bob then asked me a series of questions to qualify me. The questions ranged from how long ago the bankruptcy was discharged to how much money I could put down. After he finished questioning me, he was convinced something could be done, but he would need to look at my credit report.

I then asked whether he would review a recent copy of my credit report, which I had with me. I explained that I was trying to avoid unnecessary credit inquiries. He agreed. He read my credit report and said, "I think we can help you."

That was music to my ears. Even better, I believed him.

When I met Bob we hit it off right away. Then something really interesting happened. As we began talking about the details of financing, he told me he had also filed bankruptcy. I knew then we would be driving soon. And it gets better. Later Bob introduced me to a car salesman, Troy. Troy told me he had also filed bankruptcy!

At this point there was no question in my mind I was going to be driving a new car financed by a mainstream lender soon. There's simply no one better to have in your corner than a bankrupt person who understands what you need.

Now the only thing I needed to do was pick out the car, right? Wrong. Instead, I asked Bob to tell me which car would be easiest to finance with Ford. The only choice I wanted was the color of the car.

Bob's first choice was the ugliest car I have ever seen.

I took one look at it and quickly went back to Bob and asked whether I had any other options. His response was, "Sure, but it will increase your down payment by $500."

Troy then showed me the car. It was a brand-new 1993 Ford Escort. I liked it. Compared to the first car, this was sexy—but certainly a long way from a BMW convertible.

I kept thinking that the financing from Ford Motor Credit was more important than ego or status. This would improve my credit rating and was affordable. It was a short-term sacrifice that would have long-term benefits. Don't get me wrong, it was a very humbling experience.

I asked Bob to run the numbers on the Escort. After visiting several buy-here, pay-here dealerships I knew that my worst-case scenario would be to have to come up with $2,000 to put down on a used car at 21% interest if Bob's numbers didn't work.

As Bob was running the numbers, I called my wife, Michele. As I told her about the car her response was, "What is an Escort?" I convinced her that it was cute.

Bob and I finally sat down to discuss the numbers. The good news was that the payment on a two-year lease through Ford would be less than $94 a month. The bad news was to lease that car I would need a $1,500 down payment.

I paused.

I knew I had only $500 at the time, but the capacity to save more over time.

I then became very bold. I said to Bob, "I have $500 I can put down on this car today. Do you have the authority to allow me to spread the balance over, say, 30 to 45 days?" His response surprised me. He said confidently, "I think we can work something out. Let's submit this to Ford and see what they say."

Since it was late in the evening, he suggested that it was too late to submit it to Ford. And the following day was his day off. So he would be unable to submit it until after his day off. I agreed. I trusted my "champion" to present my case in the best way he saw fit. I would wait for Bob. I drove home and waited for him to call.

I found out later that I was working with the largest Ford leasing dealership in Indiana. They funnel a lot of deals to Ford, so they have more flexibility than smaller dealerships. For instance, they might submit a package of 100 deals to Ford for approval at one time. Of those 100 deals, 90 would be good deals, while the other 10 would be marginal. The dealership would submit it to Ford as a package, and Ford Motor Credit would take them all or nothing. It is to your advantage to work with the largest Ford dealer in your area.

Bob called back a few days later. It was a done deal. Ford had bought it. All that needed to be done was to sign the paperwork and draw up some type of agreement to pay the balance of the down payment over time. Even though we didn't have a clue exactly where the money was going to come from, we were happy. We were approved from a mainstream lender!

That day my wife and I visited the dealership and drove our new 1993 Ford Escort off the lot. The car was financed by Ford Motor Credit at 2.9% interest.

Does this mean that your Ford dealer will offer to help you with your down payment? I don't know. Most dealerships do not. Many good dealers can put bankrupt people in new cars with no money down. Every city is different. Every Ford dealer is different. It makes a difference which Ford dealer you go to.

That's how we financed our first car after bankruptcy. Bob and I have remained friends even to this day.

PRIDE

For those of you who have a hard time picturing yourself driving a Ford, you need to build a bridge and get over it. Sure, it may not be a Mercedes or Porsche, but because you've chosen mainstream credit over other types of credit you will have many more choices for your next car.

Be thankful for the opportunity to start over again, and get over your pride. It will bring many rewards in the months and years to come. We're living proof of that.

OUR SECOND CAR

When we leased our first car after bankruptcy, the new Ford Escort, the Ford dealer told us to make six on-time payments, and then come back to his dealership for a second car. We trusted him, so that's what we set a goal to do. Sharing a car can be a necessary burden, but for us it could work for only a short time.

In exactly six months we returned to the same Ford dealership. We knew exactly what we wanted. After we filled out a new credit application, Troy, our salesperson from before, made a call, and in less than five minutes we were approved for our second car from Ford Motor Credit: a new black 1994 Ford Probe.

Only six months of established credit allowed us this privilege. What was next? My next goal was a new convertible Mazda Miata.

OUR THIRD CAR

After our first two-year lease was up on the Ford Escort, we were in the new-car market again. It was time for my black Mazda Miata. We knew by calling the lease sales manager that they didn't look favorably on bankruptcies, but we hoped our reestablished credit, perfect payment history, and two excellent ratings with Ford would sway a lender in our favor. We also discovered that Ford Motor Credit owned Mazda Motor Credit.

After visiting a few Mazda dealerships and test-driving the car, we submitted our credit application to a dealer we thought could get the deal done. It was late in the evening, so we drove home with intentions of hearing something the following day. When we got home there was a message from the dealer that Mazda Motor Credit had approved our lease. After waiting for over two years, I was finally the owner of a new black 1995 Mazda Miata. We signed a three-year lease agreement. I loved it.

OUR FOURTH CAR

When our Ford Probe lease expired, my wife decided she wanted a Toyota Camry. We went to the same Toyota dealership that had turned us down three years earlier—the one that told us about the

Ford dealer across the street. We were sloppy in handling this deal. We spoke with a car salesperson first. What a mess. It turned out that she was a new salesperson in training. I didn't have the heart to request an experienced salesperson (she was trying hard), so I prepared for the worst. We were in the busy dealership two or three hours. At least I brought something to read. Always go through the finance director first.

In the end, Toyota Motor Credit approved us while we were still in the dealership. Had it not been for having leather installed in her car, my wife could have driven her new car home that night. My wife signed a three-year lease agreement with Toyota Motor Credit.

OUR FIFTH CAR

Three years is a long time to drive the same car. So we decided to sign only two-year leases going forward. This resulted in higher payments, but it still worked better for us. After being turned down by Chrysler for a lease on a Jeep Grand Cherokee, the next day we returned to Ford Motor Credit in October 1997 to lease my wife a new 1998 Ford Explorer. No money down. Two-year lease. It had everything. That's what she wanted.

OUR SIXTH CAR

I was going through withdrawal not having a convertible just before the summer of 1998. I test-drove a few different convertibles. Then I heard Mazda had redesigned the Miata, so I took the 1999 Miata out for a spin on a Saturday afternoon. By Monday, I leased a new 1999 dark blue Mazda Miata.

OUR OTHER CARS

I have honestly lost track of how many cars we have bought, sold, and leased over the years. But the one thing I know for certain is that we now ALWAYS qualify for the lowest interest rates and best terms (always with no money down) because of our high credit scores. And as our credit scores have increased, so has the quality of our cars. We've gone from being forced to drive a $97 per month economy car with no radio to now driving high-end luxury cars of our choice.

IN CLOSING

The lesson here is to start slowly and build up to what you want. After we had established excellent credit with Ford, other mainstream lenders were willing to lend to us. You need to find the captive lender that doesn't mind being first in line to give you a second chance. Ford Motor Credit is strong in some states, but very weak in others.

If you would like to be introduced to a car dealer in your area I'd encourage you to attend our free *Credit After Bankruptcy®* seminar in a city near you or on the internet. For more information on our seminar, go to: *www.afterbankruptcy.org.*

"We purchased a new car with an interest rate of 5.9%. We were treated with dignity and respect it was truly the best experience in a long time."

"My husband and I attended your Credit After Bankruptcy seminar. We walked away feeling very hopeful. At the seminar a dealership was introduced. First of all I have worked for a dealership for the last 5 years and know many of the pitfalls consumers get caught in, especially people with bad credit. So I was a little skeptical, we contacted them and we purchased a new car with an interest rate of 5.9%. We were treated with dignity and respect. It was truly the best experience in a long time. Thank you for leading us in the right direction. We are now looking forward to refinancing our home!!!"

Gwen Foster
Darby, Pennsylvania

"The tools you and your company supplied me with brings me to tears. My son asked why I cried when I was able to purchase my new SUV in August. It was my first new car. I'm so thankful that your wonder team touched my life."

"I have gone through a bankruptcy. I have been with you for about 3 to 4 years. I can't tell you enough how you have blessed my life. Following the guidelines that Stephen and his wonder team have given me. I feel self-worth again. After my divorce I couldn't finance a toothbrush. No joke. I was one of the fortunate ones who was able to meet Stephen at the seminar he did. He even signed my book. I was so excited and wanted to share the information I was learning. I let the neighbor borrow the book and he never gave it back. I know this sounds silly. But the tools you and your company supplied me with brings me to tears. My son asked why I cried when I was able to purchase my new SUV in August. It was my first new car. I'm so thankful that your wonder team touched my life. I'm not a good writer. But I've always wanted to tell you folks how wonderful you all are. The words were in my heart but I didn't know how to put them on paper. I'm sorry again my finger just went to typing. Thank you and bless all of you."

Michele Vandiver
Parlier, California

How to Get a New Car After Bankruptcy

The bankrupt person has several choices in deciding where to purchase his or her next car. Just take a look at your Sunday newspaper. It's full of car dealerships marketing to people with poor credit, no credit, slow credit, and bankruptcy.

However, the sources that speak directly to you are most likely offering the wrong kind of financing. Buyer beware. Let's take a look at a few of your options:

1. Buy-here, pay-here car lots

2. Sub-prime auto finance companies

3. Car dealers advertising creative financing

4. Credit union financing

5. Bank financing

6. Car manufacturer financing (also know as captive lenders)

BUY-HERE, PAY-HERE CAR LOTS

Avoid these companies. You will recognize them by their willingness to carry the financing. The first negative about these companies is that you're not reestablishing mainstream credit. Second, most of them do not report to the credit reporting agencies. And if they did, who wants to see Paulie's Used Car Lot on their credit report? And of course, the interest rate will be extremely high.

It's credit references like Paulie's Used Car Lot that will attract more high-interest lenders. If you think of yourself as that type of buyer, credit lenders will also think of you as that type of customer.

Most of these companies sell late-model cars. I would much prefer a new car with a full warranty. I don't have a lot of time for unexpected repairs. Time is valuable to me.

The only good thing these companies provide is hope. It's a good feeling, as you're working at getting approved by a mainstream lender, that your worst-case scenario is one of these places if all else fails.

SUB-PRIME AUTO FINANCE COMPANIES

Who in their right mind would pay 21% to 36% interest on financing a car? If you go with sub-prime auto financing, that is what you'll have to do. Not to mention you'll have a finance company account on your credit reports which lowers your credit scores.

Sub-prime auto finance companies are considered the loan sharks of the lending business. They charge outrageously high interest rates, require a substantial down payment and/or security deposit, lend on only late-model cars, and are not considered mainstream credit references on your credit reports.

Sub-prime auto credit references do not give you the power position in reestablishing credit after bankruptcy. They weaken your recovery.

Here is a list of some of the most commonly used sub-prime auto finance companies:

- HSBC™ Automotive
- Capital One® Auto
- AmeriCredit®
- WFS Financial®
- Triad Financial
- 1-800-Bar-None

You should only use these companies if it's a last resort. Even then, I'd find another solution. You're *not* going to get ahead using these types of lenders.

CAR DEALERS ADVERTISING CREATIVE FINANCING

There was a car dealership in Indianapolis that worked an arrangement with a large local bank to finance late-model cars. After noticing their ads in the Sunday newspaper, I called and asked a lot of questions.

It turned out to be a great program providing bank financing. If you can find it, bank financing is one of your best options. The only way to know if you're getting bank financing is to call and ask the right questions.

1. Determine what type of company is providing the financing?

2. Is it financing through a bank, finance company, "banc," or lease financing?

3. If bank financing, which bank?

4. What are the terms?

5. How does the program work?

6. What are their credit score requirements?

7. What down payment is necessary?

8. What is the average term of the loan?

9. Who do I make my payments to?

10. What interest rate might a person with a previous bankruptcy expect to pay?

11. What is the name of the finance company, and how will it appear on my credit reports?

12. Do you finance new and used cars?

If the financing is not provided by a bank, keep looking. No matter what gimmicks they use, it is not worth your time.

CREDIT UNION FINANCING

Credit unions have one major flaw: they usually do not report to all three of the national credit reporting agencies. If your timely payments are not reported to the credit reporting agencies, you're spinning your wheels. You're in essence delaying your recovery from bankruptcy.

There are several very large credit unions around the country. Some are even larger than banks in their area. If your credit union reports to the three major credit reporting agencies, they are just as good as a bank.

BANK FINANCING

This is one of the best types of mainstream credit. There are few things more powerful than bank references on your credit reports. The challenge is that most banks have a policy about extending credit to people who have previously filed bankruptcy. As a rule, they don't like us.

In my personal experience, I think that trying to get a car loan with a bank after a recent bankruptcy is a waste of time. The exception to the rule is if they have created a special program with a car dealership.

As for walking into a bank yourself, don't. This is better suited for someone who has several years of established credit after bankruptcy. And even then, it could be a recipe for disappointment. For the recent bankruptcy filer, bank financing is unlikely.

CAR MANUFACTURER FINANCING

Hands down, this is the perfect type of financing for anyone with a previous bankruptcy.

Car manufacturer financers (also known as captive lenders) are essentially the financing arm of the major car companies. For example, Ford dealers' captive lender is Ford Motor Credit. General Motors' captive lender is GMAC. Porsche has Porsche Motor Credit.

Using car manufacturer financing usually means you'll get the lowest interest rate with the least amount of money down financed by a mainstream lender.

A credit reference appearing on your credit reports from a captive lender is just as strong as a bank credit reference.

Captive lenders have two reasons to get you into a car:

(1) To sell you a car, and

(2) To make money on the financing.

Other types of financing companies earn money only on the financing.

Although captive lenders are ideal for someone with a previous bankruptcy, some are better than others. Some captive lenders won't work with you as long as your bankruptcy appears on your credit reports. Others don't mind as long as you've done the right things to recover.

Most captive auto lenders change their credit guidelines frequently throughout the year, so it's always a good idea to research before you purchase a car.

"Words cannot express my gratitude."

"For my entire adult life, I had perfect credit. Whenever I purchased a car or home, the salesperson always asked if I was sure I didn't want the more upscale model since I could afford it. My journey towards bankruptcy began in November 2001 when my husband of 24 years filed for divorce. I was a stay-at-home mom most of my married life, but fortunately in later years I became a legal secretary. So began my journey towards bankruptcy. My divorce was final June 2002 and I purchased my first home by myself October the same year. My ex-husband lost his job January 2003 and stopped all child support payments in March. As the loss of the child support was the greatest cause of the bankruptcy, I filed December 2003. The bankruptcy was discharged March 2004. The one positive step I took before filing was to purchase a new car in July of 2003 at 2.9% while I still had stellar credit. (Even during the bankruptcy, I have never missed a payment or have been late with mortgage or car payments.) After the discharge, I obtained one unsecured Master Card with a credit limit of $500 (the credit limit has since risen to $1,100). As I was always pretty credit savvy, I be-bopped along until I attended one of your seminars earlier this year. Since I was already hooked on the newsletters, I knew I had to attend the seminar. In fact, I brought two friends with me. It was truly amazing what I learned that day. Since attending your seminar and putting into practice what you preach, I have obtained a second car at the lowest used car financing rate of 6.5%. I also obtained a second Master Card with a $1,000 limit along with one store card (this one surprised me with a $1,000 limit that I was sure I couldn't qualify for). The last time I checked my credit scores, they were: Equifax—689; TransUnion—700; and Experian—705. My FICO Auto Score was 730 when I purchased the car in July. I can't tell you how many lenders I've screened using your techniques seeking additional credit. I think the most amazing event was last Friday when I opened an envelope which contained a new unsecured Master Card with a $6,000 limit and a very competitive rate! I have NO intention of using this card except for small purchases and emergencies, but I can't express how happy I am just having it. Stephen, you are truly remarkable in what you do. Words cannot express my gratitude. I pray God continues to bless you in this journey we call life."

Debbie Nicholson
Farmersville, California

CHAPTER **26**

How to Get a Retail Store or Gas Credit Card

One of the keys to building and maintaining high credit scores is to have a good mix of different types of credit accounts. One way to "diversify" your credit portfolio is to have two or three retail cards. However, this is not as easy as filling out an application at the store, handing it to the cashier, and expecting an automatic approval.

Here's why it has become more difficult than it used to be... there are very few independently owned retail store or gas cards anymore. This means that, despite the name of the store on the card, you are actually a customer of some other company.

Fifteen years ago, most stores had their own credit departments and banks, and they made their "approve" or "deny" decisions in-house, which is why they had a reputation for being easier to get credit with.

This has changed. Today your Best Buy®, Macy's, Gap, or Home Depot® credit application is being looked at by people at a company that has nothing to do with DVD players, dress pants, or lumber. In fact, four major companies now issue most of the retail and gas credit cards available. The four companies are Citibank®, GE® Money Bank, HSBC™, and WFNNB.

Below is a list of the top 15 retail stores and the companies that issue their retail cards:

When you apply with...	... You're really opening an account with...
1 Wal-Mart®	GE® Money Bank
2 Home Depot®	Citibank®
3 Target®	Target National Bank
4 Sears	Citibank
5 Lowe's®	GE Money Bank
6 Best Buy®	HSBC™
7 Federated Dept. Stores (Macy's, Bloomingdale's, May Dept. Stores— Marshall Fields, LS Ayres, etc.)	Citibank
8 JC Penny®	GE Money Bank
9 Staples®	Citibank
10 Gap	GE Money Bank
11 Kohl's®	Chase™ Bank
12 Office Depot®	Citibank
13 Meijer®	GE Money Bank
14 The Limited, Inc. (Victoria's Secret, Express, Bath and Body Works, etc.)	WFNNB
15 OfficeMax®	HSBC

Just like retail cards, there are very few independent gasoline credit card issuers left. Citibank is the dominant lender in this category. Below is a list of the top 10 gas cards, and their issuers:

When you apply with...		...You're really opening an account with...
1	ExxonMobil	Citibank
2	Shell	Citibank
3	BP	Citibank
4	Chevron	Chevron Credit Bank
5	ConocoPhillips	Citibank
6	Citgo®	Citibank
7	Sunoco	Citibank
8	Speedway Super America	SSA, LLC
9	Valero	DSRM National Bank
10	Marathon	Marathon Petroleum Company, LLC

For the most part, the large retail card issuers have fairly conservative credit guidelines. Remember, you have to be extremely careful when you apply for a retail card. You don't want an unnecessary credit inquiry by applying for a retail card with a lender that is going to automatically deny you simply because you've filed bankruptcy. Before you do anything, you need to call the credit department of the store or gas station you would like to apply for credit with, and ask to speak to someone in the credit department.

When you call, you may have to go through their automated services first. Be patient and persistent. When they ask for your information, enter the pound sign (#) or choose to speak to an operator. Keep entering # until they send you to a live operator. Then ask for the credit department. They may ask you for your credit card number. Just tell them, "I don't have a card yet. I am thinking about applying for a credit card, but would like to ask some questions about your terms, first." And remember—don't settle for a low-level customer service representative. Their job is to try to get you to apply for their card and get you off the phone. The first person you speak with may not have all the information you need. Try to speak to a supervisor, or someone in the underwriting department.

When you reach a person who knows what they are talking about, ask them these nine important questions. Don't give out any personal information until you are absolutely sure you're ready to apply.

1. Do you offer a credit card?
2. Does a third party issue the credit card? If so, who is it? (GE, Citi®, HSBC™, WFNNB)?
3. How does a bankruptcy affect my chance for approval?
4. Which credit reporting agency do you use to make your lending decision?
5. What is the minimum credit score that you will approve?
6. What is the credit score that is required for the lowest rate?
7. How many of the national credit reporting agencies do you report to?
8. Can I apply for the card at the store?
9. Is there an appeal process if I am initially denied?

After you get answers to all your questions, get a copy of the card's "Terms and Disclosures," and look at your options. The best cards are ones that will:

1. Not automatically deny you for a credit card because of one thing (bankruptcy, foreclosure, collection account, etc.) on your credit report

2. Offer you a comparable rate to other, similar cards (retail and gas cards typically have higher rates than other types of credit)

3. Report to all three national credit reporting agencies

4. Offer on-line bill pay

5. Regularly increase your credit limit if you handle your account responsibly (retail and gas credit cards typically have lower initial credit limits than other types of credit cards)

6. Offer their retail or gas credit through a revolving credit card issued by a b-a-n-k...not a b-a-n-c ("bancs" are nothing but finance companies masquerading as "banks")

7. Offer low or no annual fee

OTHER WAYS TO GET GAS CARDS

Shortly after we started our business after bankruptcy we decided that we needed a corporate gas card. We ended up going with Shell. They have easy requirements to obtain a corporate card. We filled out the corporate fleet card application and were promptly mailed two Shell gas cards. The key to getting approval is to have a corporation that is rated with Dunn & Bradstreet. Don't have a corporation? Start one. Call the secretary of state's office in your state for instructions. Corporate filing fees usually range from $35 to $90. There are plenty of books at the library to help you fill the form out properly. If you have an accountant, he or she could also help with this.

There's another way to get a gas card. It takes a little longer, and involves purchasing stock in the gas company. As a shareholder, some of the gas companies automatically give you a credit card.

Remember that you may not always be able to go through the front door in establishing credit after bankruptcy. Look for a window. If not a window, a back door. And with time, you will be able to walk through the front door.

"Today we were approved for a $0 down, 6% mortgage on a 3,100 square foot house. The loan is through the mortgage company that sponsored the seminar."

"My FICO scores are: 699, 650, and 706 and I owe it all to your seminar. We bought a truck one month after the seminar. I have gotten three unsecured credit cards. I have also obtained several leases on various pieces of medical equipment, and today we were approved for a $0 down, 6% mortgage on a 3,100 square foot house. The loan is through the mortgage company that sponsored the seminar. We were on the phone with them for less than 20 minutes, faxed them our income tax statements for two years, then they faxed us an approval letter for the mortgage. (And I do mean APPROVAL, not preapproved or prequalified.) I have met dozens of BK people who think that they will never get credit again. If they only knew how easy it is to access, and improve their credit."

Joe Pamplin
Timber Pines, Florida

How to Get
Other Credit

As you begin your journey to reestablish credit after bankruptcy, there may be times when you are faced with the absolute need for credit for things other than the necessities (i.e., bank card, mortgage, and car). Here are a few suggestions.

WHO YOU ASK SHOULD BE THE MARKET LEADER

For example, if you wanted to finance that motorcycle after bankruptcy...

You should start by making a list of the top motorcycle manufacturers. And if you're having trouble researching, there is a cheap and easy source you can go to...your local library. A very resourceful reference librarian can help you figure out what you need to know free of charge.

I use reference librarians all the time. Just call them up and ask a question. The best ones are usually at the downtown or main branch of your library.

Once you have a list, call each company and ask to speak to the credit department or financing division. You know the questions to ask—and if you don't you need to read Chapter 12 of this book.

After you're finished interviewing your lenders, put all of their answers together and compare what each company is offering. What you'll normally see is the market leader will offer the most financing options—because they can afford to. This strategy works whether you want to finance a motorcycle, semi-trailer truck, boat, wave runner, new furnace, furniture, airplane, or whatever.

CELLULAR PHONE

Things have changed quite a bit since I got my first cell phone. Now most cell phone providers make their decisions based primarily on your FICO® credit scores. The good news is that your bankruptcy will not prevent you from being approved. It's all about your credit scores.

For the most part, your credit scores will have the greatest effect on the amount of deposit you pay for your cell phone service. Deposit amounts can range anywhere from $100 to $1,000 (most often $300 to $500). This is usually refunded after 12 months of on-time payments. Some companies will accept a FICO score as low as 580 to 600 before they require a deposit.

It's important to call and find out what each cell phone company's policy is before you let them review your credit scores, because each of these inquiries will lower your credit scores.

LOCAL STORE CREDIT

I went to a seminar where the speaker made a statement that motivated me to action. He said, "There are three things to leave behind when you pass on: your books, your journals, and your pictures . . ." It made me think. My wife and I didn't own a camera. I was suddenly inspired to go out and purchase a camera. And since I was up for the challenge, I decided I would purchase it on credit and pay it off in two months.

My search for credit to purchase a Nikon camera system began. I knew that my chances of being approved through normal channels were bleak, so I got creative. I remembered my father having a credit account with the local camera store when I was a kid. After making some initial calls to local camera stores, I decided the best way for me to get credit for a Nikon camera system was through a camera store that held its own credit accounts.

I began the project like any other, with lots of telephone calls and asking plenty of questions. I found a large camera store close to Indianapolis that had a reputation for working with professional photographers. After talking with a sales associate about the different types of financing for a camera, I quickly discerned that the credit programs offered by the camera manufacturers were not the best option for a recent bankruptcy, and in any case they were certainly the most expensive.

I then inquired about in-store credit with the ability to pay it off in two or three months. They faxed me a credit application. I was right: no fine print, no credit verification, and no review of my credit report. All they wanted to know was the names of a few companies I did business with, called trade references. Within a few days I was approved to purchase a Nikon camera system.

When looking for in-house credit, do not be too generous with information. My "sound bite" was that I wanted to avoid high interest lenders. I did not say it was important that they not review my credit report. By looking at a credit application, it's easy to tell by reading the fine print just how far they go. If the fine print does not disclose that they will review your credit report, this is a good indication that this is the company you are looking for.

HEAT PUMPS AND WATER SOFTENERS

It is easier to get approved for this type of credit if you go through the company offering the product. They have more leverage than going directly to the bank on your own. Few of these programs are funded by banks, and those are the best ones. Steer clear of programs offered by finance companies or bancs. Not only does a finance company credit reference lower your credit scores, but their interest rates are also too high.

Another option is to find a small heating and cooling company that will extend credit to you. That's what we did when our heat pump went out. We talked with the owner, and he agreed to put in our heat pump based on a payment plan we mutually agreed upon.

Sometimes you have to get creative. Don't be afraid to ask.

Have you had success getting credit for other items? If so, go to: *www.afterbankruptcy.org/othercredit* and let me know.

"Over the last six months my credit card company has doubled my line of credit and offered me another credit card with a matching line of credit."

"I attended your seminar [and] it was one of the best things that ever happened to my wife and I. We were 18 months into a chapter 13 bankruptcy, living in a house that we DID NOT like, and our 11 year old van had just blew the engine. Even after reserving our place at the seminar, I was considering voluntarily dropping out of the bankruptcy and dealing with our creditors myself. You see even though we filed bankruptcy 6 months before I received an unexpected promotion and doubled my salary, no one would help us and we could not do anything without approval from our trustee. I felt like a little kid in time out for having bad credit. After I attended your seminar, I felt like there was hope. Here's my success story. We started to apply some of the things we learned from you. Within 3 months my median FICO score went from 545 to 620 with my high score at 640. After 5 months I contacted the suggested lender and applied for a refinance mortgage on our property to use the equity to pay off our bankruptcy. I just received confirmation that we are approved for a mortgage at 6.75% and all the needed steps that the trustee requires the lender to do have been completed. All we are waiting for is the courts to process the paper work. I had one unsecured credit card when I started. Over the last six months my credit card company has doubled my line of credit and offered me another credit card with a matching line of credit. I'm sure that we have only seen the tip of the iceberg with all that has happened for us since attending your seminar. We appreciate so much all the advice you have given and I will be adding to my success story shortly."

Gilbert Fluker
Atlantic City, New Jersey

How to Increase Your Credit Limits

Once you have established credit, it's important to keep increasing your credit limits with them. While this may not be practical for an auto loan or home mortgage, it certainly applies for credit cards, department store credit, and other types of revolving credit. Every six months, consider calling to request an increase.

WHY BOTHER TO INCREASE YOUR LIMIT?

Raising your limit is important for several reasons.

1. Your revolving credit (the type of credit where the amount you owe fluctuates with your balance such as a credit card) weighs heavily in the composition of your FICO® credit scores. And if your lender reports that you're using a high percentage of your available credit, your credit scores will suffer.

For example, let's say you're giddy with your Capital One Visa card with a $500 limit. Your son's birthday is on Friday, so you have to buy gifts and plan a party for him. Then, as luck would have it, your car breaks down on Saturday and you have to get new brakes. Between the gifts, party and getting the car fixed you've charged $450 to your credit card. And that's just one weekend.

Here's the problem—you're nearly maxing out your credit limit. In this example you've used 90% of the available credit limit. That's not exactly ideal. In a perfect world your utilization (the percentage of your credit limit that you owe) should be 5% or less a month.

2. The larger the amount a lender is willing to trust you with, the more it may influence another lender to grant you a similar line of credit.

A credit lender looks at several things to evaluate your credit-worthiness. For example, let's say you have a Visa credit card with a $300 line of credit. You've paid on time for 6 to 12 months. Your water pipes burst and you need to repair them fast. The plumber gives you an estimate of $1,000. But no bank will extend you a $1,000 credit to repair your pipes. By taking the time to raise your credit limit over a period of time, this emergency could have been covered.

Sure, you will reach a point where higher limits are of no significance to you. But keep raising them.

HOW TO INCREASE YOUR LIMIT

All you need to do is ask. Simply call the lender's customer assistance department and request a credit limit increase. That's all there is to it.

Many companies review credit limits every six months. Make it a habit to call for a credit limit increase every six months. Schedule it in your calendar so you don't forget. Remember, when you request a credit limit increase it counts as an inquiry that lowers your credit scores, so avoid these calls if you are getting ready to make a major credit purchase (i.e., house, car).

When you call you may experience the joy of talking with customer service people who do not understand the meaning of "customer SERVICE." They may tell you they don't know when your limit will be raised, or that it happens automatically. In this case, simply ask when the last time the credit limit was increased, and cheerfully end the call. Immediately mark in your day planner to call back six months from that date to request a credit limit increase.

And when you call, don't ask for any specific amount of increase. Let them decide the amount.

A word of caution—if you didn't include the card in your bankruptcy because it had a zero balance, it may be best to let the credit limit increase happen automatically. You run the risk of the company canceling your credit card once they know about your bankruptcy.

THE RIGHT TO ASK

You are entitled to ask for a credit limit increase only if you have paid your monthly payments early or on time. Timely payments are what the lender is looking for, and they will determine whether your request is approved.

IMPROVE YOUR CHANCES

Most stores will be more eager to grant your request if you are either calling from the store ready to make a purchase or you request an increase during the busiest season—the Christmas holiday. Be careful, you run the risk of being embarrassed if you are turned down at the register. I prefer using the telephone in the store's credit department, or calling from home.

DON'T TAKE NO FOR AN ANSWER

If you've done all the right things, and they still say no, ask to speak to a supervisor. This happened to us with both of our credit cards after bankruptcy. Our credit limits were $2,000 each. I asked for an increase. They turned us down. I asked to speak to a supervisor. Both credit limits were raised to $2,500 and the interest rate was lowered by 4%.

If you've done all the right things, don't take no for an answer. Politely ask to speak to a supervisor.

Now that you know why you should increase your credit limits, here's how to do it and what you need to watch out for.

SEVEN STEALTH STRATEGIES TO INCREASE YOUR CREDIT LIMITS ON ALL YOUR CREDIT CARDS

A few important tips on increasing your credit limits...

1. Remember, when YOU initiate a credit limit increase, it will cause a credit inquiry—the kind that lowers your credit scores. Plan accordingly.

2. When the lender reviews your credit on their own (meaning you don't authorize an inquiry, sign a credit application, or give them your Social Security number), the credit inquiry doesn't affect you. Many lenders review for credit limit increases every six months. Call first to see if you have an automatic review coming up.

If so, you may get the increase without wasting the credit inquiry. In addition, if your creditors are banks or credit unions, group your limit increase calls all within a 14-day time frame to minimize credit inquiries that count against you. Depending on how each bank or credit union codes their inquiries there's a chance you could minimize any damage.

3. Some banks will give you a choice when you call for a credit limit increase. For example, Citibank will offer some of their customers the option of a lower credit limit increase without a credit review or the chance of a higher credit limit increase with a credit review. What you do depends on your circumstances. If you feel that your credit scores are not high enough yet to get a larger credit limit increase, you may want to take the lower amount and avoid the inquiry.

4. Remember, if you deserve the increase because you've managed the account well, don't settle for a, "No." Always politely ask for a supervisor and plead your case respectfully...not as a threat. You attract more flies with honey than vinegar.

5. Sometimes timing is everything. If you don't succeed the first time, try again at the end of the day...at the end of the month...at the end of the quarter...or during the holiday shopping season. Just be careful of how many times you do this—remember, each time you ask for an increase, you will initiate a credit inquiry that can lower your credit scores.

6. Most retail stores will be more eager to grant your credit limit increase when you're in the store ready to make a purchase.

7. Have a competitor's offer in your hands when you call. Tell them "so-and-so bank just mailed me an offer today that says, 'blah blah blah.'" Sometimes this motivates them to action. It's more expensive for them to find a new customer than it is for them to make an existing one happy.

One final warning, remember that when you do get a credit limit increase on your credit card(s), make sure you don't go out and use the increased limit. You want to increase your credit scores, not increase your spending habits, which lowers your credit scores.

"Your books and seminar were not only a GREAT single point of reference of information, but inspiring and reassuring in the fact that we ALL have the ability to recover and get back to a semi normal life style..."

"I had the privilege of attending your seminar on 2/25/06. Let me first say this: after all the research I have done since my discharge two years ago, your seminar and book included it all. I cannot tell you the countless hours spent in the library and on the internet, gathering information, talking to bankers and mortgage brokers, attempting to put a recovery plan in place for my family's future. I wish your foundation was better advertised two years ago. Your books and seminar were not only a GREAT single point of reference of information, but inspiring and reassuring in the fact that we ALL have the ability to recover and get back to a semi normal life style, all to which gets better with time and proper credit management. Thank you for what you do for others. I have recommended your books and seminars to a few people in a similar position."

Steven Pine
College Park, Georgia

"After 2 years in bankruptcy I bought a house. I was pre-approved for $143,000 dollars. I got a fixed rate at 5.85% with no points, that was great."

"I have followed your book to the letter, it really works. My biggest problem was the IRS. I received an offer of compromise from the IRS. All I had to pay was $769 and file my taxes on time for the next five years. After 2 years in bankruptcy I bought a house. I was pre-approved for $143,000 dollars. I got a fixed rate at 5.85% with no points, that was great. I went to car dealer you recommend and bought a new car. I also applied for a credit card. It worked! Thank you."

Cardell Torney, Sr.
Longboat Key, Florida

Standing Up to the IRS

Where there is smoke, there is fire. Where there is a bankruptcy, there are usually unresolved problems with the IRS. Dealing with the IRS can seem intimidating. It doesn't have to be. With the proper advice, a whole new world of options can be brought to your attention.

The key to improved relations with the IRS is either becoming a tax expert yourself or locating a person experienced in handling these matters for you.

Do not take the threat of tax liens and levies lightly. You need to avoid federal tax liens and levies at all costs. They not only damage your credit reports, but they may also slow you down from obtaining new credit until the liens are paid or subordinated. In our case, tax liens forced us to wait before we could mortgage a larger home. Today, this is no longer a problem when applying for a mortgage. However, if you do have difficulty because of this, you may be able to get around it with a signed installment agreement with the IRS and a 12-month payment history.

The goal of this chapter is to lead you to professionals who can help you resolve your tax problem. For a complete understanding on the topic of working with the IRS, I recommend reading *Stand Up to the IRS* by Frederick W. Daily. Be sure to request the most recent version, since it is frequently updated to stay current with tax law.

IT HAPPENED TO US

Within three weeks of receiving a letter from the IRS stating their intent to levy on us, it happened.

My wife called from her cellular phone. In tears, she shouted at me, explaining that 100% of her next paycheck was going to be levied by the IRS.

The IRS had officially garnished her wages. She was very embarrassed and worried that we would not be able to make ends meet.

The good news: days before her next paycheck, we had a signed release of the lien and a $50-a-month installment agreement with the IRS on an alleged $188,000 debt.

If we hadn't had a tax professional waiting in the wings, we might have become the latest victims of an unfair IRS tax levy. Before you do anything else, be sure to get your tax professional working on your case. Do not let any excuses hold you back. Because when the IRS moves, it moves, and you must be ready. This is even more true today, as the IRS has only become more aggressive in their collection practices as government spending and deficits have increased.

MY MISTAKE

I was always successful in buying extra time with the IRS. But the mistake I made was neglecting to do anything constructive, like finding someone to help me after I bought the time. I always procrastinated in taking the time to find quality help.

What triggered our levy was my failure to call back the IRS at a specific time to update them on our situation. I had written the call-back day on the wrong month in my day planner!

The best thing to do is to seek competent, specialized help from people who have a background in working with the IRS, as early in the process as possible. Our entire levy could have been avoided if I had found our tax pro earlier.

TAX PROS

There are professionals who specialize in helping people with tax problems. They are known as tax pros. They understand what the IRS wants, and they can represent you or give you advice on how you can represent yourself. Some tax pros used to work with the IRS. As in any other profession, there are good tax pros and bad ones. A good one is worth his or her weight in gold.

Tax pros come in three flavors. You can choose a(n):
1. Enrolled agent $
2. Certified Public Accountant $$$
3. Tax attorney $$$$$

ENROLLED AGENTS (EA)

An EA is usually a full-time tax advisor and tax preparer who is permitted to practice before the IRS in all matters. Most EAs cannot represent you in tax court, however.

They earn the designation "enrolled agent" by either passing a difficult exam or having at least five years of experience working for the IRS. They also must participate in continuing education programs to retain their EA designations.

There are approximately 40,000 EAs in the United States, 11,000 of whom are members of the National Association of Enrolled Agents. EAs are usually the least expensive of all tax pros. For a cost-effective approach to handling a tax problem, or if your tax problem involves less than $10,000, consider an EA.

A lot of EAs I've met around the country used to work for the IRS. There's something about these individuals that compels your trust. All the EAs I've met who were IRS employees are very experienced. I would hire any of them to handle a tax matter under $10,000.

What you need to watch out for are former IRS employees who are still loyal to the IRS. I've seen it firsthand. One of our seminar tax pro sponsors from Michigan years ago carried the IRS tax code around like some folks carry their Bible. Very competent fellow. Highly knowledgeable in the tax code. But would he fight for me, and present my case in the best light? My feeling was he was still answering to "The Man."

CERTIFIED PUBLIC ACCOUNTANTS (CPAS)

CPAs are licensed and regulated in all states. They do sophisticated accounting and business audit work, and prepare tax returns. To become a CPA, an accountant must have a college degree and work experience with a CPA firm, and must pass a series of rigorous examinations. Some CPAs have a great deal of IRS experience, but many do little IRS work. Of those who do, many are as good as tax attorneys and charge about the same or even a little less. Some CPAs, however, are not as aggressive as tax lawyers when facing the IRS personnel.

TAX ATTORNEYS

Tax attorneys are lawyers who do various types of tax-related work, including complex tax and estate planning, IRS dispute resolution, and sometimes tax return preparation. To assure competence, look for a tax attorney with either a special tax law degree or a certification as a tax law specialist from a state bar association. If more than $10,000 is at stake, if the IRS is accusing you of committing fraud, or if you're headed to tax court, call a tax attorney.

We've met a few tax attorneys. I think they have what it takes to represent you well. They have the balance of knowledge and sales skills to present your case. The downside in using a tax attorney is the cost. In Indianapolis, it's five times the cost of using an enrolled agent.

HOW A TAX PRO CAN HELP

Most auditors and collectors prefer dealing with experienced tax pros. It makes their job easier. Good tax pros know what the IRS wants, and they don't waste time.

If you face an audit, collection of a tax bill or a tax court hearing, and you've decided to at least consult a tax pro, here are the ways an experienced tax pro can help:

Consultation and advice: A tax pro can analyze your situation and advise you on the best plan of action. Rarely is there only one way to handle an IRS matter. He or she should describe your alternatives so you can make an informed choice.

Negotiation: Tax pros often possess negotiating skills. And an experienced tax pro should know what kinds of deals can't be made with the IRS.

Representation: Experienced tax pros know IRS procedures and how to maneuver around the IRS bureaucracy. Tax pros can neutralize the intimidation factor that the IRS knows it holds over you. And if you have something to hide, a tax pro usually can keep the lid on it better than you can.

DO YOU NEED HELP?

Under the taxpayer's Bill of Rights you have the right to have a representative handle any IRS matter for you. This means you never have to face the IRS if you don't want to.

In general, you can safely go it alone in the two most common, but serious, IRS situations:

- You are being audited and your records are in order, you can substantiate everything on your return, and you have nothing to hide, or

- The IRS is seeking to collect an overdue tax bill of $10,000 or less and you can pay it off within 36 months.

But before making any decision on proceeding alone or with a tax pro, weigh the pros and cons of each.

Going-It-Alone Basis

Pro: You save professional fees.

Con: It takes a lot of time.
You may find it very stressful.
You may say or do the wrong thing.

Consulting a tax pro before facing the IRS

Pro: You get the information you need and gain confidence.
It's cheaper than actually going for it and hiring a tax pro to represent you.

Con: Most tax pros charge for consultation.
You still have to ultimately face the IRS on your own.

Hiring a tax pro to represent you

Pro: The IRS respects knowledgeable tax pros.
You don't face the IRS.
Tax pros know tax issues.

Con: The best tax pros can be expensive.
You understand your tax records best.
You lose some control over your case, and risk hiring someone who is inexperienced or incompetent.

WHERE TO FIND A TAX PRO

There are several ways to find a good tax pro. Asking the IRS is not one of them. Here are some practical ways to find the right tax pro for you:

- Ask your tax advisor or accountant. They might have a good recommendation of a tax pro who can help you deal with an IRS problem.

- Look in the Yellow Pages under Tax Consultants & Representatives. Most tax pros offer a first consultation by phone or in their office at no charge. Look for the words "enrolled agent" or, "licensed to practice before the IRS." Some tax pros boldly state in their advertising they used to work for the IRS.

- Ask experienced realtors. These people deal with all sorts of financial situations every day. Good ones know a lot of people.

- Refer to professional associations and referral panels. Most local bar associations will give out the names of tax attorneys who practice in your area. But bar associations don't meaningfully screen the attorneys listed. Those who are listed may not be experienced or competent.

To find an EA in your area, call the National Association of Enrolled Agents at: *(800) 424-4339*. To find a CPA, try calling a local or state CPA society.

WHAT TO LOOK FOR IN A TAX PRO

Once you have the name of a tax pro, call and ask to speak with him or her directly. If the person is too busy to talk to you—and your call isn't transferred to another tax specialist—assume that the office is too busy to handle your case, and call the next person on your list.

When you speak to a tax pro, try to develop a rapport. Mention how you got his or her name, especially if it was a personal referral. Then get to the point: tell them your tax problem. If he or she doesn't handle your type of situation, ask for the names of some people who do.

Here are some other suggestions for making a good match:

- Don't be in a hurry to hire the first tax pro you speak to. It took over 13 months to find ours. Your decision is important, and rarely is there only one person for the job. Talk to a few. Choose the one you communicate with best. Ask to speak to a few recent customers.

- Question the tax pro carefully about his IRS experience. No matter how well he or she knows the tax code, prior IRS dealings are key. Previous IRS employment is not always a plus. It may have forever impressed the IRS point of view on him. Also, be skeptical if he hasn't been in practice at least five years.

- Does the tax pro seem to be aggressive or timid in discussing your case? If he seems awed by the IRS, find someone else.

- Does the tax pro give you a feeling of confidence? Ask him the likely outcome of your case. While no one can predict the future, his answer should create trust. Look for an honest response, not necessarily a rosy picture.

If you lose faith in your tax pro, find another one fast. But don't dismiss the first one until you get a second opinion on what he or she is doing. And don't fire a tax pro simply because nothing is happening. Frequently, inaction is because the IRS is dragging its feet. Remember, delay often works to your advantage in dealing with the IRS.

TAX PRO FEES

Be sure to get an understanding about the tax pro's fees at your first meeting. Does he or she charge by the hour or work by a flat fee? Most professionals charge $25 to $250 per hour, depending on where you live, the type of case, and exactly what you want the tax pro to do. Our tax pro charged us a flat fee of $2,000.

To some extent, you can control costs. Tax pros can be either hired as consultants, meaning you handle your own case and ask for advice as needed, or hired to represent you from start to finish. In other words, going to a tax pro need not be an all-or-nothing affair.

Although uncertainty about costs leaves most folks uncomfortable, many good tax pros shy away from quoting flat fees. When they do, it's usually for straightforward matters. But even if the tax pro won't give you a firm estimate, he or she should be able to "ballpark" a range of hours necessary for your case.

Most tax pros require a retainer paid in advance, often equal to the minimum time estimated as needed on the case.

TIPS ON CONTROLLING A TAX PRO'S FEES

- If you like the tax pro but not his or her fee, ask whether it can be done for less. If he or she isn't very busy, he or she may be flexible on fee and payment arrangements. Small tax firms or solo practitioners are more likely than professionals in large offices to negotiate the fee.

- Consider asking for a written fee agreement and monthly billings with itemized statements of time and services rendered. This will keep the tax pro honest. In many states, attorneys are required to give you a written fee agreement before starting work.

- If you disagree with a bill you receive, call your tax pro. If the firm is interested in retaining your business, he or she should listen to your concerns, adjust the bill, or work to satisfy you. If the tax pro won't budge, call your state or local CPA society or your state's bar association. Many groups have panels that help professionals and clients mediate fee disputes.

"The information you shared has given us our lives back...We got an invitation to your seminar, which changed our lives forever. Our scores are now in the low 700s. We just closed on a beautiful tri-level home at 6.375% with no money down. I was able to buy my dream truck last year at a great rate..."

"I wanted to write and thank you so much. The information you shared has given us our lives back...We got an invitation to your seminar, which changed our lives forever. Our scores are now in the low 700s. We just closed on a beautiful tri-level home at 6.375% with no money down. I was able to buy my dream truck last year at a great rate, and just as important, you said something so profound, you said to learn to give away 10%, save 10% and invest 10%, and I thought how could I ever do that? We actually are doing it all in just 3 years, and I can't even describe the awesome blessings we have received and the feeling of security. We are so grateful for all your time and effort you have devoted to helping people like us."

Rob Derho
Ojus, Florida

"My husband and I were able to purchase a brand new spec home, get a great fixed interest rate, no money down and get a tax lien paid for all through escrow in less than 30 days."

"I attended your seminar and immediately took action. My credit scores increased and my middle score is 690 with the highest at 700. I felt brave enough to contact your preferred lender and she was great. My husband and I were able to purchase a brand new spec home, get a great fixed interest rate, no money down and get a tax lien paid for all through escrow in less than 30 days. I told her if the loan did not close it was definitely not because of her as she did everything she could and I mean everything to get me approved, funded and closed with a Chapter 7 being discharged in August 2005. I recommend this lender to anyone. Thank you!"

Elea Sherrod
Altus, Oklahoma

What We Learned While Dealing With the IRS

When it comes to paying the IRS the taxes you owe, you really have four options:

1. Pay in full. An obvious choice.

2. Pay a monthly installment agreement. Nearly one million Americans are on an installment agreement with the IRS each year. I wouldn't recommend filling out the paperwork yourself unless you are a master negotiator or do significant reading on the subject. Otherwise, hire a tax pro. They know what the IRS wants and can negotiate the best deal for you. My tax pro negotiated a $50 monthly installment agreement on an alleged $188,000 tax bill, with an understanding that an offer in compromise was forthcoming.

3. Reduce, eliminate, or pay debt through bankruptcy. Bankruptcy can possibly reduce your total tax liability. Not always the tax itself, but the penalties and interest. Very rarely are taxes completely eliminated. If bankruptcy attorneys were more savvy at knowing the rules, more people might qualify. If my wife and I had waited two more months, the majority of our tax bill would have been dischargeable.

4. Offer in compromise. This is where you basically say to the IRS that you can afford to pay them X number of dollars to resolve your tax bill. The amount they accept has nothing to do with the amount you owe, and everything to do with your offer in compromise proposal.

SEIZURE POWER

The IRS has far greater powers than any other bill collector. The agency has the power to take your wages, bank accounts and other property without even first granting you a hearing. If you're successful in buying time, don't rest on your success. It's only temporary. The sooner you develop a strategy, the more soundly you will sleep at night.

THE "AUTOMATIC STAY"

The beauty of the "automatic stay" is that the moment you filed your bankruptcy petition, virtually all your creditors were stopped in their tracks. The automatic stay even prevents federal and state tax collectors from seizing your property and issuing lien notices —for a period of time. There are restrictions, however (even more with the most recent update to the bankruptcy law).

The automatic stay does not stop a tax audit, the issuance of a tax deficiency notice, a demand for a tax return, the issuance of a tax assessment, or the demand for payment of such an assessment. In addition, some types of debts cannot be erased in Chapter 7 bankruptcy:

1. Certain tax debts

2. Recent student loans

3. Child support

4. Debts incurred by fraud

The issues surrounding the discharging of debts listed here are very technical. A tax professional should be retained for a complete and thorough understanding as to how it applies to you. The bottom line is that the rules for discharging penalties and interest are less stringent than for discharging the underlying taxes.

SUSPENDING YOUR TAX BILL

If your finances are bleak and you have no job, little or no money, and no immediate prospects, you can ask a revenue officer or other IRS collector to "53" your case. If he or she agrees, it means that he recommends to his supervisors that your tax account balance be deemed "currently not collectable."

Once your account has been declared a "53," you won't hear from the IRS concerning your tax bill for up to one year. The IRS stops bothering you, but interest (and sometimes penalties) still accrue. At the end of your "53" period, the computer brings your account back up and you start the process over again.

The IRS doesn't take the "53" procedure lightly. You must persuade the IRS that you are almost destitute—that even a $25-a-month installment agreement is beyond your means.

Having your case classified as "currently not collectable" doesn't solve your tax problem either. It does, however, let you delay dealing with it. The "53" process simply buys time.

OTHER WAYS TO BUY TIME

I was very concerned about having anything negative show up on my credit report. I told the collection officers that I felt I might be able to get a loan after two years. Telling them this not only bought me time, but also prevented tax liens from posting to my credit report for a time. It wasn't until I dropped the ball in communicating with the IRS that the bottom fell out of my strategy. From that point on, my tax liens were reported to the credit reporting agencies.

Explain your situation. Even though the IRS has become more aggressive in collecting their debts, they are still willing to work with you (they're more lenient when the government doesn't have a war to pay for). Tell the IRS that you filed bankruptcy and need time to get back on your feet. If you don't have a job, tell them. Tell them anything truthful to buy time.

Question the accuracy of your tax bill. If there is ever a question about the accuracy of the tax bill, you could receive an automatic extension of more time.

File an amended return. Filing amended returns is evidence that there may be a question about the accuracy of the tax bill. This helps the delay process.

Submit an offer in compromise. Once your offer is submitted, the IRS usually does not harass you if it's legitimate. Offers in compromise can take anywhere from 4 to 12 months to be accepted or denied.

BEFORE YOU SPEAK WITH A TAX COLLECTOR

Never lie to the IRS. It's a crime.

Become a tax pro, or hire one fast. If you don't have a tax pro yet, and a tax collector calls, tell him that you are in the process of retaining a tax professional and would like to reschedule this conversation. Then proceed to arrange a time for your tax pro to call the collector back or give the tax collector your tax pro's name and phone number.

Have an action plan. If you don't have a plan, the IRS will. You can develop an action plan by reading *Stand Up to the IRS* by Frederick W. Daily, or hiring a tax pro to advise you.

Communicate. People who hide from the IRS will some day be sorry they did. It's so much easier to communicate. You're a fool if you tell them too much, though. It's like playing poker and showing your opponents your cards.

We used a day planner to keep track of dates and conversations. It is very important to remember your call-back dates with the IRS. If you miss one of these dates, their computer will automatically proceed to the next step. If you don't own a day planner, run to the nearest Franklin Covey store and pick one up.

Another option is to use a software program with a calendar like Outlook Express, which can sync to your cell phone or PDA.

WHAT IS A TAX LIEN?

A tax lien is a notice to the world that you owe taxes. The IRS cannot collect any money by just filing a tax lien. If the IRS sends you a tax bill and you don't contest or pay it, the IRS has a right to inform the public that you owe taxes. This is done by recording a Notice of Federal Tax Lien at your county recorder's office (where real estate transactions are recorded).

The practical effect of a tax lien is to scare off potential lenders or buyers and to warn others that you are a tax deadbeat. The tax lien notice will be picked up and reviewed by the credit reporting agencies such as Experian®, Equifax®, and TransUnion™.

Tax liens are not easily resolved once recorded, unless you pay the taxes, penalties and interest in full. And even then, they could remain on your credit reports for years.

WHAT IS A TAX LEVY?

A tax levy is how the IRS must seize your property—by way of levy—to collect what you owe. Usually this means taking money held from you by others, such as your bank, stockbroker (in an investment account), or employer.

Before the IRS seizes your money or property, you must be sent a Notice of Intent to Levy. This gives you 30 days from the date of the notice to pay what you owe in full. The law only requires that the IRS send the notice—not that you actually receive it.

If you are unemployed, have only the clothes on your back, and no money in the bank, you are a poor levy target for the IRS. If and when your financial situation improves, you'll have to worry about the property-seizure power of the IRS.

WHAT IS AN OFFER IN COMPROMISE?

An offer in compromise is a one-page written proposal to the IRS that basically proves you are unable to pay the debt, but are willing to pay a fixed amount either in one lump sum or over time, then call it even.

These offers are very common, and are best handled by a tax pro on your behalf. The problem is they can take from 4 to 12 months to get approved or denied. They are handled on a case-by-case basis, so there is no typical deal. Everything varies, based on the facts surrounding each individual's situation.

Offers in compromise have nothing to do with the amount of taxes owed, but they have everything to do with your ability to pay.

The IRS accepted our offer in compromise on June 7, 1999.

On an alleged debt of $188,000 they took $8,250 as payment in full. Does the IRS accept offers? Yes. Would I submit an offer on my own? No. I highly recommend hiring a tax pro to fill out the paperwork and negotiate on your behalf.

You can go to: *www.lifeafterbankruptcy.com/backissues/issue85* for the contact information of the best tax pros I know (who also helped me).

"It's the proudest moment I've ever had."

"In December of 2004 my Chapter 7 bankruptcy was discharged. I was heartbroken that I had to go through it and I had cried the entire time when I had the actual hearing. Once it was over I swore that I would never get myself into another mess again. It wasn't until May of 2006 though that I heard of the Credit After Bankruptcy seminar. I was eager to attend and wrote so many notes throughout that my hand was tired. I absorbed it completely and began to follow the advice that was given. My middle FICO score has raised to 688. Next week I'll be closing on my first home. When I went in to get financing the loan officer even commented on how great my scores were considering that I had filed bankruptcy. I had no problems whatsoever in securing my home loan. It's the proudest moment I've ever had. I've come very far! Thank you Stephen for all the useful information you provide to people such as myself. I may not have been able to do it without you!"

Stacy Ewen
Huntington Park, California

"Two years later we bought a $200,000 house, and kept our old one and rented it out. We also bought a new pickup and a car."

"Almost three years ago my husband and I went to your seminar. My husband didn't want to go but I talked him in to it and we have been happy ever since that day. Two years later we bought a $200,000 house, and kept our old one and rented it out. We also bought a new pickup and a car. We have all the credit we need and our scores are 670. I am sorry it took me so long to thank you, but better late than never. Thanks again."

Sandy Bradley
Mendota, California

How to Start Investing After Bankruptcy

*The next few pages are excerpted from an amazing book (*A Kick in the Assets*) by Tod Barnhart. Reprinted below is what I consider the most powerful part of the book. If you don't know much about investing, there may be some parts that seem too technical. If something doesn't make sense to you, don't be afraid, just move on to the next heading. This book really changed the way I think about investing.*

THE BEST-KEPT SECRET ON WALL STREET: THE TOP TEN METHOD

People tend to complicate something in direct proportion to its importance.
—Michael O'Higgins, author of Beating the Dow

In the next few pages I'm going to share with you a summary of the single best stock market investment method I've seen. The reason it's such a secret, I think, is this: using this method, you can achieve better results than most of the pros, with only one minute of homework per year.

THE PHILOSOPHY

As the most popular market index, the Dow Jones Industrial Average (DOW) is a weighted average of thirty of the largest and most profitable companies in the world. You probably recognize most of the steady companies that make up the Dow; they're household names.

The "Blue Chip" 30 Dow Industrials—A sample listing

- Allied-Signal
- Alcoa
- American Express
- AT&T
- Boeing
- Caterpillar
- Chevron
- Coca-Cola
- Disney
- Du Pont
- Eastman Kodak
- Exxon
- General Electric
- General Motors
- Goodyear
- Hewlett Packard
- IBM
- International Paper
- Johnson & Johnson
- McDonald's
- Merck
- J.P. Morgan
- Philip Morris
- Procter & Gamble
- Sears Roebuck & Co.
- 3M
- Travelers Group
- Union Carbide
- United Technologies
- Wal-Mart

Together, these thirty companies employ nearly five million people worldwide, have combined assets of over a trillion dollars, and combined sales that exceed the gross national product (GNP) of every country in the world except the United States, the former Soviet Union, Japan, and China. To me, it just makes sense to select a portfolio from these quality issues. So, our initial philosophy is that of regarding the Dow issues as far as our total investment universe; we'll only consider investments from within this index.

THE METHOD

Our portfolio selection method is based on the following premises:

1. Common stocks are the smartest long-term growth investment alternative.

2. Dow stocks are enormously important; all tend to make good long-term investments.

3. A portfolio of out-of-favor Dow stocks could be constructed (allowing minimal risk) that could outperform the Dow as a whole—a feat that has eluded the majority of professionals.

Q: How do we decide which stocks to select out of the Dow?
A: The Top Ten Method simply uses one indicator of value— YIELD.

Q: How does that work?
A: First let me explain the concept of dividend yield, or just yield, as we'll refer to it. Most companies in the Dow (twenty-nine out of thirty at this time) pay a return to their shareholders in the form of a dividend, which usually comes from the company's earnings. It can be $1, $2, or $5 per share, or more, or less. But the dollar value doesn't matter that much. What's important is the dollar value of the dividend as it relates to the company's share price. This relationship is expressed as a percentage called the dividend yield.

For example: Let's say that XYZ Company is trading for $20 per share, and the dividend they pay to the shareholder is $1 per share. Regardless of how many shares you own or how much money you have invested, your percentage return, on dividends alone, would be 5% (1/20 = .05). That's clear enough, right? On the other hand, let's say that XYZ Company has dropped to $5 per share, and the dividend they pay to the shareholder is still $1 per share. Now your percentage return, on dividends alone, would be 20% ($1/5 = .20$). Clear again?

The point I need to communicate is this: There is an inverse relationship between yield and price. As the share price moves up and down the yield fluctuates equally in the opposing direction, like a child's see saw: when the yield is down, the price is up; when the yield is up, the stock is down. We use this mathematical relationship to our advantage and buy only those companies with high yields and consequently, relatively low prices. It's like discount shopping. Choosing a portfolio of ten high-yield/low-price stocks forces the investor to "buy low and sell high"; it's a contrarian approach that avoids guesswork in knowing when to buy and sell.

PORTFOLIO OPERATION
Three steps:

1. Buy ten stocks. Invest equal dollars in the ten Dow companies that paid the highest yields in the past year.

2. Hold for one year. Long enough for some growth, plus receiving the entire annual dividend.

3. Repeat. Then readjust to include this past year's ten highest yielders (only three or four will differ).

Q: Why does this simple strategy work so well?
A: There are two parts to the return a dividend stock investor realizes:

1. Dividend yield, which we're maximizing by choosing the companies with the highest yield.

2. Price appreciation, which we're likely to achieve by buying the issues that are low-priced.

Together these two forms of return create a measure of performance called total return. Instead of shooting for one over the other, the Top Ten Method aims to maximize the sum of them both. Neat, huh?

Also, the method buys out-of-favor stocks. Buy low, sell high is an old idea, but how many people really do it? This system tells you exactly when to sell; after twelve months, you recycle your money back into undervalued securities, based on yield.

Q: How well has the Top Ten Method performed over the years?

A: 1. The Top Ten Method has outperformed the DOW sixteen of the last twenty-one years.

2. The Top Ten Method has had an annualized return of 16.58% since 1973—50% higher than the 11.04% the DOW itself posted.

3. The Top Ten Method has never lost money over any three-year market cycle.

4. The Top Ten Method performs well in up and down markets.

By using the Top Ten Method your money would have increased over twenty-fold in the past twenty-one years.

That's the method. It is simple, but logical and powerful—and it works, without the gurus. Most of the large brokerage firms offer a unit trust (similar to a mutual fund) that employs this strategy, and the charges are substantially lower than they would be if you tried this on your own by buying individual stocks.

So your next step is to pick an online brokerage firm, set up an account, and start investing!

Here's a list of online brokers to choose from:

- *TD Ameritrade:* www.tdameritrade.com
- *Charles Schwab:* www.schwab.com
- *E*Trade:* www.etrade.com
- *Interactive brokers:* www.interactivebrokers.com
- *Scottrade:* www.scottrade.com

"I am still in bankruptcy, not even discharged and I have bought a new home, the one I wanted not the one I could settle for."

"I attended your meeting, but I was real skeptical and almost didn't go! I sat in the back as I wanted to get to the door without making a fuss. I listened to your talk and almost left, but then something caught my attention: scores. I did not know that they were used to check on so many things. About half way through you had my attention. I used several of your ideas to start my comeback from two bankruptcies after a major life threatening illness, a bad divorce, and a child custody battle which ended with identity theft, and had put my credit in the bottom of the trash can! I decided right there that with your ideas on how to do things to find out what my credit actually showed! My biggest need was a home for myself and my son. I had a place that I really wanted but knew I could never have with my credit situation! I met a young lady at your seminar who was the rep of a mortgage company. I spoke with her for a few moments and she said it would not hurt to try. I contacted her after few days and she sent me the forms and got the ball rolling. After a lot of hard work by two dedicated young women and some work on my own three months after your seminar I will be closing on my new house, 100% VA at a very competitive 30 year loan. This could not have happened without your seminar and introduction to the mortgage rep. Believe it or not, I am still only three years into my chapter 13. That's right, I am still in bankruptcy, not even discharged and I have bought a new home, the one I wanted not the one I could settle for. I have also been given a Master Card with a $1,000 limit at very good rates. My bank has also approved a $15,000 home equity line of credit. It seems that I have been able to improve my FICO scores thanks to your method and the contacts you introduced me to. I found that I climbed out of my hole and learned to make things work for me and not against me. I don't know how to thank you and those great ladies at the mortgage company. It has changed my life so much, you can't believe the change in just three months! It is finally my turn to recover and move ahead with my life, thanks to you and great people you have introduced me to! Oh yes, I am also disabled and no one else would look at me. I have been able to return to the office of the fat cat who told me to get lost or come back with cash! I left him with his mouth still open! NEXT is great advice! One of your patients that has been cured, and educated and will never be run over again! Keep up the good works as you are saving people's lives and giving them hope to fight back!"

Roger Turner
Hanover, New Hampshire

How to Get Credit During Chapter 13

If you filed Chapter 13 bankruptcy and are still paying your trustee, this chapter will arm you with the knowledge you need to recover the right way. You can use it, along with what you learned in this book, to start your recovery before your bankruptcy is even discharged. You'll learn the best way to work with your trustee to get the loans you need, and how to make sure you get the best rates and terms on all the credit you apply for—before and after your discharge.

HOW TO GET CREDIT DURING YOUR CHAPTER 13 BANKRUPTCY

First, let me tell you that I respect you for filing Chapter 13 with the intent to pay back a large portion of your debt. I really do. It's very honorable on your part. You're making a huge sacrifice that many of us who filed Chapter 7 bankruptcy didn't make...including Michele and me.

However, as you probably know by now...you're treated the same by lenders as if you filed Chapter 7 bankruptcy (in my opinion, you're treated worse).

You see, from a credit scoring standpoint, you don't earn any brownie points for agreeing to pay back a large portion of your debt. In fact, the FICO® scoring model considers a Chapter 7 and a Chapter 13 bankruptcy with the same level of severity...and so do most lenders.

As a Chapter 13 filer you have to make monthly payments to a bankruptcy trustee for 3 to 5 years. Your trustee basically controls your financial decisions.

And when you finally complete your payments, you have to wait up to six months for your discharge letter. Then and only then do you experience the same freedom as a person who has been discharged from a Chapter 7 bankruptcy.

In other words, if two people filed bankruptcy at the exact same time, one filing Chapter 7 and the other Chapter 13, the Chapter 7 filer would have a HUGE advantage.

By the time the Chapter 13 filer gets discharged, the Chapter 7 filer has probably already bought a home, financed a new car, and acquired a couple of credit cards...in other words, the Chapter 7 filer is on their way to being fully recovered, while the Chapter 13 filer is still at the starting line.

It doesn't seem fair. You do the right thing by filing Chapter 13 and get penalized for it.

This is the part the credit card industry missed when they wrote the new bankruptcy "reform" bill. Instead of offering incentives for people to file Chapter 13, they tried to write the law so people would be forced to file that way.

Even before the new bankruptcy law, the math didn't add up for me to file Chapter 13. I didn't have a house to save—which seems to be the number one reason people file Chapter 13.

Saving a house that has a lot of equity with a house payment you can afford makes a lot of sense. But saving a house with no equity or with a payment you can no longer afford is a decision based on emotion and should be avoided.

Since we've covered the basics, let's see how we can potentially make the best of your situation...

SHOULD YOU CONVERT YOUR CHAPTER 13 TO A CHAPTER 7?

First you must understand that I am not an attorney (nor do I play one on TV). My expertise is helping bankrupt people recover from bankruptcy—not giving legal advice. So whether you should convert your Chapter 13 is really a question for your attorney.

A "conversion" is when you switch an existing type of bankruptcy to another. In this case, you'd be converting a Chapter 13 to a Chapter 7.

A conversion is not the same as having your Chapter 13 dismissed then filing a Chapter 7. That's actually two different bankruptcies.

Here are some things I would consider if I was thinking about converting a Chapter 13 to a Chapter 7:

1. How much longer do I have until I finish my Chapter 13 payment plan?

2. Can I afford the monthly payment as it is now?

3. Can I finish my payment plan?

4. What does my bankruptcy attorney advise me to do?

5. What will I lose by converting to a Chapter 7?

6. What will I gain by converting to a Chapter 7?

As you can probably tell from this line of questioning, I'm personally against converting...unless you have no other choice.

You see, from a credit scoring perspective, having one bankruptcy appear on your credit reports is the equivalent of an atomic bomb. Converting to a Chapter 7 could be the equivalent of 2 atomic bombs.

However, having said that, time can heal most things. And depending on your specific circumstances, it can sometimes make sense to convert—especially if you're very proactive about your recovery.

MANY PEOPLE CONVERT FROM CHAPTER 13 TO CHAPTER 7

According to a famous study done by Elizabeth Warren in her book, *The Fragile Middle Class: Americans in Debt*—about 1-in-3 Chapter 13 filers convert to a Chapter 7. I think the conversion rate is much higher...probably two-thirds of Chapter 13s convert.

The bad thing about converting is that even though a converted bankruptcy may seem to be just one bankruptcy, many lenders consider a conversion the same as two bankruptcies. So you double the damage.

In addition, there may be things you wanted to keep that you end up losing when you convert to a Chapter 7. For advice specific to your situation, talk with a bankruptcy attorney.

There is one type of lender that doesn't view a conversion as two bankruptcies—mortgage lenders—making them the only lenders lenient toward converted bankruptcies.

The good news is: whether or not you decide to convert, you can still recover from bankruptcy.

WHAT YOU CAN DO WHILE YOU'RE STILL PAYING YOUR TRUSTEE DURING A CHAPTER 13 BANKRUPTCY

Everything during a Chapter 13 starts with your bankruptcy trustee.

This is so important I'll say it again...

Everything during a Chapter 13 starts with your bankruptcy trustee.

You need to find out what they will allow you to do. Each state (and every trustee) is different in what they will and will not allow. That's the not-so-fun part. But before you go straight to your trustee, my advice would be to run the idea by your bankruptcy attorney. He should act as a sounding board to determine if your idea has merit (i.e., you need a new car, bigger house, credit card, etc.) and if it's something the trustee might allow.

By first going to your bankruptcy attorney, he may be able to give you some advice that will help you present a stronger case to your trustee. Remember, it's usually about numbers, not emotion.

PURCHASING A NEW HOME WHILE IN A CHAPTER 13

You can purchase a new home while in a Chapter 13—if your trustee allows.

First of all, you need to know that your options are limited. FHA and VA will allow you to purchase a home while you're still in a Chapter 13, but for the most part all other lenders won't even come close to helping you until you're discharged or your Chapter 13 is paid.

If you want to get approved for an FHA or VA mortgage, these programs require that:

1. You've been in your plan at least 12 months.

2. You've made all of your trustee payments on time.

3. You qualify for the monthly mortgage payment.

4. Your monthly debt-to-income ratio must be less than 43%—if it's more, you'll need to wait until you either reduce your monthly debt or you're within 10 months of paying off any installment debt.

For example, let's say your annual income is $60,000. That breaks down to $5,000 a month. Multiply $5,000 x .43 and you get $2,150. Your total monthly debt in this example could not exceed $2,150 per month.

"Debt" would include:

- Mortgage payment
- Monthly property taxes
- Homeowner's insurance
- Car loans
- Student loans
- Other installment loans
- Your trustee payment

Your revolving debt is also figured into your debt-to-income ratio. There is a glimmer of hope though...only the minimum monthly payment is calculated on revolving accounts (such as credit card accounts).

Now let's talk loan amounts.

With a VA loan, the maximum loan amount on a purchase is $417,000 nationwide.

The maximum loan amount from FHA varies by county. You can get more information about your county's maximum loan amount on the purchase of a home by visiting this website: *https:// entp.hud.gov/idapp/html/hicostlook.cfm.*

USING EQUITY IN YOUR HOME TO PAY OFF YOUR 13 AND GET DISCHARGED SOONER

If you have equity in your home, it may make sense to use it to accelerate your discharge.

If your trustee approves, a skilled mortgage banker can tap the equity in your home through refinancing to pay off a Chapter 13 bankruptcy early. It could speed up your recovery...help you break the chains that bind you to your trustee...and free you from the financial prison you're currently in.

FHA will refinance up to 95% of your home's value (less your mortgage balance) as long as you meet the 4 qualifications previously mentioned. Any mortgage financing other than FHA or VA will require you to pay off your Chapter 13 before having access to your equity.

That is unless you live in Texas. If you do, the only way you'll be able to get equity out of your home is to sell it.

Unfortunately, no matter where you live trustees are becoming more feisty about allowing filers to pay off a Chapter 13 early.

The potential glitch is each state views paying off a Chapter 13 early differently. Some states will allow it after 36 months in your plan...others require you pay the entire debt of what is owed to your creditors. Yes, I said entire debt, not just the balance on your plan.

It's best to discuss these options with your bankruptcy attorney to assess what is acceptable in your state. If you can get your trustee's approval, then contact your mortgage lender to proceed.

ANOTHER OPTION FOR REFINANCING A HOME

If you've been paying on your Chapter 13 for less than 12 months or have a delinquent payment history—a non-conforming refinance is another option.

However, late mortgage payments or late trustee payments will affect your interest rate and how much they'll loan based on your home's value.

The interest rate and amount a lender will loan is based on...

- Your Chapter 13 payment history

- Your mortgage payment history

- Your middle FICO® credit score

For more information about what you can do with your mortgage while you're in a Chapter 13, contact a mortgage lender with experience working with Chapter 13 bankruptcies.

CAR FINANCING DURING YOUR CHAPTER 13

Can you finance a car while in a 13?

Yes, but it won't be through a mainstream lender at a normal interest rate. Until you're discharged, financing a car will be expensive.

In fact, there are only four lenders nationwide that I know will provide that type of financing. Just be aware—you'll be forced to accept some high interest rates. I personally would pay cash for a car, or drive a rental car before I paid a double-digit interest rate on a car.

In most cases you should never settle for auto loans at 8% or higher...however there are times when necessity overrides your plans, but this should be a last resort. I just wanted to make you aware that there are options out there, if you absolutely have to get an auto loan while you are still making payments on your Chapter 13. Also remember, if you want to apply for a loan you'll have to be approved by your trustee first.

CREDIT CARDS DURING YOUR CHAPTER 13

When it comes to credit cards, you have a choice between applying for a secured or unsecured credit card.

An unsecured credit card will be extremely difficult to get before you're discharged...if not impossible.

So, since Plan A (an unsecured credit card) is probably out of reach for you at the moment, you should focus on Plan B— a secured credit card.

A secured credit card is very similar to an unsecured credit card. The only difference is that you must put money on deposit and the amount of your deposit becomes your credit limit. The money you have on deposit allows the lender to recover their money if you default.

For example, let's say you put a $500 deposit on an unsecured credit card. This means you can charge up to $500 on the card. If by chance you do charge $500 on the card, and you don't pay your bill, the card company keeps your deposit—and you won't be able to use the card anymore. The deposit acts as a safety net for the card issuer.

Believe it or not, even these types of credit cards can be difficult for Chapter 13 filers to acquire before they are discharged.

That's right, if you're in an open Chapter 13, and you go to a credit card company with $1,000 in hand and say, "Here's $1,000 in cold hard cash, can I please open a secured credit card," most banks will still say, "No!"

However, there is one bank that shows Chapter 13 filers some love. In fact, it's one of the only bank secured card programs that I know of that accepts people in a Chapter 13 who are not discharged yet...and I've looked at a lot of secured card programs.

If you want more information about the card, contact Mary Ann at: *maryann@afterbankruptcy.com*.

THE 4 MOST IMPORTANT ACTIONS TO TAKE DURING YOUR CHAPTER 13 BANKRUPTCY

Even if you're not discharged yet, there are steps you can take now to improve your credit rating. And if you're sharper than the other tools in the toolbox, you'll heed my advice.

The four most important things you can do are:

1. Dispute inaccurate information appearing on your credit reports. Do this yourself or hire someone to do it for you. The law firm I mentioned in Chapter 7 has years of experience disputing such items.

2. Learn how to manage your credit differently to increase your credit scores. These are actions that you must do yourself. For more help with increasing your credit scores, subscribe to the FREE *Life After Bankruptcy*® newsletter. Just go to: *www.lifeafterbankruptcy.com*.

3. Continue to make your Chapter 13 payments on time. Here's why...lenders can use your trustee payments to show a good payment history.

4. If possible, pay off your Chapter 13 sooner. You'll recover faster.

Using these strategies while you're still in your Chapter 13 bankruptcy will put you well ahead of the crowd that does nothing to improve their credit while in bankruptcy.

With higher FICO® credit scores, once you're discharged you'll hit the ground running...while others will hit the ground crawling...or limping. The difference between you and them was that you began increasing your credit scores.

Testimony

I filed bankruptcy when I was a Christian. I knew about God, but I didn't know God. There is a big difference.

I'm convinced that my success was and is a direct result of following His ways, as illustrated in the pages of our instruction manual—The Bible.

One of His instructions is the principle of giving God the first 10% of whatever you earn. This was very hard for me. I finally came to the realization that my way wasn't working, and it would be wise to listen to someone else's plan.

Let me tell you that ever since my wife and I put God first in our lives with our money, everything changed. I would encourage you to do the same. Find a local church and plant your giving there. Be sure to give cheerfully, and base your giving on His promises, which you will find in the Bible.

I believe Jesus Christ is the Son of God, was crucified, died, and on the third day rose again. And now sits on the right-hand of God the Father. His Holy Spirit lives in me and in all true believers.

In closing, you do not need to be a Christian to use this book. But, I believe that having God on your side is the best possible partnership anyone could have.

Most people do not know that the only prayer God answers from people who do not know Him is a prayer to ask Him to come into their hearts. Please consider asking Him into your life today.

If you are interested in learning more about what the Bible says about practical everyday living, I encourage you to call Bible Study Fellowship, commonly known as BSF. BSF is a worldwide Bible study organization that can be called the Mercedes Benz of Bible studies. It's free. And there's a local group that meets near you.

The entire world is learning the same lesson every week. So if you travel a lot, you can always find a local meeting. The group I used to frequent when I lived in Indianapolis was one of the largest, with nearly 600 men meeting every Monday for two hours. There are women's groups too.

This Bible study group helped do what few churches have done for me: take me from a part-time Christian to a full-time Christian. Call BSF headquarters at: *(877) 273-3228* and look for the BSF men's or women's group nearest you.

The single greatest cause of atheism in the world today is other Christians who say it with their mouths and deny it with their lifestyles.

My best friend was born in a manger.

STEPHEN SNYDER

Stephen Snyder

January 2008

Index

Learn directly from the nation's leading bankruptcy recovery expert during the Credit After Bankruptcy® Internet Seminar... it's FREE!

Discover How to Get Perfect Credit After You File Bankruptcy

Stephen Snyder's credit building techniques have been featured in...

Stephen Snyder, Founder of the After Bankruptcy Foundation

A proven system to get approved for any type of credit or loan you want—at low interest rates—even after filing bankruptcy

The secret to recovering from bankruptcy

Are you ready to change your life? Are you sick and tired of being told it's going to take 7 to 10 years to recover from bankruptcy...that you'll have to settle for double-digit interest rates whenever you borrow money?

Soon after I recovered, I got Visa credit cards at low interest rates...a new home mortgage (at only 6%)...a car loan with almost no money down at an interest rate of 2.9%...and personal and business loans at low interest rates. All of this in less than 8 months after my bankruptcy!

Use my experience as your guide

How did I recover so quickly? Simple, I developed a system. It's a system anyone who's filed bankruptcy can use. After my recovery, I founded the nonprofit After Bankruptcy Foundation. Through the foundation, I present the Credit After Bankruptcy seminar 61 times per year.

Strategies you can use right now to get the credit you need

During the seminar you'll discover specific steps you can take right now to rebuild your credit so lenders will want to work with you and offer you low interest rates with favorable terms. Specifically, you'll learn how to buy a new car...buy a new home...and get approved for credit cards—all at low interest rates—even after you've filed bankruptcy.

Works for Chapter 7 and Chapter 13 filers

These strategies work regardless what type of bankruptcy you filed. And it doesn't matter whether you filed yesterday, last week, last month, or last year. By simply following my system, you can recover and get approved for mainstream credit more quickly than you ever thought possible, just months after filing or being discharged.

Take a step toward regaining your good credit

It's no secret that the system I used to recover from bankruptcy works. Over 200,000 people have already used the strategies revealed in the seminar to recover from bankruptcy. Now it's your turn. Your recovery can start the moment you reserve your spot for the seminar.

You'll Learn More About How to Recover From Bankruptcy In 4 Hours During the Seminar Than You Will In 12 Months on Your Own...

The seminar is presented on the internet. No special software is needed. It's just like watching TV. Best of all, it's FREE to watch. But, due to bandwidth limitations, viewership is limited. So you must reserve your spot immediately.

www.CreditAfterBankruptcy.com/free

If You're Bankrupt, Then This Will Be the Most Important Website You Will Ever Visit...

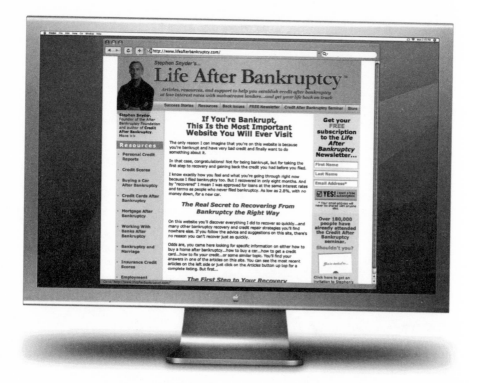

www.LifeAfterBankruptcy.com

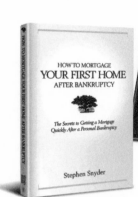

Imagine how much faster your recovery would be if you could get...

Specific, step-by-step instructions for every important credit decision you'll ever make...

I hear it all the time...

"Stephen, I love your newsletter and books, but I need help buying a car now."

"Stephen, you have great information in your newsletters and books, but how do I get the best rate on a mortgage? I'm buying a house next month."

Not a day seems to go by that I don't receive seven or eight emails seeking ultra-specific advice about how to buy a car...buy a home... refinance a home...get a credit card...etc. When it's time to make a major purchase, you want more specific guidance geared toward your individual situation...and you want it all in one place. In other words, you want someone to walk you through the process step by step.

Announcing the world's most powerful credit library

Now, with the introduction of the Credit Power Library, you can discover how to get whatever credit you need—when you need it. Each book in the library will focus on one specific topic, so you'll get instant help for every credit-based decision you need to make—from how to buy a car at a low interest rate with little or no money down...to how to get approved for a single-digit interest rate on a mortgage...to how to open a checking account even if you're in ChexSystems℠.

Every month I'll release a new, detailed book and audio CD on a credit-specific topic. The Credit Power Library is the ultimate credit-building resource.

Sign up today!
For more details and topic descriptions, go to:
www.CreditPowerLibrary.com